THE RAINMAN'S THIRD CURE

PETER COYOTE
THE RAINMAN'S THIRD CURE

An Irregular Education

COUNTERPOINT

BERKELEY

Library of Congress Cataloging-in-Publication Data

Coyote, Peter.
The rainman's third cure : an irregular education / Peter Coyote.
pages cm
ISBN 978-1-61902-496-0
1. Coyote, Peter. 2. Actors—United States—Biography. 3. Motion picture producers and directors—United States—Biography. I. Title.

PN2287.C64A3 2015
791.4302'8092—dc23
[B]

2014044879

Cover design by Kelly Winton
Interior design by Megan Jones Design

COUNTERPOINT
2560 Ninth Street, Suite 318
Berkeley, CA 94710
www.counterpointpress.com

Printed in the United States of America
Distributed by Publishers Group West

10 9 8 7 6 5 4 3 2 1

Now, the Rainman gave me two cures,
Then he said, "Jump right in."
The one was Texas Medicine
The other was just Railroad Gin.
And like a fool I mixed them
And it strangled up my mind.
And now people just get uglier
And I have no sense of time.

—BOB DYLAN
"Stuck Inside of Mobile with the Memphis Blues Again"

One of the most important things to do is to keep cutting deliberately through political lines and barriers and emphasizing the fact that these are largely fabrications and that there is another dimension, a genuine reality, totally opposed to the fictions of politics. . . .

—THOMAS MERTON

For **all my teachers**, but especially for:

Susie and Ozzie Nelson—there are no words to express my gratitude.

My sister, **Elizabeth West**, the person I'd most have liked to become.

Gary Snyder, my first model of a fully-dimensional life.

Nino Cerruti, who offered me a second chance at a father.

Chikudo Lewis Richmond, my Buddhist teacher.

And **Stefanie**, for the deepest lessons.

ACKNOWLEDGEMENTS

T HIS BOOK HAS passed through a number of iterations, beginning as a political screed that effectively smothered the true book inside it. Once again, I am grateful beyond measure for the acuity and unvarnished honesty of my old friend and fellow writer, Terry Bisson, for helping me carve away the dross. The same credit needs to be shared with Stephen Molton, another fine writer who applied his intelligence and encouragement tirelessly to help me, and my dear friend Terry Strauss for her close read and comments. My sister, Elizabeth West, was an indefatigable ally who read and reread subsequent drafts, asking cogent questions, pointing out confusions and ambiguities that helped me clarify my intention in every case.

Once again, I am indebted to Counterpoint Press and Jack Shoemaker. While agents were dithering about how to "position" this book, Jack stepped up immediately to claim it. As with *Sleeping Where I Fall*, the process of transforming the manuscript into a book has been an author's dream from the beginning to final publication. I have to single out Kelly Winton's fine editing; Megan Fishman, director of publicity; and her able staff, Sharon Wu and Claire Shalinsky, who have been diligent and dedicated allies in their attempts to bring this book before the public. I would also like to thank Megan Jones for an attractive design, Irene Barnard for an excellent copyedit, and Matthew Grace and Joseph Goodale for proofreading the book carefully and accurately. Every author should have such a team.

I beg the forgiveness of anyone I have overlooked. This book has taken six years to finish and I'm sure I sought the aid of others during that time that I cannot recollect at the moment. I offer them the deepest apology if they have been overlooked.

—PETER COYOTE
    DECEMBER 11, 2014

FOREWORD

THE TITLE OF this book plays off the verse from Bob Dylan's "Stuck Inside of Mobile with the Memphis Blues Again" quoted above. Whatever Dylan's intent, I had personal referents when I first heard it in 1966. "Texas Medicine" was, for me, peyote, the hallucinogenic cactus. I'd taken it often, and had received my new name, Coyote, under its influence, liberating me in unexpected ways.

For the purposes of this book it represents the Ecstatic, the Transcendental, the inclusive, the collaborative and utopian possibilities of life—a shorthand for the world of Love. It is directly linked in my imagination to the democratic and spiritual intentions of the 1960s counterculture.

"Railroad Gin" was the lubricant of the Robber Barons, and the tonic of my parents' generation; the "go-juice" of those who compete for wealth, fame, and status. I enlist it here as a trope for the world of Power.

Those two options appeared to be my only available choices when I was younger and what seemed key was to get the mix right. Love without power was flaccid and Power without love was cruel. Love and Power were the frames through which I perceived the world and within them, sought to fashion a life. I pursued them both with a passion and diligence often more impulsive than strategic. Despite the mentors and teachers who appeared at each stage of my evolution and are chronicled in these tales, it is the folly of a young man to believe that he can pick and choose between what Love and Power offer him, keeping only the Light and leaving behind the Shadows.

The Third Cure came late, though it was there all along.

THE FIRST TWO CURES

T HE ROHATSU (the Great Cold) *sesshin*—a week of intensive Zen meditation—takes place in early December ending on the 8th, the day
commemorating Buddha's enlightenment. At Green Gulch Zen Center,
near my home on the fog-shrouded slopes of Mount Tamalpais in
Northern California's Marin County, meditation begins at 5:00 AM
and lasts until 9:30 PM each day punctuated by service, meals, walking
meditation, and several short rest periods. Talking, except for essential
communication, is discouraged, as is eye contact and any behavior that
might distract others from their concentration. It takes enormous collective effort to organize a *sesshin*, with volunteers cooking, serving,
and maintaining the Temple on behalf of those sitting. Consequently,
great care is taken not to waste the opportunity or the gift of their service. I knew none of this when I signed up for my first *sesshin* after only
a year of meditating, sitting, at most, two 40-minute periods a day at
the San Francisco Zen Center.

Nor did I know that in *sesshin* meals would be eaten in place at
one's sitting cushion, in the same painful cross-legged position one
had been meditating in. They are served in a highly efficient manner,
done precisely this way for hundreds of years. Each monk's eating

utensils—chopsticks, a wooden spoon, a cleaning apparatus called a *setsu* (resembling a doctor's tongue depressor with a cloth pad sewed on the tip)—are laid across three nesting bowls called *oryoki* (meaning "just enough")—covered by a napkin and cleaning cloth, the whole wrapped in a bandanna-sized cloth that, when unwrapped, is efficiently used as a place mat.

Because Zen Buddhism is not precisely a religion like the Abrahamic trio—Christianity, Judaism, and Islam, (Buddha was a normal man—neither supernatural nor a prophet)—behaviors that appear to the uninitiated as worship of a Deity are actually expressions of gratitude for the Buddha's compassionate teachings. By the end of the first highly ritualized meal, I was convinced entirely too much gratitude was being displayed and began wishing harm on the officiant whose chants and offerings had to end before I would be allowed to leave my seat and mercifully straighten my paralyzed legs.

There were chants of thanks when food was offered, chants after it was served, and more when the first bowl was raised. Before the servers entered bearing the food, the wooden bar in front of the sitters' places had to be cleaned. A damp towel was introduced and then either passed from hand to hand down the length of the room, or if one was graced with an elevated seat, propelled by a runner racing down the aisle between sitters scrubbing the "table" (the edge of the raised platform) as he went.

The servers moved quickly, but no matter how efficient they were, I wanted to scream with frustration, impatience, and pain, because until the meal is over and one's bowls washed and put away and the last chanted syllable uttered, you cannot rise from your seat. Furthermore, it is an arduous and delicate maneuver to change the position of crossed, cramped insensate legs without sending the delicate bowls in front of you skittering into the lap of the person sitting opposite you. The frustration was akin to being trapped behind a comatose driver at a stoplight that changes once an hour for twenty seconds and the moron in front of you misses it while texting. Imagine this occurring repeatedly, while you are on fire, and you'll have a clear idea of my state of mind.

Every task proceeded at its own agonizing pace. You cannot simply eat, wash your bowl, and leave to go fart and pick your teeth. At the signal of clacking wooden sticks we wait while the food is brought in to the *zendo* (meditation hall), served into each outstretched bowl (the serving bracketed by stately bows) and then, before it can be touched, a complex grace is offered reminding us where the Buddha was born, taught, and died, and what virtues each portion in our bowls is dedicated to. Then (still on fire), we are asked to consider "whether our virtue and practice deserve this offering" of food. I was deranged with frustration at the slowness, the waiting, the ritualized cleaning of the bowls and the collection of the last scraps of food for "the hungry ghosts." ("Fucking ants!! They're feeding *ants* while I'm dying here!") All of these ritual steps were inserted between my wretched self and the post-meal relief I desperately needed. I was furious. Every cell in my body was intent on inhaling my food as quickly as possible so that I could flee the *zendo* and straighten my legs. This was day *one*. By 7:00 AM I had forgotten that I had chosen to be there because I was desperate for help.

It's quite normal in *sesshin* for one's knees to be in pain, and muscles in the upper back and shoulders to be burning with tension or in spasm. It matters not. The pace of meals and services is glacial, and from my perspective that day, pitiless. The older monks sat quietly erect and maddeningly patient with no evidence of discomfort. By the second period of zazen, compounding my discomfort with embarrassment, my body began shaking violently, twitching and jerking as if I were experiencing a grand mal seizure. The shaking enervated my muscles, made me gasp for breath, and it was distracting, exhausting, and embarrassing. The monks on either side of me were still as oil paintings while I writhed and flapped like a landed fish between them. Restarting my recently abandoned use of heroin began to appear tantalizingly preferable to another sixty seconds of Zen.

In such a situation one is forced face-to-face with one's body and mind and their discomforts. There are no distractions and no places to hide. There is no way to pretend that your suffering is not occurring nor is there any way to philosophize it away. The *sesshin* demands everything you have and then takes a big gulp of more. An old Zen adage states, "Pain in the legs is the taste of zazen."

Even after a year of regular zazen, I was completely unprepared for the rigor and determination required by a *sesshin*. By lunch of the second day, my body was trembling and shaking and tears were spilling over the edges of my eyes. "I can't do this," I thought. "I have to get out of here." Internal narratives chronicling previous failures and self-betrayals were flashing like neon signs in my psyche and I began rehearsing excuses that might offer me the cover to flee; *anything* that would afford me the opportunity to rise from this odious, smug, self-satisfied *cushion*, and move spontaneously again.

Unfortunately for my craven and indulgent self, I was pinioned firmly in place by pride. There were a number of Zen students in the *sesshin* whom I had previously dismissed as fools, certain that my spiritual development exceeded theirs by a comfortable margin. I would never be able to maintain this imagined sense of superiority if I crawled out of the *zendo* on the second day. My ego dictated that I stay put.

Miraculously, near the end of the third day, my physical pains began to diminish. Though still shaking, I could investigate the pain in my knees more attentively, and noticed how investigation actually changed the quality of the pain. I continued my St. Vitus dance, but a certain amount of the emotional charge my shaking carried diminished as well. It was simply shaking.

On the very last day's break period, walking up the dusty road in a high, chilled wind, I had the distinct feeling that the entire center of my body had disappeared or become transparent. I could feel the wind whistling through it. I felt feather-light and momentarily problem-free; as if the back of my head had disappeared and the space behind my eyes opened out onto the universe. Before me, the world was extraordinarily vivid and alive, shimmering intensely. I had not taken a drug and yet I was truly "high." I thought, "This is nice! I'm gonna check Zen out a little further." Forty years later I'm still checking.

—◦—

I AM STANDING in a crib. I cannot see myself, but in the corner of my vision a small, plump hand grips the white plastic railing, and I "know" it as my own. The upright bars of the crib have rounded edges and the paint is enamel-smooth and glossy. The crib rests opposite a large window through which I can see a broad expanse of dun-colored, rippled water and a far shore, flanked by cliffs that are topped by trees. I am not conscious of any sound.

Between my crib and the window, on a low daybed, I see two human heads, some shoulders and arms, writhing on a rumpled white sheet. A man is lying on top of a woman, covering her with a back so broad it might be the shell of giant turtle. The woman is my young mother. She could be floating, or sleeping. Perhaps I made a sound of recognition. The man lifts his head and locks eyes with mine. His face is contorted into a mask of rictus; lips compressed and grim; his eyes unsettling in their intensity. I have no words for what I am observing, but it frightens me.

I learned years later that until I was eight months old, my parents lived in an apartment on Riverside Drive in Manhattan, overlooking the Hudson River. Their apartment window would have offered a clear view of the dramatic vertical cliffs, the Palisades, on the far shore in New Jersey.

My father, in this memory, if that is what it is, is the age he would have been when I was crib-bound, his hair black and un-silvered. The woman's face is turned aside and obscured by coils of rosy-gold hair, my mother's color when I was young. Her eyes are closed and the long lovely lashes are those I remember from later in life. Her body is barely visible beneath his. My father's strained expression might have been due to exertion during sex. Equally plausibly, it might have been a warning— his silent command not to disturb him. I would become familiar with this visual insistence later in life, always transmitted from his eyes with the force of a slap. It is my earliest image of my father, and it saddens me to acknowledge that this first impression was not love, but fear.

MY FATHER, MORRIS Cohon, was only five feet nine inches (a giant to a child) but his nineteen-inch neck and fifty-four-inch chest gave him a formidable solidity. He was handsome, with a virile, charismatic manner, a witty man capable of immense charm and extravagant generosity. However, a stratum of something molten lay just below his surface, leaking most visibly from his eyes.

Normally animated by a cool, appraising steadiness, those eyes were so dark the irises often appeared as black as his pupils. His gaze communicated a restless, barely sublimated irritation, as if its subject had already claimed more of his attention than it deserved. When he was angry, his regard could sting like a paper cut. His eyes moved in small calculating arcs like a blade, expressing an unmistakable intention to dominate what they measured. He was not incapable of love and sometimes-lugubrious Victorian sentimentality, but his more tender feelings were not easily expressed and only rarely in a form I could comprehend.

Even as a child, Morris possessed extraordinary physical strength, which he developed as a boxer, Greco-Roman wrestler, and black belt in judo. In a sepia-toned snapshot from his college days, he is lifting the front end of a Stutz Bearcat car off the ground for the amusement of his friends.

Morris made his first money anticipating the Depression and selling short for a boss who made a killing and rewarded him. He possessed an unusual facility with numbers, a skill that gained him entrance to MIT at fifteen and later served him in establishing his own stockbroker's firm and several other business concerns, all of which thrived for a long time. By the time I was able to follow his conversations, it became apparent that he possessed encyclopedic knowledge about a broad array of subjects, claiming that such breadth was required of him to be good at his various occupations.

His activities were indeed varied. He owned his own investment firm, Morris Cohon and Company, on Wall Street. Family friends credited him with "inventing" the over-the-counter stock market—the market for smaller companies not yet trading on the New York Stock Exchange, and he made a fortune bringing a number of them public. He became an expert in museum-quality American and English Colonial antiques and silver and bankrolled a famous antique dealer in Manhattan, a half-Cherokee Indian named John Walton, whose clients included DuPonts and Rockefellers.

Morris and his partner in the cattle business, Harl Thomas from Raymondsville, Texas, introduced French Charolais cattle to the United States, evading the legal ban on the breed initiated by Angus and Holstein breeders, by painting black spots on the magnificent white animals they had imported into Mexico and running them across the Rio Grande as Holsteins. Other business interests included the Phoenix-Campbell Oil Company and the Hudson and Manhattan Railroad and he served as president of both institutions. He was not Warren Buffett–rich perhaps, but he was rich enough to do damn near anything he wanted . . . except relax.

Morris's will was obdurately focused on winning—in the gym, in business, and in life. He wanted all the toys, privileges, and accoutrements that winners accrue. He set his sights on surrounding himself with "the best"—imitating English baronial traditions in his bespoke Dunhill suits and Prince of Norfolk jackets, dressing as if he were as tall, slender, and elegant as Lord Mountbatten, and not the swarthy half-Kazakh half-Spaniard he was. He took his possessions seriously, and felt comfortable only if he had assured himself that there were none finer; as if a lapse of taste might indicate some tainted strain of mediocrity within him. Consequently, Morris's furniture and silver were museum quality and featured in the magazine *Antiques*; his floors beautified with 18th-century silk Persian rugs. He hunted raccoons on his farms with hounds bought in Mississippi and Alabama, some for thousands of dollars. He was my earliest model of power; and for a young boy who sought a niche in his father's life and required his recognition and attention like a parched plant requires water, his focus rarely seemed to fall on me in any way I hoped it might.

MY MOTHER RUTH Fidler's family was a drop in the tidal wave of Russian and Eastern European Jews that crested and broke on the shores of America in the earliest days of the twentieth century. Fleeing lethal anti-Semitism abroad, many of these immigrants expressed their understanding of Old Testament justice as Socialists or Communists—a number of my relatives among them. They packed these ideas, along with their few clothes, hand-wrought copper teakettles and sooty pots, samovars, books, and culture and brought them to New York, eager for new beginnings

My mother's parents, Nat and Rose, and their relatives, the Fidlers and Adlers, had been raised in the cloistered ghettos of Eastern Europe. The elders spoke primarily Yiddish, kept Orthodox kosher homes and lived with the closeted reserve and suspicion of outsiders common to *shtetl* people. In the nutrient-rich broth of their closed community and culture, they tended to be warm-hearted, gregarious, and social, unlike Morris's people—who were wary, solitary, and high-status.

Morris's family—Cohons (K'han in Kazakhstan), DaSilvas (Silvers), Bartolomeos, and Mendeses—were immigrants like my mother's people, but wealthier, more secular, and cosmopolitan. One cousin, Pierre Mendes France, was the prime minister of France during whose term the French withdrew their forces from Vietnam. Morris's mother, Rae, came from a long line of Sephardic Jews who had thrived in capital cities in Morocco and Spain (until they were expelled in 1492 after the Reconquest of the Moors). Migrating to France and England, they made their living as skilled artisans, and chefs. Her people were proud and clannish, convinced of their superiority over all others, and especially the Eastern European Jews known as Ashkenazim—my mother's people.

Ruth's father, Nat, ran a little four-seat soda fountain/candy store in the Bronx, where he sold notions, penny candies, and magazines. Ruth had her eyes fixed on grander vistas. Tall and slender, naturally refined, with high cheekbones and warm, empathetic eyes, as soon as she was able to she migrated from the Bronx, working as a model in Manhattan, an aspiring jazz singer, and later as a secretary for Walter Winchell, the notorious gossip columnist at the *New York Daily Mirror*. Before and after matriculating from Hunter College, she absorbed social information and cues from glossy weeklies and films, assiduously polishing the Yiddish, the rough accents, and nasal Bronx resonance from her speech until she spoke as if she were performing in her own *film noir*. (My mother confessed to me once that she had named me "Peter" because she had heard Bette Davis utter the name in a movie. "It was impossibly elegant dear, and I knew in that moment that if I had a son, I would name him Peter.") This genetic heritage may also explain the exaggerated role imagination came to assume in my life, as well as my predilection for sometimes allowing fantasy to alter unpleasant facts.

Ruth absorbed Manhattan style, elegance, and manners by studying fashion magazines, the customers, and salesgirls in fine stores as if she was consciously preparing herself for the wealthy and elegant life she eventually secured with Morris.

They met through a mutual friend in the silvery glitter of New York nightlife. Morris moved fluidly and authentically between polymorphic identities: a chess-playing intellectual, a financier in white linen suit and Panama hats, or a rugged working farmer on his ranch. Ruth loved the gloss and finish of his butter-soft chestnut-colored shoes, his flair and panache, and even the slender Romeo y Julieta Cuban cigars he favored. Traipsing among prizefighters, gangsters, professors, chess masters, cattle ranchers, and businessmen, Morris squired Ruth through shimmering evenings at the opera, theater, and ballet as well, laying before her a world she had previously admired only across the divide of class and status. She was an eager student, absorbing everything, noticing the assured conversations and languid manners of the entitled men and women she met, marking names she recognized from the daily papers. Morris must have appeared to her as a virile, bulletproof embodiment of America's opportunities and promises and she wanted them all. Ruth was a prize, a true beauty and Morris pursued her with relentless ardor until the two were soon married. They produced me and then nineteen months later, my sister, Elizabeth, known from my earliest memory as Muffet.

WHEN I WAS eight months old, Morris and Ruth moved from Manhattan to the stately town of Englewood, New Jersey, on the far side of those cliffs I had observed in my crib-bound memory. In the early years of the century, Englewood had been a millionaire's playground. Gloria

Swanson owned a gated estate on Woodland Street, up the hill from our house, a broad avenue running perpendicular to my own at the hill's crest, dotted with impressive stone mansions.

Our house at 90 Booth Avenue was an ample, three-story brown shingled home with spacious, high-ceilinged rooms, a generous front porch, and a screened-in side porch. Booth Avenue itself was a broad street shaded by large, mature maples and its homes were usually fronted by generous lawns. The neighborhood felt solid and calm and immune to disaster. Directly behind my uphill neighbor's house was a dense wood and year-round brook where I spent many days exploring and playing.

◄○►

THE NEIGHBORHOOD MIGHT have felt immune to misfortune, but the inoculation failed for my household. When I was two and a half or so, my mother suffered an incapacitating breakdown and became unable to care for me and my sister. Her weight plummeted to ninety pounds and she was lobotomized by depression. She disappeared from my sight and consciousness. I don't know many details because neither she nor my father ever once discussed or alluded to it. This period, which lasted for about two and a half years, remains vague to me, like observing events through dimpled glass, but it is characterized in my memory by a sense of anxiety and loss. Ruth was a shadowy, uneasy presence muffled in an impenetrable solitude. My father was gone all day. The job of caring for my sister and me fell, by chance and good fortune, to one of the most remarkable women I have ever known.

A year before my mother's breakdown, my father's sister, Aunt Ruth—an artist who designed textiles and linoleum—was browsing in a fabric store near her home in Paterson, New Jersey. A Negro woman in her early thirties, her teenage son, and a tall, teenaged black girl with her were the only other customers. The boy was bored and fooling around and his mother began reprimanding him stridently. The teenager, sixteen year old Susie Howard, had recently arrived in Paterson from Henderson, North Carolina, seeking opportunities not available to her in the South. She had been fired that day from her job sewing coats for the Army after they discovered her age. She was far from home, broke and out of work, and rooming with a family friend, the older woman, she had accompanied to the store. Sixteen and broke or not, she was also Susie Howard, and would face down the Devil at the crossroads before she would quit or retreat. Sue's landlady was exasperated with her son and resorting to threats of the "Shut up! Stop foolin' around or I'm gonna whup you" variety.

The harangue chafed Sue's sense of right and wrong and she spoke up. "Shut up?" she said. "Tone down *yourself*. If you want your child to behave, you have to *show* him how you want him to be. And if you want him to say 'please,' you got to say 'please' when *you* talk to him."

In the face of such effrontery, Susie's landlady was momentarily speechless, but as I was to learn, it was like Sue to lay everything on the line. She had been taught "how to be" and by God, as a descendant of the Coley and the Howard clans, she was damn sure going to *be* the way they taught her. Never one to surrender an advantage, Susie pressed on with a lecture about kindness, courtesy, and modeling good behavior.

Aunt Ruth, heretofore half-listening, now studied the outspoken girl. She visually catalogued her clear, light chocolate–colored skin and almond-shaped eyes. She noted her high cheekbones, open, amiable features, her good humor and ready laugh, and she particularly appreciated her courage for standing up for what she felt was right.

Acting on impulse, Aunt Ruth approached Susie and placed her hands on her shoulders (something I cannot imagine happening between black and white strangers today) and said, "Do you have a job?"

"I just *knew* something would work out," Sue said to me years later and her laughter's overtones of sandpaper on wood still reflected that early self-confidence. Answering my Aunt boldly, she said, "No, but I'm sure *looking* for one." Aunt Ruth offered her a job helping her care for her children on the spot.

Susie was a perfect fit for Aunt Ruth's household and the two women grew close. Susie knew about children. At fourteen she had begun caring for other people's kids in Henderson, and for that work received what, was to her, the astounding salary of $13.00 a week, working for the white family who ran the town's tobacco-processing operation. Thirteen dollars was a *lot* of money in that place and time. Sue's father made $1.50 a *week* at the bag factory, and her mother made $1.00 a day picking tobacco, at which she so excelled that she was paid twice the going rate of fifty cents a day. Susie had abundant good sense, and was smart and shrewd, as plucky as if she had survived a lightning strike. She had been diligently trained to cook and keep house by her grandmother and another local woman and had been working at that trade since she was ten years old.

One day shortly after my mother's breakdown, Aunt Ruth approached her and said, "Susie, you're never going to get ahead on the twenty-five dollars a week I can afford to pay you. My brother needs help. His wife is *really* sick and they need someone to care for their kids. He can pay you eighty-five dollars a week *and* give you free room and board. You'll be able to send a lot more money home. I hate for you to leave my house, but I think you should do it. It's better for you, and he'll be good to you." And that is how Sue Howard entered my life.

When she came to work for my family Sue was, at first, just another in a succession of anonymous caregivers, but she did not remain anonymous for long. Her job was to care for my sister and me. There was a housekeeper who would see to cleaning, cooking, and household chores. I was around three when Susie moved in. My dad was gone all day and when he was home, aside from mealtimes, he continued working after dinner in an upstairs office with Mrs. Whitehead, his after-hours secretary, a plump dry woman who reminded me of a large-breasted, blue-serge turkey. My mother was confined in the locked ward of her depression, removed from me as certainly as if she were encased in glass. Both of my parents were distracted and often upset. Dark moods flickered through the house like heat lightning, and, adding insult to injury, my sister Muffet had recently appeared, claiming half the minimal attention previously available to me. I was not happy about it.

I was wave-tossed through these disturbing years of early childhood until Susie Howard became my emotional anchor. Before long, she had inserted herself seamlessly into our daily life—displacing the housekeeper who'd been caught stealing and dismissed—and was instantly promoted from nanny to majordomo. Along the way she became my surrogate mother, a stabilizing force in my daily life, and so critical to the stability and functioning of our home that her absence became inconceivable. She deserves a book of her own, but for this tale, suffice it to say, the combination of my love for her and my marveling at her personal power—palpable to everyone who met her—was a source of enduring fascination to me.

Within a year or two my mother Ruth reappeared as a presence in the household, though memories of her as a distracted wraith lingered. My mother was quiet. She was sweet. She talked to me, she shopped, she read, she played solitaire, she drank Cutty Sark and soda, but all without apparent purpose or commitment. The problems that had driven her to collapse were still present—Morris was still an obdurate, uncontrollable, demanding force and she had not devised effective defenses against him. While I was relieved to see her up and about I don't remember that it changed the dynamics of the household much. The sun around which I orbited was Susie. I cared about my mother certainly and remember worrying about her and wanting to "fix" her—an impulse I carried forward into too many adult relationships with women—but my affections for her were tangled with old hurts and a child's blame for "abandoning me" to her illness and later my father's predations.

Ruth must have understood that she was damaged. She adored Susie and appreciated her role in running and stabilizing the household, but she would not have been human if her respect had never been tinged with jealousy about having been displaced as a mother. She had offered her sanity as a buffer between her children and Morris and while we were now safe and well cared for, her sacrifice had been enormous. Unaware of the details of her struggle, my sister and I transferred our loyalties to Sue with barely a glance over our shoulders.

SUSIE HOWARD HAD burst into our troubling and unpredictable environment with the insistence of morning sun burning off frost. To a small,

confused boy, she was an awesome, smiling, playful, trumpet-voiced giant; a force field of positive, can-do energy; a whirlwind delicious to be swept up by. Once I adjusted to the shock of the freedom she displayed, in short order I was clinging to her like iron filings to a magnet. The problems that confounded me with my parents disappeared when I was with her, and consequently I chose to be with her often.

For the next ten years Susie Howard was the North Star around which my solar system revolved. She included in her orbit an extended family of black friends, black music, black speech, and black perspectives—a world I wanted to and was allowed to join. Sue, her boyfriend (and later her husband) Ellsworth "Ozzie" Nelson, and their friends Jules Cowl—an upholsterer who was, like Sue, part Cherokee—John and Violet Ellerbee, and my father's chauffeur Melvin Christopher, whom everyone called Chris, lit up the house like flashes of black lightning. With Sue "in charge," the otherwise silent days were now punctuated by music—Errol Garner, Billie Holiday, and Sue herself singing "He Takes Me Off His Income Tax" along with the radio. Instead of long, quiet, dull hours alone in my room, laughter and raucous arguments made the days convulse and breathe. Susie and Jules pursued long, impossibly convoluted arguments about civil affairs, politics, and the Bible, while Ozzie mocked their seriousness by making quizzical faces that collapsed me with laughter. Ozzie's friend John Ellerbee was like Ozzie, short and low-waisted, but where Ozzie's skin was the color of coffee with plenty of milk in it, John was inky-black, with an outsized head and muscles stacked along his body like cordwood. He was fascinating as a tiger, intimating danger.

Life with Sue was not emotionally complex. My feelings around her were uncomplicated—usually happy and without anxiety. Black speech was a captivating new music. Its range of pitches and rhythms, punctuated and underscored by expressive physical posturing and gestures, cascaded through ranges of notes I had no idea were available to conversation. Expressed with the entire body, speech became musical, more alive than the measured cadences and utterances of my parents' white friends and shopkeepers.

I drank it in and must have absorbed much, because I remember my mother once saying to me with a subtly critical edge, "My God, darling, sometimes you sound just like a little black boy." I knew that she was signaling disapproval, but I couldn't have cared less. If that was how Susie spoke, that was how I spoke.

Black people sang, laughed, danced, argued, teased, and shouted. Everything appeared to be on the surface and transparent to me. There were no uneasy silences or fermenting emotions. When they spoke, they were loud and self-assured; like Morris their voices made the air vibrate. When they were quiet, they were just quiet, and I did not fear that they might be angry and ready to explode. They introduced me to a sense of play and, most importantly, how to laugh at my own suffering. *Life*, with all its flowers, fruits, and brambles, bloomed in the previously sterile soil of my house. I observed in black people possibilities of being I could not have imagined, and spontaneously adopted them wholeheartedly as my role models and new family, as a child does: without guilt, confusion, or regret.

Sue brooked no arguments, but neither was she normally angry, irritable, moody, or unhappy. She had heaved the entire deadweight of our family onto her back and carried it around as if it were weightless as a sack of promises. That accomplishment alone lent substance to my conviction that she was magical. When she warned me that if I misbehaved she would know because she could "hear a mouse pissin' in cotton"—I never doubted her supernatural abilities.

Sue Howard would become my most profound early teacher, the prism through which other strata of power and the mysterious frequencies of "race" were made comprehensible. Under her influence I was offered a safe perch outside "white" culture, to view it at a remove—a life-altering perspective unappreciated at the time, but which I later came to appreciate as her most valuable gift. She had invisibly and innocently offered me the option of escaping "whiteness"—at its root an identification with "white" culture and the political and extra-legal systems designed to protect and perpetuate its dominance. "Whiteness" is a creation of power that has little to do with being a Caucasian. Just understanding that there was a way to be *outside* of it and to claim commom humanity rather than race was my first experience, unconscious though it might have been, of liberation.

—◁◦▷—

I POINTED OUT earlier how Morris inhabited each of his protean identities—banker, rancher, corporate president, chess and Go master, antiques expert—fully and authentically. What was most vexing and puzzling to me as a child, however, was his ability to bury all other contradictory aspects of his personality so deeply that when one appeared, it felt as if the others had never existed.

He could be a loyal, generous friend—a compassionate man who wept at the misfortune of others. Correspondence and records uncovered after his death revealed a number of young people whose college educations had been charitably underwritten by him. He was honorable in business, and loyal to a fault. He surrendered to laughter like no other force on earth, slapping his legs, weeping with joy, and sobbing for breath in an amazing display that never failed to delight my sister and me.

But he was also quixotic and changeable as blustery weather. His emotions were undependable, anarchic, and often violent and explosive. On a good day he might tousle my hair and laugh at something I did or failed to do. In the next moment he might be distracted, irritable, threatening, or angry. Never sure of what to expect, I galvanized my attention to him, studied his moods and proclivities so thoroughly it made it impossible to attend to myself. I studied his certainty and his forcefulness as if he were a textbook of manhood, trying to determine how he managed it. I also studied him as a textbook of threat.

◄○►

TURKEY RIDGE FARM was the great love affair of Morris's life, more important than his marriage, his business, or his relationships with his children. He was attached to it in a deep, mystical way and offered the most creative, selfless part of himself to it. Besides loving it myself as a source of endless adventure and play, it was also the place where I came closest to receiving what I needed from my father.

Turkey Ridge was a two-hour drive from Englewood, west on Highway 46, which brought us to the Delaware River—the shared border with Pennsylvania. We crossed the river through a stately old wooden covered bridge and emerged on the desultory main street of Portland, Pennsylvania, a one-stoplight town a few miles south of the Delaware Water Gap, the deep notch in the Appalachian Mountain

range carved out hundreds of millions of years ago by the abrasion of
the river and collisions of tectonic plates. Perhaps Morris loved this
place so much because of the evidence of massive force so clearly visible there.

In the 1930s Morris had bought the old 150-acre homestead from
a family named Williams. It was situated on a broad flat just below
the crest of the hill, three miles uphill from the town. A working farm,
its solid early-nineteenth-century house had a stone foundation and
waist, wide yellow-pine floorboards, three fireplaces, and clapboard
sides, topped with a roof of locally mined slate. Next to the house was
a small shed and beside that was a large barn with an upper story at
driveway level reserved for hay, and a lower level reserved for cattle.
The barn let out to a large pasture, and where the gate to that pasture
was hinged, a clear, cold spring-box oozed into a bed of wilo fresh
mint frequented by snakes.

Opposite the barn Morris constructed a generous machine shop/
garage that could easily hold four vehicles. Just below it, terminating
the driveway a large aluminum gate contained the cattle as they moved
between the barn, an upper pasture, and new bull-barns and hay-barn
Morris also had constructed. On the far side of the cows' causeway
was an old manager's cottage my dad used as an office. Like the barn
and shed it was painted red with dark green trim and like every building on the property save the tin-roofed shop, it was topped with local
slate.

In the first years we began going there as a family, Morris's manager was an old, unshaven man named Art Donovan, who lived in
the cabin's one room. He, his clothes, and the room smelled of wood
smoke and liquor. One day he was no longer there, and when I inquired

about him Morris answered simply, "He shot himself," and said no more. Later details from the farm's new manager confirmed that he had crawled into a hollow log in the woods and killed himself there— an image that haunted me for years.

Morris spent every moment he could spare at Turkey Ridge, building his burgeoning cattle business, and designing and drawing the blueprints for additional barns and sheds. His new manager, Jim Clancy, and two hired hands, Walt and Bill, milled the lumber from our forests on a portable sawmill, constructing these new buildings, pens, and fences from the fragrant oak and hickory timber. They cut and tended the crops, livestock, and performed the myriad chores required on a working farm.

Morris acquired property like an addict, until, by the time of his death, he owned five or six farms comprising nearly 3,000 acres. Besides summers, we spent as many weekends there as my mother would bear and when she could bear no more, or if the weather was slightly moody—cold, icy, or rainy—Morris would go by himself, leaving the Englewood house at the slightest excuse, at any hour of the night, sometimes taking me with him. A patter of rain on the roof in Englewood would move him to leave immediately for Turkey Ridge so that he could sleep in the rain there. On snowy mornings, I often found him in a sleeping bag on the open farmhouse porch, huddled against the stacked cordwood and drifted over with snow, sleeping like a baby.

I received his best there because as soon as we reached the farm, his mood lightened. The tensions and pressing concerns of Wall Street and Englewood evaporated and his posture seemed to straighten, his shoulders rise. He'd change into his long-sleeved Henley undershirt, his black hat, ripped sheepskin vest, and boots, and dive into the life of the place, often working at his blacksmith's forge, forcing cherry-red iron to his will.

I was free there as well, released from his hypercritical observation of me, his criticisms and corrections, and abandoned to my own entertainments and whims. While Morris worked with the men planning, repairing, branding, and medicating the animals; deciding which fields would be for hay and which for grazing; assessing the equipment and deciding about repairs and purchases; I was free to wander the woods, hunt for snakes, fish, and daydream to my heart's content.

During the heavy summer rains, when the thunder cracked and rumbled, lightning flickered through the clouds and the ozone-rich air felt dense as a damp wool shawl, Morris would sometimes gather me under an arm and climb to the top of the hay-loft in the tin-roofed bull-barn. He would position us directly beneath the roof, and wrapping us in a rough horse blanket as the rains began, nursed a bottle of pear brandy until he fell asleep. I lay beside his enormous chest, towering over me like a cliff face, enveloped by the sound of drumming rain. Since then, there has never been a rainy day in my life when memories of that simple happiness have not returned to me as a balm. My father had *chosen* to be with me, and at such moments my heart would drop its guard and open to him as only a boy's can. I loved him totally, without measure or reproach in those moments, as if I had been blessed by the attentions of a god.

ONE AUTUMN WEEKEND just past my tenth birthday, my dad and I were en route to the farm. Morris pulled the car over and parked in downtown Englewood. Commanding me to wait, he disappeared into a sporting goods store. When he returned he carried a single-shot Stevens .410 shotgun. "This is for you," he said, laying it across the backseat. I was stunned. My father had just bought me a real gun! I imagined him teaching me to shoot rabbits, quail, and grouse, as he did, and spent the two-hour journey imagining long hours with the two of us hunting the stone rows, wood-lots, and fields together. I barely watched the road that trip, but spent most of it hanging over the back of my seat (before seat belts), studying my new weapon, reveling in its potency and imagining the altered relationship with my father it implied.

The instruction I had hoped for did not materialize. It was beyond Morris's temperamental capacity. I was disappointed, but that disappointment in no way diminished the grandeur of the gift. After rigorous safety instruction, I was left to my own devices with it, and it is a testament to an earlier, carefree age, that at ten years old I was allowed to wander free and unsupervised with a loaded shotgun.

◄◦►

JIM CLANCY WAS Morris's foreman at Turkey Ridge. A calm, self-contained and confident man with a classic Scotch-English "cowboy face" featuring flat planes, high cheekbones, and a dashing aquiline nose resembling the movie heroes I admired in the Saturday matinees. Jim favored checked wool lumberjack shirts and carried a sheathed hunting knife on his belt. A beaten-up cap perched on his head at a jaunty angle. He was everything that books, movies, and imagination demanded a man should be: handsome, unflappable, cool, strong, and best of all, friendly and accessible to me. Starved for adult male company, I began dogging his footsteps when I could.

Jim's and his wife Ellie's cabin, a half-mile down the dirt road from our house, was just out of sight around a bend in the dirt road that ran past Turkey Ridge (always referred to by us as "The Farm"). It was the first place I was allowed to walk by myself at a very early age and every walk there was an adventure spiced by heady feelings of independence.

Jim's small kitchen was overheated by a large beige enameled wood-stove trimmed in pale green. Over the lintels of his doors, rifles and fishing rods rested, ready for use, and the outside walls bore clusters of leg-traps and split-wood backpacks. The interior walls were hung with paintings by Ellie, who created naïf oils of local landscapes, creeksides, and forest glens. Until I was nearly grown, Ellie always greeted my arrival with a shrill hog-caller's cry—"Peeeetey . . . Peeeetey-*rabbit!*"— emphasizing the last word abruptly. In those days, I suppose I was a sweet little bunny-boy.

I liked the Clancy cabin, which was small enough to be quickly comprehended: One bedroom, a kitchen, bathroom, and living room comprised the whole, much closer to child-size than the four-bedroom farmhouse or the brown-shingled, three-story Englewood house and its expansive porches, lawns, garage, and storage shed. I was content to watch Jim oil and clean his revolver or organize his fishing tackle— arranging the shiny lures and colorfully feathered fishing-flies in small metal cough drop and ginger tins. I preferred helping him categorize and separate his lures or feed his dogs, chickens, ducks, and pet raccoons than returning home for lunch. Besides, if I lingered, Ellie, a true backwoods mountain woman (a "Cunnerman" as she referred to herself), would make me egg and bacon sandwiches on thick slices of homemade bread and offer me pie, hot from the warming oven. The only task required of me to receive this largesse, was to whirl the crank on the black wall telephone and ask the local operator to ring my house. When the two longs and a short ring brought my mother to the phone, I would announce proudly, "I'm staying at Ellie's, mom. 'Bye!" Only then was I allowed to eat.

Everything about Jim was fascinating: his encyclopedic knowledge of nature, the smell of wood smoke in his clothes, the careful preservation of his tools and personal items. Perhaps most important to me, was that I knew him for many years before I ever saw him angry. Unlike Morris he never splintered the kitchen chairs or kicked the dog so hard it had to be taken to the vet. He did not shout and curse and make me flee the house in fear. His self-discipline marked him to me as a superior being.

Jim's life was modest but completely adequate, and its scale sometimes raised uncomfortable issues with me. There was a showiness about Morris that could embarrass me and make me uncomfortable, interfering with my admiration for him. I wished he could be more restrained and heroic, like Jim, but Morris left large footprints where he passed, moving as if tearing a hole through space, insisting that whatever he desired be "the best," whether appropriate to his level of skill or not. He might buy a brand new tool, or farm implement on impulse, and abandon it to gather dust once his curiosity had been satisfied.

Jim, on the other hand, owned little, but what he did possess was well cared for and kept in the same perfect order as he maintained our farms. His clothes were carefully patched and stylish to me in their functionality. The evidence of his careful repairs indicated an aspect of Jim's character I admired and have tended to emulate from then onward, incurring criticism from two wives. From every perspective he was my first idea of the man I thought I might want to be one day. My father was simply too exalted to consider emulating.

MORRIS ASKED JIM to teach me to fish, and from that request and what followed I received a profound and confounding lesson. I could not have been more than six or seven when Jim began by teaching me to thread a living worm on a hook. "Does it hurt the worm?" I asked nervously. Jim looked at me then asked me what I thought. I regarded the writhing creature on my hook, understood that it could not feel good and said so. "That's right," Jim said. "But we have to do that to catch and eat fish. We don't hurt things for no reason."

After worms, Jim began instructing me in the use of a spinning rod and how to cast the shimmering lures out into our lake; to jerk the rod once to set the spinner moving and then retrieve it at the right speed—reel the line in too quickly and the fish would not expend the energy to chase it, too slowly and even the dumbest bass sunfish, or perch could discern that the lure was a mechanical toy. Jim taught me to tie knots that would not come undone, and how to imagine being in the water and looking up like a fish, to "see" the lure against the sky from underneath and to adjust my choice of lure depending on the light.

After I had become proficient with a spinning line, Jim began instruction on the rudiments of fly-fishing. He patiently drilled me in the rhythm of waiting for my line to straighten out behind me on the back-cast before flicking it forward, and how to lay the fly lightly on the water's surface without splashing the line or leader first and scaring the fish. He taught me to turn over rocks to discover what insects were about to emerge, notice flying bugs, and how to read "the hatch" of insects and match them to appropriate flies. Most importantly, he taught me to slow down, to relax, and meter my youthful enthusiasm. Forty years later, I transmitted those same skills to my son.

ONE AUTUMN DAY, perhaps a year after Jim's fishing instructions began, I was working on a piece of pie in his cabin and grazing through a back issue of *Fur-Fish-Game*, a trapper's magazine Jim subscribed to. I saw photos of boys only slightly older than myself posing proudly with muskrats and beavers they had caught and I thought it would be grand to be one of them. I wanted to master that skill, to be such a boy, and I asked Jim to teach me to trap.

We peeled thin strips of maple bark and boiled them into a broth to lubricate the metal leg-traps and also disguise any scent of humans. After boiling, Jim, wearing the canvas gloves that had been stored outside in the split-oak backpack, loaded the prepared traps and gloves and shoes that he wore only for trapping. He added an old canvas ground-cloth, some thin wire, a small hand-spade, and a section of coarse screen. With everything in order, we set off for the woods together early one morning, our breath steaming and the hoarfrost thick on the fallen leaves crackling and crunching underfoot.

We tramped through the timber, which Jim kept thinned and clean of deadfalls. The trees were resplendent in autumn rusts and gold, and like me, I thought, quivering with anticipation. Jim identified good locations for my "sets"—explaining the way different species of animals thought, foraged, and fed. He taught me to read signs and notice where the animals went to root and scratch. He began in the most rudimentary fashion, constructing a little stone shelter about ten inches by ten inches, closed off at one end, and employing a large flat stone for a roof. We buried a trap at the mouth, being careful to lay all the removed dirt on the canvas cloth, and returned it by shaking it lightly over the trap through a screen. Then we shook leaves over the dirt. In the back of the lean-to, I placed a half a sparrow I had shot for the occasion with my BB gun.

The next morning I was up early and waiting when Jim arrived. We returned to check our sets, shushing through the leaves in air crisp as a green apple. I was nervous with anticipation and overjoyed, in the woods with my hero—life could not have been finer. Perhaps I was going to see a wild animal alive and up close. The first two sets were empty, and as we approached the third, a flutter and rustle in the leaves prompted goose bumps on my arms and legs. A weasel, already half-transformed into his white winter coat (which would make him an ermine), was held fast by a rear leg. He sat up in the leaves, regarding me intently and gazed directly into my eyes. I "heard" him (in my mind) ask me, as clearly as if he'd spoken aloud, "What are you going to do to me?"

I was stunned. I hadn't anticipated anything like this. I looked to Jim for guidance. I could see the weasel's hind leg was bloodied and raw from the jaws of the trap. I hadn't anticipated causing pain either. I was conflicted and suddenly guilty and I did not know what to do. Without hesitation, and before I could protest, Jim killed the weasel with a blow from a fallen stick.

I sublimated my unease while he taught me how to skin it and stretch the skin inside out over a narrow board he had me whittle to a point at one end. I did this soberly and in silence, no longer certain that what had transpired was what I had originally intended. Jim said nothing. Perhaps he had not heard the weasel speak to me, or perhaps he had and chose to leave me alone with my own reactions and feelings. I could not be sure, but I was definitely thinking about what had just transpired.

A day later, we visited another set, and an immense raven was held fast by one leg, regarding us as we approached. He was as still as if he were carved from slate, fearless and apparently unperturbed. He surveyed Jim calmly and then turned his head and regarded me. Inside my mind, as before, I heard or in some way "saw" a clear plea not to kill him. This time, on the verge of panic, I spoke up quickly, "Let's let him go, Jim."

"We've injured him," Jim said. "We can't," and dispatched it with a blow. Killing creatures that could communicate, that bled and suffered, was unnerving and pierced me with remorse. Perhaps this was the lesson that Jim had intended for me because as we walked home through the woods together, he began the first of what would become a long series of teachings about what he referred to as "The Laws of Nature"—the interconnectedness of everything.

"It looks like just dead leaves, doesn't it?" Jim queried, indicating the leaf-litter carpeting the forest floor. "But together, all those leaves make a blanket that protects the roots of the trees from freezing under the snow. Everything has a purpose, even death, even if we don't understand it. Nature operates for its own concerns, not man's." He continued, explaining how flowers could not exist without bees, or we humans either, tracing the relationships simply and clearly; cinching the connections of my personal life to microbes in the soil required for plants to grow, to sunlight and to water. As he continued to link apparently disparate living forms together I received an image of the world like a tangled ball of yarn with every object and species caught in its wrap. Jim spoke to me in a patient manner, waiting for my understanding to settle before proceeding. I had no idea at the time that I would never forget anything he ever told me.

After heavy snows, we would sometimes walk out together and thread ears of dried corn with baling wire, tying groups of five or six around tree trunks so that they radiated outward like jets of flame. "When the snow is too deep, the deer can't feed," Jim explained. "Sometimes we have to help them." As we headed out dragging our bag of corn that morning, I realized that other than fishing, I had never seen Jim hunt or kill anything. Except once.

It was after a deep snow and Jim wandered out carrying his rifle. He had noticed a large pack of feral dogs in the area, dogs brought out to the country and abandoned by their owners. Normally they were not a problem, but the deep snow could trap deer, and the apparently "harmless" mutts, light enough to be supported by the snow's crust, could maim or kill immobilized deer. Meticulously and methodically Jim shot the pack of feral dogs. "What'll we do with them, Jim?" I asked.

"They won't go to waste," Jim said. "Foxes, coons, skunks— everything'll eat 'em." Then he muttered, "Sons-of-bitches," as we turned for home.

"The dogs?" I asked, thinking that he didn't like them.

"No, the owners," he said. "People who would turn a pet loose to fend for itself." I had seen those dogs in summertime, making heart-breaking efforts to catch the receding cars that had abandoned them; had felt their desperation and fear, but in that moment, walking away from the bodies splayed in the snow, I couldn't figure out who was worse, those heartless owners, or Jim and me.

After the raven's death, I let the subject of trapping lapse and Jim did not bring it up again either. I wish I could testify that due to my innate sensitivity I abandoned hunting after those early encounters, but that would be false. I loved guns and the power they afforded me and I became skilled at using them. Later in my life, during the hard-scrabble 1960s, I became a successful poacher, bringing home much appreciated meat for the communes I lived on. However, Jim's lessons were never far from my mind, and even as I hunted, true to his instruction I sought out the runts, the wounded, the outliers, culling the weak as a predator would and by observing "the laws of nature," helping the healthy and vigorous to transmit their genes forward, keeping the species strong.

During that same period in the Sixties, when a drive for spiritual insight and specific knowledge of place drove me to seek out Native American elders and teachers, I was not surprised to discover that their stories and perspectives reinforced Jim's early lesson and understood my good fortune in having had such a mentor as a boy. In some manner, all the stories that follow are as concerned with my teachers as they are about the knowledge they bequeathed. Each became a part of my sense of self, and whatever I may be today that might be worth emulating is made of these men and women and of what I took away from them.

-◦-

THE EASY TIMES with Morris disappeared when we returned to Englewood. Changes in me as I aged also exacerbated tensions between us. Experiences with Jim and Ellie Clancy had afforded me a safe perch outside my family and that perspective had been helpful in clarifying differences between life inside and outside my house. This period, between five and eight or so years old, was marked by the discovery that I was a distinct personality and definitely separate from my parents, but this knowledge also appeared to provoke and challenge my father in some way.

I remember a clarifying incident vividly. I was running on my front lawn one balmy summer evening after dinner, distracting myself about some situation that had disturbed me during the course of the day, but that I had been unable to articulate. As I whirled and twirled through the odors of fresh-cut grass and blossoming flowers and danced among the winking fireflies, I remember "seeing" the inexpressible dynamic as images in my mind's eye and comforting myself by thinking, "Oh, my *mind* knows what I mean." It is my earliest memory of a conscious "self," an awareness of awareness co-existing with my physical body.

Knowledge of this separation prompted a fascinated curiosity and I began to move through the world with the sensation of being somehow split; one eye was looking out probing the generally accepted public reality and the other was gazing in, probing the mystery of my interior responses and feelings. It changed my behavior to a degree, making me spacey and distracted, preoccupied by the tension between the two. These changes appeared to affect Morris negatively. What had previously been a relationship of benign neglect, random displays of affection, toleration, advice, and occasional anger on his part, began at this time to feel more stressed and suffused with an underlying irritation; as if I were teetering dangerously away from his control, a situation he appeared to find threatening; as if I had discovered a secret refuge to which he was denied entrance.

Around this time too I also began to observe Morris's intemperate behavior more clearly. He appeared to be throwing tantrums more often, enraged at telephone operators, at the fact that he could not find his glasses, at the dog, at my leaning back in one of his antique chairs. "That chair's worth fifty thousand fucking dollars," he'd snap, turning on me with physical menace. The causes of his perturbation changed from moment to moment and day to day, making life unpredictable and unnerving. And for the first time, daily life became increasingly confrontational, filled with inexplicable threats and danger. Perhaps it had always been this way, and I had simply become conscious of it.

Morris possessed so many demonstrable skills, which were honored and recognized by the world; he exhibited such certainty and competence and could be so charming and dazzling, that as a boy I felt impossibly diminished beside him. I felt that I could never approach the scale of his accomplishments. Because of the respect he received from so many adults, I assumed the faults he often highlighted in me— "Watch what you're doing!" "How can you be so fucking stupid?" "What've you got, shit-for-brains?"—*were* mine and I accepted his criticisms and disapproval as both descriptive and deserved. From this perspective, even his lack of daily attention seemed justified.

Learning to read Morris's moods became critical to my survival, not to mention household stability and order. One had to understand when "Yelling from room to room," talking on the telephone (when he wanted it), being depressed when he returned from work in a good mood, or being overly playful when he returned in a bad mood might ignite a conflagration, blazing through the house like a gas explosion, making home precarious and tense for hours.

Luckily for all of us, Morris's violence towards his family was verbal. To his credit he never laid a hand on my mother, sister, or me in anger. However the deeper threat—the certain knowledge of his violence, the lore of peers and family of the harm and beatings he had administered to others—was a dominant feature of his reputation. My anxiety as a child was predicated on the observation that his violence was only precariously restrained . . . and by what? That question came to dominate my concerns with him.

ONE AFTERNOON, I could not have been over six, Morris arrived home from work with two pairs of purple boxing gloves, holding them aloft like prize eggplants. He announced that he was going to teach me "to take care" of myself. I was thrilled.

Excited by seeing the gloves and the prospect of learning to be a fighter, I began hopping around the room sparring and jabbing like the boxers I had observed training at Bothner's, Morris's gym. I imagined myself already well down the road to invincibility.

"Stop fooling around," Morris barked, his voice clanging like a starting bell. "Somebody'll *kill* ya if you fight like that," he said and the word "kill" came off his lips like a shard of glass, sobering me into attention. Some of the fun had just slipped away from the afternoon.

He took a sip of his Scotch, set the glass down, and tied my gloves on. I tried to pay close attention as he instructed me on the fine points of posture, balance, and guard, but by this time my imagination had already run off with me. He held up his hand, palm out, and instructed me to hit it, which I did, with all my energy and zeal. "Good!" he exclaimed. "Again." He showed me how to push off my back foot and put my hip into it and I repeated the blow over and over again. It must have amused him, because he chuckled at my diligence. Then we began to spar.

Morris admonished me repeatedly to keep my guard up, becoming increasingly irritated and impatient when I forgot—"Don't drop your fucking hands, Goddamnit!"

I was so concerned with *looking* like a fighter that most of what he said went right over my head, but Morris, perhaps forgetting that I was a child, knew what such posing could cost a man in a real fight.

"Keep 'em up, for Christ's sake, somebody'll . . ." and his frustration was involuntarily released through a short, straight jab to my chin and that's all I remember.

I woke up on the library floor, with my mother cradling my head in her lap and screaming at my father. "Are you out of your goddamned mind, Morrie? Are you totally *insane*? He's a little boy, for Christ's sake." Either Morris's inability to check himself or my mother's outrage must have frightened him, because from that day on, boxing lessons were never mentioned again. Instead, he transferred lessons in "self-defense" to Greco-Roman wrestling.

Morris was an accomplished wrestler who actually reached some level of Olympic trials, losing his berth when an opponent dislocated his knee. Later, in the 1950s he sponsored the Russian wrestling team on a tour of the Eastern U.S. and still wrestled weekly at the gym with much younger men. One story will afford the reader a clear view of Morris's internal dynamics in the realm of competition.

Morris's younger brother, Bert, who accepted Morris's violence as a matter of course, related the following story to me. Bert was a gifted mimic and wildly zany man who often made me laugh. We both shared a combination of pride and terror where Morris was concerned, and Bert related the following as a humorous tale:

"We were in the changing room at Bothner's," he began. Bothner's was a no-nonsense fighter's gym Morris frequented in New York. Grimy by today's standards, it was filled with medicine balls, wooden bowling pins, trapeze and bars, the floors covered by thick mats. There were no men and women flirting and sizing up dates as there are in today's gyms—in fact there were no women at all. It was a men's domain. There were no rugs and no chrome, no polished equipment and no gesture whatsoever at aesthetics.

The gym was run by Morris's pal, George Bothner, an ex-lightweight champion of the world, who had beaten over fifty heavyweights, and consequently was a celebrity draw. Ernest Hemingway had showed up there one day, looking for a match, and after having been asked by George to spar with him, Morris dismissed the famous author as "a fucking pansy." Because of the disparity between Hemingway's public persona as a "two-fisted man'" and his ineptness in the ring, Morris refused to even read his books.

Bert continued his story. "Your dad was wearing his normal ratty long underwear and a pair of baggy swimming trunks. He was searching for his handball partner, but the guy wasn't around. A chesty kid wearing a Harvard wrestling team sweatshirt turned around from another locker—a well-built guy, carrying himself like he was hot shit. Your father asked the guy if he'd like to wrestle, so they could both get a good workout."

"That's when the kid made a mistake," Bert said, with a rueful grimace. "He looked your father up and down, kind of . . . *dismissively*—I mean Morris *did* look like a fucking bum, you know—but the kid could have been a little subtler about it. I thought, 'Oh Holy Shit, here it comes.' Moish (Morris's nickname) never changed his expression, never moved a muscle. Just kind of *wheedled* the guy in a kindly way to give him a workout. The kid looked bored, but he agreed. He also made it obvious that this was a complete waste of his time. He walked out first and Moish followed. As he passed me, your dad gave me that little mischievous grin." Bert continued, "I shook my head and thought, 'This kid has no idea.'

"I knew what was coming and didn't want to leave the locker room, but your dad insisted. The kid was about thirty, light-heavy-weight material, athletic looking, you know, those sloping shoulders. He was taller than Moish by four inches, and almost half his age. Morris had these spindly little legs and enormous gut that made him appear comical. They got out to the mat, and Morris put his hands up, like you do," and Bert imitated the wrestler's crouch, one hand on the back of the opponent's neck, the other on the guy's arm—"and, well, everything might have been okay, but the Harvard guy, *hesitated* . . . he hesitated, like he was having second thoughts. He *sighed*, the stupid kid sighed, like it might not be *worth his while* to do this. He had no idea . . ."—and here, Bert's comic distress at what was about to tran-spire made me laugh—"because I know what's coming." He grinned at me broadly. "And you do too, right?" I was hopping up and down in anticipation as he continued.

"In the next second, your father has taken this kid off his feet and smashed him to the ground like a phone book. Moish has his legs scis-sored around the poor bastard's neck. The kid is gagging and thrashing and trying to get away. He's terrified! He's turning blue. He is fucking

dying! I'm yelling, 'Moish, Moish. You're gonna kill the guy. MOISH!'
Just before the kid passes out, your father relents, hops up, and turns
on his heels, leaving the kid puking all over himself on the mat. As
he walks away, I swear to God, he mutters, 'Harvard *that,* ya little
cocksucker.'"

Given Morris's penchant for violence, perhaps I should not be
blamed for listening too literally when he was angry with me and
threatened to snap my "fucking legs and send you to reform school."
I heard "reform" as "*re-form*" and imagined some stained and grimy
abattoir where unacceptable children were somehow reconstituted
into more acceptable beings. I had no idea *how* that might be accomplished, but neither did I want to learn . . . ever!

Given that this tale was only one among many chronicling Morris's
barely sublimated violence, my hesitation might be understandable as
many an evening, waiting to be called in for dinner, Morris might sidle
into the living room and suggest that we "have some fun together and
wrestle a little."

Like most boys I was initially delighted by any opportunity for the
uninterrupted attention of my father, however these "lessons" were
not pedagogical in any sense of the word. He would begin by showing
me how to stand or kneel beside him, but from the moment I made
my first move, he would close on me like a Venus flytrap. From that
instant, wrestling became a painful endurance contest involving the
wrenching of my body into extremely contorted positions where gasping for a full breath became claustrophobically difficult. While exe-
cuting these holds, Morris maintained a running patter of informed
pedagogy about how one softens an opponent's resistance and will by
increasing their suffering.

"See?" he'd say. "See what I mean?" as he compressed and torqued my body, crimping my neck or crushing my chest, explaining calmly over my rising panic how clever it was that he was "forcing me to carry his weight."

At the slightest sign of my resistance or struggle he would demonstrate the advantage of "leverage" by increasing his efforts minimally enough to reinstate his complete mastery. I soon realized that Morris's "lessons" had less to do with preparing me to be competent in self-defense than they did in affirming his alpha status in our house—warning me of the potential costs that would accompany any rebellion. Eventually I accepted that there was nothing to be done but hibernate in my interior until he either lost interest or dinner arrived. His pedagogy was not good training for facing life with energy and confidence, or developing self-esteem and optimism. As we walked to the table, I would, with false *bonhomie,* agree with his assertion it had "been fun" and sit, stuffing my humiliation and anger out of sight along with my dinner. Unfortunately, those submerged feelings were never far from my mind.

ONE DAY, AFTER a particularly painful and debilitating "lesson," storming through the house in high dudgeon, I tracked my mother down in the library. Usually, my first impression on seeing her was to be transfixed by her beauty. This day, she was backlit by the glow of the pale gauze curtains, relaxing in a high-backed leather chair, smoking and reading her equivalent of the Bible—a book on Sigmund Freud. The tumbler of Scotch and soda beside her was nearly empty.

"I'm mad at Daddy," I announced, making a bid for her attention.

"Oh darling, I'm sorry," she said, inhaling her cigarette. "He can be rough, can't he?" she continued absently.

"He *really* hurt me, Mommy." I said. "I don't want to wrestle with him anymore, ever! I don't even *like* him and I'm going to *tell* him!"

In an instant my mother focused the totality of her attention on me and her body went into high alert, as if I had slapped her. Grinding her cigarette into the ashtray, she set Dr. Freud aside, snatched me close to her, whispering conspiratorially and with great urgency, smoothing my hair obsessively, "Darling, you *mustn't!*" she exclaimed in a whisper like a hiss. "You *mustn't* tell your father that. It would *kill* him. I'm serious, darling, he would *die!*" She asserted this with startling emphasis, gripping my arms painfully.

I was angry with him, but not *that* angry. I didn't want to kill my father, I wanted him to stop hurting me and I wanted to express my feelings to him. In my confusion, I didn't know what to say and my mother pressed on, "Yes, honey, if you hurt your father's feelings, he'll *die!*," offering this as an incontrovertible fact. "He can't take it. Really. You see, darling, you and I are different from Daddy. We're the *gentle* people, sweetheart. We're the *losers!* Your father *has* to win, don't you see? You and I can "lose" and it's all right." (She expressed this last assertion with gaiety, as if inviting me to celebrate good news.) "It's what makes us stronger, in a way. Don't you see?"

I did *not* see. What I saw was that in a moment of pain where I sought some succor for the repeated humiliation of wrestling my "lessons" with Morris, my mother was informing me that not only would she not help me but that "losing" was to be my permanent fate. Furthermore, and more galling was her implicit instruction that it was not only incumbent on me to lose but *to assume the responsibility of tending my father's feelings*—as if that were to be my appointed task in life.

I may have been only seven or eight, but I understood that I had been offered a completely unacceptable future and placed in a paralyzing double bind. My mother was so committed to what she had expresed, had made her wishes so vividly clear, that my refusal meant risking her disaffection. I had been placed in a situation that had no acceptable alternatives. Furthermore, if my winning meant making another boy feel as bad as losing to Morris made me feel, I wanted no part of that either.

What happened next was a watershed moment that I could not fully understand at the time. I made a decision then with such conviction and commitment, with the entirety of my being, so that it became a vow, a commitment to which I would remain bound from that point onward. In the frustration of that moment I vowed "never to play"— I did not understand my decision any more fully than that—but as a consequence, from then on I eschewed *all* sports and competitive situations, any endeavor that might present me with either *losing* or *winning* as options—both of which were unacceptable.

I rejected these two options totally and with no idea of what the consequences might be. I could not have understood at that age that I would be carving a large portion of normal life away from my own; the nourishment that sports and competition offers by creating bonds, friendship, and respect between contestants. I did not understand that I would be denying myself the opportunity to test myself in certain ways that makes male society comprehensible and, in a certain way, compensates for the pain loss with the camaraderie of participation. As a result, I never learned to play football, baseball or basketball, tennis, soccer, or even golf. I know (and care) less about sports, sports stars, sports scores, or statistics than anyone I know. My practices

SCAN GETS CUT OFF ON THE LAST EDIT

became singular—riding my bike and horse, shooting, fishing, being in the woods, daydreaming, and *always* reading—reading compulsively as if I were trying to compensate my imagination for victories denied my body; reading until my imagination assumed the dimensions of a safe and empowering alternate reality. It was in that same imagination that my unresolved anger and unexpressed aggression gained gradual potency and mass, assuming the shape and qualities of an unloved junkyard dog that would haunt and wound my later life, hunting my tender self as if it were a deer immobilized and trembling in deep snow.

IT IS SHAMING today to admit the degree to which this rash promise sealed in a long period of anger and estrangement from my biological mother, an anger I justified to myself by inventing the notion of her "deserting" me first during what was her nervous breakdown and later her inability to protect herself from or control my father. I sealed her guilt by compounding the charges of failing to protect me from Morris with conscripting me as her unwilling neighbor in Loser-ville. Later, adolescence and other circumstances offered my predisposed, critical eye numerous faults to extend the sentence against her. My pique with her lasted in some form until I was in my early thirties. My intense feelings about being identified as a loser and being forced to weigh that identity against losing her affections felt like a toothed and clawed beast inside me trying to chew its way out. I blamed my mother for those feelings and transferred my affections and respect more passionately to Susie and Ozzie Nelson. With the cruelty and ignorance of a child I created an unbridgeable moat between us for the next twenty-five years; turning my anger on the only parent it was *safe* to fight with; the one with no defenses against me. The one who was unable to save herself. Had my own children ever treated me as badly, I am certain I would have perished, and today, reviewing my belief that my mother was my enemy fills me with remorse and an inexpressible pity for the pain and estrangement she suffered at my hands.

CURIOUSLY, MY SISTER Muffet appeared to be immune to either the consequences or fear of Morris's threats. She was an athletic tomboy who often had to be called down from the tippy-tops of the immense pines that towered over the roof of our house. She would leap fearlessly from our garage roof, leaving me behind, paralyzed and seeking the resolve to follow her until she grew bored with entreating me and left for other diversions. Most embarrassing to me however was her ability to turn on Morris like a miniature terrier facing down a maddened bull.

One day, when she could not have been over eight, he was hollering at her about something and she got snippy. He snatched her up by her shirtfront and hauled her face up to the level of his own, muttering some threat at her. Uncowed, she yipped back, "Go ahead, hit me. I'll sue ya!" I was expecting her to be broken like a match, but Morris grinned broadly, then laughed aloud. Inconceivably, he hugged and kissed her, despite her struggles, tousled her hair affectionately, and set her down, immensely pleased by her spunk. Such behavior from me would have received immediate retribution. I envied my sister's courage and comparing myself to her invidiously delivered one more lash to my inner dog. There seemed to be no way for me to win on any front. Perhaps my mother was correct.

◄◦►

SEVERAL YEARS LATER, my parents developed a new friend who had moved to New York from "down South," a white man named Burgher "Buddy" Jones, a bebop jazz bass player. He appeared one day when I was around ten and in short order became (and remained) an important and trusted person in my life. He would become my most trusted adult friend and know more about me than either of my parents. The most precious gift he transmitted to me was that life could be improvised.

On the day I met him, I bounced into the house after school and stopped short because it was swollen with music. Notes were ricocheting off the walls, and the energy was intense. Four strangers were in our living room playing an up-tempo and complicated song. Two men were interweaving melodies between their saxophones as if they shared a common mind, braiding intricate parts of an exhilarating conversation. A third man was playing light, quick, percussive piano, with different melodies on each hand. The fourth turned out to be Buddy Jones, a rumpled-looking fellow bobbing his head over a stand-up bass, marking the time insistently with a right hand missing two digits of his first finger. Sometimes, when one played something especially appreciated, the others laughed and called out to one another, or sang a phrase back. It was festive and joyful and I had never seen white adults having this much fun.

This encounter changed my life. I decided on the spot, that somehow, some way, I wanted to be like them; wanted a life that felt like pure communication, liberated from the misunderstandings and contradictions of words. I was lost in it. I especially loved that they called it "bebop"—a perfect kid's word. I wanted to be heard too!

Morris was laughing and filling glasses with whiskey, slapping his leg, demanding, "Goddamnit, Ruthie, can these guys play or what?" He was happy, and pulled me close to listen with him. My mother was smiling and bobbing her head. Susie was dancing in and out with food, and leaning up against the wall to listen. She had a word she'd utter when she was particularly happy—"*Aleesha*"—and it meant something like "slow and easy." When I heard her say it during a blues tune, I knew that these guys had passed Susie's test and that they were all right in her world, knew indisputably that this was good, and decided impulsively that one day I would be like these men. I would make people happy too.

I loved my dad in moments like these. All my admiration usually suppressed by self-pity or resentment came to the fore at such times. These musicians were in *his* house, because they admired and liked him. He did many things and did them well. He was kind to (most) people, funny and charming, and people regarded him as special. His friends were people I did not meet in other homes, and life with Morris had made them available to me.

The day turned out to be an introduction to jazz of a high order. The two saxophone players were Al Cohn and Zoot Sims, an already famous duo. The piano player was named Dave McKenna and though not as well-known as Al and Zoot, he was appreciated by jazz folks. All were friends of Buddy's and part of a network of jazzmen and women that Buddy introduced me to in the coming years.

Within a year of meeting him, I was so under Buddy's influence that I began to study jazz drums with his friend "Cozy" Cole, a well-respected big band drummer from the 1940s who, along with jazz giant Gene Krupa, operated a drum school in midtown Manhattan.

Every week the chauffeur or my mother would drive me in and wait while Cozy himself, a tall, lanky, laconic man with a large head and enormous hands, gave me patient lessons—drilling me on rolls, paradiddles (singles, doubles, and triples), flams, and other rhythmic figures. He taught me to free my hands and feet to operate independently of one another—most of this demonstrated (and to be practiced) on a disappointingly silent rubber practice pad. The cherished part of the lessons occurred in the final ten minutes of the hour, when he would let me sit at one of the studio drum kits, a bass drum played with the right foot, a hi-hat cymbal operated by the left foot, a ride cymbal floating over the bass drum, and tom-toms mounted to it.

Cozy was a charming, very relaxed man. Apparently made out of patience, he pointed out my errors but never fussed over them. Quite the opposite, he urged me always to "jus' keep goin'. Don't build yourself a habit of stoppin' every time you make a mistake." Under his tutelage, I discovered that I had been blessed with solid time and a good feel for "the pocket" of a song—the place in the beat where everything feels right. However, as a beginner I had no idea of what to do with them.

In my free time in the drum room at Cozy's studio, I smashed, crashed, and blasted around his drum set and big, brassy Zildjian cymbals, imagining myself driving a thirty-piece orchestra. Cozy would let me burn off some of steam before resting an enormous hand across my forearm. "Slow down, Peter," he said. "Don't put *all* your ideas out there at once. Leave yourself some space to grow in and to *feel* what comes next." (Wonderful advice for any artist.) Then he took the sticks and beginning with a simple figure, would create a simple rhythmic "floor," embellishing and expanding it, adding an idea here and there until he had constructed an elegant structure on a solid foundation that not only possessed drive and power, but the feeling that there was always more on tap he could summon.

After a year of diligent practice my parents bought me a drum set that I established in our finished basement. I practiced assiduously, making the house vibrate until Morris bluntly threatened to kill me one day if I didn't stop. "Practice when I'm not home, for Christ's sake," he shouted down the stairs. "Jesus!" His fussing did not bother me that day. I was becoming a jazzman.

—◁◦▷—

ALMOST IMMEDIATELY AFTER meeting Buddy, I began dedicating my allowance to collecting records, seeking recommendations from him, Susie, and Ozzie. It didn't matter if it was Bobby Blue Bland or Charlie Parker—it was all new and exciting, as fresh to my ears as black speech. I cannot overstate how important music became to me during this period of my life. It was such pure expression, free of the confusing tangles of language, where you could express multiple meanings simultaneously, express things that were forbidden to be put into words. It was a language of *feeling*, and once liberated from the iron rules of grammar and logic there *were* no contradictions or double binds. In the same way that I once understood, "My mind knows what I mean," I understood now that within the formless world of creativity, I was free. It would be many years before I would experience pure formlessness itself.

In another year I became attracted to folk music—generally blues, but also the high keening harmonies and blood-tingling banjo and stopped speaking suddenly when I entered the room or appeared overly concerned with what I might or might not think about something they said. Rather than protecting me from complex or difficult issues, as my parents often tried to do, they included me and answered my questions, protecting me from spinning off into imagined terrors by explaining events and facts clearly. I never felt responsible for the social injustices or persecutions they discussed. How could I have been responsible? I had no power! I identified with them as victims of forces beyond our control. I certainly understood that. The fact that both these sets of adults felt that I could "handle" whatever came up in conversation made me also feel more competent and adult.

BUDDY JONES WAS not black, but to me nearly so. He had the same rich speaking voice with a similar accent, timbre, and pitch as black people. He possessed the same unselfconscious sense of play and spontaneity they did. There was nothing I could not discuss or share with him, and today, there was much more I wish I had been able to share with him and several things I wish I had not.

One morning, at Turkey Ridge, Buddy and I were the first awake. When I came downstairs, Buddy was walking around the kitchen in his long johns, wearing an old straw cowboy hat, smoking his corncob pipe and refilling it with a pleasant-smelling green herb, shaken out from a 35mm film can, which I later learned was marijuana. Buddy informed me several years later that he had been high every day of his life since he was seventeen. His love of pot approached the worshipful. It was my first introduction to the existence of marijuana, and I was not particularly curious about it. That would change in due time.

percussive mandolin of Appalachian music and bluegrass. Before long I had followed this trail and discovered chain-gang songs, shave-note singing, authentic cowboy music, and Tex-Mexican *conjunto*. I began tracking down original 78 rpm records of old blues singers—Bukka White, Lonnie Johnson, Robert Johnson, Blind Willie Johnson, and Blind Lemon Jefferson. My aural world was expanding.

By the time the folk-music craze spread to a broader public, I had become a dedicated aficionado, able to knowledgeably discuss styles and players the way my school friends discussed sports figures and statistics. I joined the swelling numbers of my generational peers pursuing those bewitching sounds to wherever they led and wherever that might be, the path definitely led us away from the safe and orderly suburbs. The rawness and authenticity of that music, the pungent tastes of life beyond the borders of Englewood and Portland were magnetic. Furthermore these songs did not sugar-coat America's shadows. The poverty, racism, class distinctions, and vulnerability to power I had been introduced by Susie and Ozzie and their friends, or my parents' friends and family who were crushed and ruined by McCarthyism during the 1950s, were augmented by sagas of life on the road, the tales of death by overdose and car crash recounted over kitchen tables between songs by jazzmen. They were all expressions of the powerless, the disenfranchised, the disappointed—those who did not count—and I identified with them. If we were the "losers" our music promised fair compensation for the world's prizes we would be denied.

IT WAS THEIR unvarnished acceptance of the truth—wherever it led—that made both Buddy and Susie easy for me to be around. Neither until he had constructed an elegant structure on a solid foundation that not only possessed drive and power, but the feeling that there was always more on tap he could summon.

After a year of diligent practice my parents bought me a drum set that I established in our finished basement. I practiced assiduously, making the house vibrate until Morris bluntly threatened to kill me one day if I didn't stop. "Practice when I'm not home, for Christ's sake," he shouted down the stairs. "Jesus!" His fussing did not bother me that day. I was becoming a jazzman.

—◁○▷—

ALMOST IMMEDIATELY AFTER meeting Buddy, I began dedicating my allowance to collecting records, seeking recommendations from him, Susie, and Ozzie. It didn't matter if it was Bobby Blue Bland or Charlie Parker—it was all new and exciting, as fresh to my ears as black speech. I cannot overstate how important music became to me during this period of my life. It was such pure expression, free of the confusing tangles of language, where you could express multiple meanings simultaneously, express things that were forbidden to be put into words. It was a language of *feeling*, and once liberated from the iron rules of grammar and logic there *were* no contradictions or double binds. In the same way that I once understood, "My mind knows what I mean," I understood now that within the formless world of creativity, I was free. It would be many years before I would experience pure formlessness itself.

In another year I became attracted to folk music—generally blues, but also the high keening harmonies and blood-tingling banjo and

Every week the chauffeur or my mother would drive me in and wait while Cozy himself, a tall, lanky, laconic man with a large head and enormous hands, gave me patient lessons—drilling me on rolls, paradiddles (singles, doubles, and triples), flams, and other rhythmic figures. He taught me to free my hands and feet to operate independently of one another—most of this demonstrated (and to be practiced) on a disappointingly silent rubber practice pad. The cherished part of the lessons occurred in the final ten minutes of the hour, when he would let me sit at one of the studio drum kits, a bass drum played with the right foot, a hi-hat cymbal operated by the left foot, a ride cymbal floating over the bass drum, and tom-toms mounted to it.

Cozy was a charming, very relaxed man. Apparently made out of patience, he pointed out my errors but never fussed over them. Quite the opposite, he urged me always to "jus' keep goin'. Don't build yourself a habit of stoppin' every time you make a mistake." Under his tutelage, I discovered that I had been blessed with solid time and a good feel for "the pocket" of a song—the place in the beat where everything feels right. However, as a beginner I had no idea of what to do with them.

In my free time in the drum room at Cozy's studio, I smashed, crashed, and blasted around his drum set and big, brassy Zildjian cymbals, imagining myself driving a thirty-piece orchestra. Cozy would let me burn off some of steam before resting an enormous hand across my forearm. "Slow down, Peter," he said. "Don't put *all* your ideas out there at once. Leave yourself some space to grow in and to *feel* what comes next." (Wonderful advice for any artist.) Then he took the sticks and beginning with a simple figure, would create a simple rhythmic "floor," embellishing and expanding it, adding an idea here and there

With Buddy and his friends Morris was relaxed and in good humor. He was appreciative of their ability and creativity and always passionate about his delights. When he was engaged with Buddy's music, he was so rapt that I could move around him with the same alert ease a zebra might manifest in the presence of a fully fed lion. Morris respected musicians in particular and creativity in general. He often helped them with their business affairs, giving advice, arranging loans, and sometimes even cosigning them. It was a side of him I had not been previously aware of and began to hope that this common affection might bring us closer to one another.

MORRIS HELPED BUDDY secure a farm near ours and after that we saw Buddy and his wife Betty quite often. Betty was an olive-skinned Sicilian with opulent and unruly black hair. She resembled the actress Anna Magnani, and possessed a soft musical voice and effortless hipness. She was nonjudgmental and easy to be around. As I came to know them better, I developed a familial love for them.

When I was around thirteen Susie and Ozzie married, and moved downtown into their own house and had a child. Consequently, Sue was no longer as readily available to me as she had been. At thirteen, I was also becoming more independent and less needy, so Buddy and Betty filled much of the space previously reserved exclusively for Sue.

Buddy was born somewhere in Arkansas, but when he was six or seven, his family moved to the town of Hope where he attended school. On his first day, as he stood in the strange grade-school classroom nervous and unknown, a young girl named Virginia Kelly befriended him, sliding over on the bench of the two-seat desk and inviting him to sit beside her. He and she became the best of school chums through high school. Virginia's expansive, generous spirit was duly recognized later in life after she became famous as the mother of President Bill Clinton.

My upbringing and development was not Buddy and Betty's responsibility and consequently in their home I was liberated to the status of a carefree person. I did not have to be overly cautious or overly concerned with their moods. Times spent with Buddy and Betty were further holidays from anxiety and I relished them.

--◂◦▸--

BY TWELVE, I had discerned within my family's values the rough outlines of a three-sided matrix involving "money," something referred to as "taste," and the unequal and invisible distribution of something felt but never overtly identified as "power." I had absorbed this system before I knew that it existed, and living in my house made it invisible to me in the same way that water is probably invisible to a fish. However, upon leaving the fragrant, light-filled Englewood house and its spacious lawns and massive trees to visit my mother's parents, Nat and Rose in the noisy, tumultuous Bronx, this matrix became visible as if I had slipped beneath the surface of a muddy pond.

The apartment building of my maternal grandparents was grimy and dark. The hallway floors, composed of tiny white octagonal tiles, were stained and gritty underfoot. The air was an unpleasant amalgam of scents I associated with the word "poor." I linked them mentally to ugliness and choking odors—liniments, burnt cooking oil, kitchen wastes, and the throat-closing mustiness of unloved, airless interiors.

Their window glass was embedded with chicken wire and the light seeping through it lay dim as dust on the dark furniture.

Nat and Rose's apartment was claustrophobic and smelled of cabbage, tobacco smoke, sweet wine, airless closets, and upholstery dense with enough dust to lock my windpipe. The rooms were cramped with overstuffed graceless furniture and the whole so lacking in light and beauty it made me physically uneasy.

There was nothing for me to do while my mother and grandmother visited. Neither appeared to be happy. They conversed in impenetrable Yiddish, which sounded like conversations between people clearing their throats. They drank dark tea with jelly stirred in tall glasses, and puffed endless cigarettes, filling the house with clouds of roiling blue smoke. I could do little there except twitch and fret with restlessness, drumming my heels against the base of my chair in frustration. It was difficult for me to accept that the mother I thought so beautiful had come from such shabby people.

Grandma Rose scared me. She had pitiless eyes, minimal warmth, and an irritable restlessness like my father's. (Which might explain why they got along well.) Why, I wondered, fretting internally, did we have to visit them *here* instead of in our house? Being confined in the dim boredom of their apartment was like being immobilized in one of Morris's wrestling holds.

My mother might have felt as I did. There had been much bitterness between Ruth and her mother. Rose was an inveterate gambler who had sent her daughter to work early, charging her rent, even as a child, to secure her gambling stakes. There was a quality of the dutiful attending Ruth's visits and I observed that even as an adult she remained subtly under her mother's thumb, as I remained under Morris's. Perhaps I was receiving my mother's aversions to and resentments for the world she had fled subliminally, transmitted to me like radio signals through the ethers.

I loved my maternal grandfather, Nat. When he visited us at Turkey Ridge he taught me to care for our chickens, which he loved. He taught me to carve whistles from sections of willow branches, tapping the bark gently to slide off an unbroken tube, reinserting it after he'd trimmed the pith to the correct shape. He loved the peace and ease of the country and relaxed at Turkey Ridge. Like Morris, signs of his age and the stresses of running his marginal little business in the Bronx fell away from him there like feathers from a molting bird. He was a spiritual man who had trained to be a rabbi before fleeing the Czar's draft in Russia, and today I think the immersion in nature Turkey Ridge afforded nourished something deep and hungry within him.

◄○►

THE YEAR I turned twelve, my mother announced to me that I was going to be Bar Mitzvahed at thirteen and that I would have to begin studying Hebrew for the occasion. This edict was an unwelcome shock and I protested, because I had never been exposed to a single day of religious training. My home was unambiguously secular. We celebrated Christmas unless my mother's parents visited, because I suppose my parents wanted their children to "fit in" with the unquestionably Christian influence of the dominant culture and did not care enough about religion to be loyal to Judaism.

Morris and Ruth were secular humanists, a maligned appellation among politically conservatives circles today. I knew much more about rock 'n' roll, jazz, folk music, and hot rods at twelve than I did about the Torah, even though my last name, Cohon, placed me within the Cohainem—the priest's tribe.

The Bar Mitzvah celebrates the moment when parents can no longer be held accountable for their children's sins, and it signifies the age at which a boy becomes subject to Jewish law and able to participate in all rituals. None of that mattered to me, but my mother's parents were orthodox, and kept a kosher home with all the consequent complexities of separate tableware for meat and milks. This ancient ceremony was important to them. There was no discussion or dispute available to me and I was, in my own mind, to be sacrificed on their altar.

Shortly after my mother's startling announcement, I began weekly study of Hebrew text with a dry, studious, and charmless man named "Mr. Fineman" (not his real name), the most soporific individual I have ever met to this day. His carefully articulated two-syllable "Hel-lo" engendered in me an immediate and overwhelming desire to sleep. Upon hearing his voice my eyelids felt like steam irons were attached to them. Mr. Fineman appeared to have been born without passion, humor, or animating influence other than the (laudable) aim of preparing young boys for their Bar Mitzvah. Consequently, it was my fate to spend several afternoons a week of my twelfth year sitting alongside him in our library, learning to recognize and follow the black Hebrew letters with my forefinger while chanting the ancient and impenetrable prayers I would be called upon to recite. Fairness to Mr. Fineman demands confessing that 60 years later I still remember them.

During our lessons I would gaze out the window at the sun-drenched leaves and lawns and *will* the minute hand on my watch forward. I attempted vain pleas with the Lord that should he free me from this room, I would at some indeterminate future date become the most observant of Jews. (What kind of a boy lies to God?) I would indicate my desire to be freed to enjoy my bike by sighing, fidgeting, and gasping, but no matter how much I fretted, Mr. Fineman never faltered in his obdurate snail's pace, and the hour crept along as if he had willed time to slow down.

On one of our study days, the library had been conscripted by my parents. They invited Mr. Fineman and me to join them in front of the television, where they were engrossed by a documentary film about the Nazi death camp at Auschwitz. It was on that couch in that room, safely ensconced between my parents, among the comforting shelves of books and records, insulated from the sullied world by thick walls, spotless white curtains, sparkling porcelain, and the luster of silver, that I first absorbed the flickering images of power's unrestrained potential. In grainy, quivering 16mm black-and-white footage, bulldozers pushed the naked, emaciated corpses of men, women, and children into mass graves, tumbling them over the lip in a ghastly, slow-motion choreography of waving arms and tangled legs, gaping mouths and vacated eyes turned skyward as if struck down in mid-thought. It was simultaneously horrifying, fascinating, and confusing.

When it was explained to me that they had been killed for no other reason than their being Jewish, I was perplexed. That's what *we* were. If this was their fate, why were my parents preparing me to become *more* Jewish than I was currently when there were people in the world waiting to do *this* to me? Why would I want to prepare myself to become dead? This confusion was shot through with dread.

MORRIS WAS EXTREMELY proud of being Jewish, at least *his* version of Jewish. He was fond of saying, "While the Angles, the Celts, and the Gauls were painting their faces blue and hanging from trees, the Jews had created Justice and God and were writing poetry." He relished their exploits as the superlative warriors who had held off the entire Roman Empire at Masada for seventeen years and how "we" revered learning, wisdom, and intellectual achievement more so than others. To hear Morris tell it, Jews were like a combination of Einstein and Superman, but if that was true, how was it that on my television they were being shoveled into mass graves?

My experience of Jews was different than Morris's. At the Englewood Jewish community center, where I was taken to roller-skate or swim on occasion, the children were loud and pushy, intimidating and uninteresting to me. They wore boring clothes and bragged about their parents' wealth with competitive fervor. I could not connect Morris's Jews to mine, could not balance what I liked about Judaism (the food, the humor, the skepticism, the curiosity) with those elements I did not like. Now, my studies with Mr. Fineman had made it irrefutable that, like it or not, I was one of them and could be shot and pushed into a ditch for something I barely cared about. How was it that no one had warned me about this? Or had they? Might that have been why Morris was so insistent on "toughening me up?"

That afternoon in the library absorbing the ballet of the dead, my mother's eyes brimmed with tears, certain that relatives were among them. My father was grim, growling deep in his throat as he often did before an explosive outburst. Their intensity made me afraid to puncture the silence with any questions, and absent information, my world became suddenly much less safe. Television had introduced me to irrefutable proof that even large numbers of adults could not always protect themselves or their children from danger. Ruth must have been aware of that early in her life and in all likelihood, that knowledge may have contributed to her marrying such an apparently indomitable force as Morris. It was obvious to me however that I was witnessing something that even frightened Morris.

—◄○►—

MY FATHER'S OFT-REPEATED admonition to me, beginning when I was six or seven, was to "never, ever, under any circumstances sell the farm." By my teens, Turkey Ridge had become the site of Morris's highly profitable cattle-breeding operations as well as the focus of his creativity. He had built it to be even more profitable than his Wall Street firm. It was infinitely more pleasurable, and possessed totemic importance for him. Turkey Ridge remained primary among the five farms he had amassed within two hours from Englewood. I loved it there as much as he did, and so never understood why Morris lectured me so insistently (particularly when he'd been drinking). Why would I sell Turkey Ridge? How could I ever *own* a farm if I did not receive his as a gift? Despite the fact that I had no idea of how I would take care of it, feed the cattle, or pay the men who worked there, I dimly understood that it would always be my future and assumed that he would work out the details at an appropriate time.

"The details" arrived when he informed me that I would spend my coming tenth summer working on the farm. I was put out because my sister was allowed to attend sleepaway camp, swimming, canoeing, singing around campfires and eating s'mores, while I was to be retained at home to "learn to work."

I protested loudly, but the issue had been decided. There was no appeal. He did not have to shout or threaten. He simply removed his attention from my complaints and placed it elsewhere. It was permissable for me to be angry because I was not challenging his will directly. He tolerated a modicum of whining before a sharp "Enough!" stoppered my complaints.

IT WOULD HAVE been consistent with conventions of the 1940s and 1950s that Morris assumed that my sister would marry and stay home tending children and have no need to enhance her capacity for employment. I am sure that he was also concerned about my dreamy vagueness and lack of focus and in trying to explain why he felt this work was important for me, referred to "standards of quality" and "endurance," and would not be moved. I am doubly grateful for his insistence today. Morris understood that he was incapable of the patience required to teach me, and in the same way that indigenous people the world over send daughters to be raised by aunts, and sons to be raised by uncles, he placed me under the supervision of Jim Clancy, the ranch foreman, and our two "hands," Walt Poliski and Bill Jelinek. These three men transmitted lessons and skills to me that have remained useful my entire life.

Morris's mandate to Jim Clancy was, "Teach that kid to work." To that end, Jim harnessed me to Walt Poliscewicz (pronounced *Pol-i-shev-its*, but shortened in Pennsylvania vernacular to Poliski) and Bill

Jelinek, and they began the process of training me to accept the harness of discipline and the requisite endurance for work. Walt was "Mr. Slow-and-steady" personified. He did everything—driving a fence-post, stretching barbed wire, hammering nails, feeding cows, taking a smoke break, or stopping for a beer—at the same unhurried, deliberate pace. He never rushed, never stalled, and never slowed down. His pace was frustrating to a boy with energy to burn and an eagerness to prove his worth.

It didn't take long however before eight-hour days of farm labor certified the wisdom of Walt's measured tempo. I was soon stretched to my absolute capacity, clearing rock; mucking manure; wrestling heavy bales (fresh oat-hay bales weighed about ninety pounds—my body weight); and tamping rock with a heavy steel bar a head taller than I was; lifting and dropping the bar so that its flattened head tamped gravel around fence-posts until my back and shoulder muscles burned from the strain. On some days, it felt as if all of life was reduced to driving fence staples and cinching fencing to the cedar posts I'd spent days tamping into place. Difficult as the work was, the idea of a tantrum, or quitting and losing face before these men, was unthinkable. The problems, the fatigue, the frustration of physical work were actual, direct, and simple compared to the mental wrestling required of me in my family environment. It was not long before hard labor had burned away my youthful ardor (and much baby fat) and slowed my pace to match Walt's.

Bill Jelinek was Walt's polar opposite, spry and quick with a high wit and nimble mind. He teased Walt to a degree that sometimes made me anxious for Walt, who did not appear to possess the wits to defend himself. Bill was a polymath who could do nearly anything: carpentry, welding, auto repair, machining, gardening, and canning. He was also extremely verbal and ran rings around Walt, who at times resembled a fighting bull after being exhausted by the *picadors* who had set steel barbs in his neck muscles to weaken them.

Bill had served with the Seabees in the Pacific during World War II and I was absorbed by his stories about rolling his bulldozer onto the Pacific island beaches, blade up to deflect Japanese machine-gunfire as he rolled over their gun emplacements, crushing and suffocating the soldiers to death. He laughed easily, and his eyes twinkled, but some vestiges of war must have remained to gnaw his guts because in all the years we worked together he ate only bottled baby food and drank goat's milk for his lunch.

Working with us often but not always was my hero, the taciturn, rock-solid outdoorsman, Jim Clancy, a man of acute observation and few words. Jim's most dreaded pronouncement when reviewing some task I had been assigned was, "Boy work"—meaning careless, thoughtless, and unacceptable. Fear of receiving this judgement of my efforts spurred me to do my best. These men became my favored alternative to school. Smart, capable, and each gifted in his own way, they taught never to confuse book learning with intelligence. More importantly, I learned to recognize different varieties of intelligence and hold them in equal regard with the academic skills that conferred high-status pedigrees.

—◦—

LEARNING TO DRIVE meant crossing a threshold of freedom, even though my first vehicle was a homely Ford-Ferguson tractor with a manure fork extending in front of it. It had a top speed of about nine miles per hour, but it made mechanical power available to me and extended my reach. In short order I was adept enough with it to be trusted driving on the dirt back roads connecting Turkey Ridge to my friends' homes.

It is no easy chore for a young boy to plow or harrow a fifty-acre field, and it requires sustained concentration. The compensating balm was the isolation of the tractor seat, which afforded me uncluttered space to think and dream without interruption or criticism. Each new skill I identified in the world of men became a goal to master and the fact that I could learn them produced positive alterations in my self-esteem.

After the season's last harvest, when fall announced itself in cooler mornings, and umbers and reds began to flush the face of the forest like a blush, I assisted Walt in disassembling the tractors—cleaning, lubricating, repairing, and repainting them, fixing leaks, and checking for damaged hydraulic hoses and fittings. I loved transforming the muck, grime, and disorder of a summer's work into perfectly running, repainted machinery, in stolid Ford-Ferguson grey or industrial Allis-Chalmers orange.

The farm shop was new at that time, a heated building with a cinder-block base, and a low wooden superstructure with a shallowly sloping flat tin roof. It was amply stocked with useful tools including a rolling overhead chain-hoist powerful enough to lift an engine, arc and oxy-acetylene welders, and a ten-foot-long workbench covered with sheet tin. At one end of the bench was a massive vise and at the other a twin-wheeled grinder driven by a powerful electric motor that made the building tremble when it ran at high speed. On the far wall, fifty-gallon drums of petroleum, solvents, grease, and diesel fuel were stacked sideways on wooden racks.

There was no mechanical task within my capacities that could not be accomplished here. The shop was a perfect classroom, and unlike school I was never bored in it. By the time I was twelve, I could clean and pack wheel bearings, change brakes, and help with the disassembly and reassembling of mowers, rakes, harrows, front-loaders and a variety of farm equipment. I had also attained middling arc and oxy-acetylene–welding skills.

A year after I began driving the tractor, I graduated to the farm's World War II surplus Jeep and the intoxication of driving a real car. I appreciated the implied trust my parents showed by allowing me to drive without supervision (or driver's license) as much as I enjoyed mastering the skill. As driving age appeared on the conceivable horizon, I began focusing my shop skills on becoming a fledgling hot-rod mechanic. My intention was to provide myself with a nifty set of wheels when I reached legal driving age. These new skills stood me in good stead when I returned to Englewood for school, because automania had become an epidemic in teenage circles.

Fulfilling my desire to possess the power and freedom a car implied led me to seek out new teachers: mechanics, grease monkeys, hot-rodders, and sports car aficionados. These fellows had their own culture and while they might not have passed the style-manual regulations of the private school where I was enrolled, I appreciated them and the time they were willing to dedicate to instructing me. My preferred professors favored ducktail hair combs and elaborate sideburns, greasy jeans and stained coveralls. In their company I learned to appreciate cleverness, creative problem-solving, and intelligence packaged very differently than what was on offer in school. Increasingly, my education was being transmitted to me by people my parents would have considered a waste of my time—had they known what I was doing.

◄◦►

THE FIRST ENGINE I ever assembled without help had only one cylinder. I no longer remember how I came to possess the large bushel basket of engine parts, a frame, wheels, and the requisite extras to complete a British AJS 500cc single-cylinder motorcycle, but I stashed everything in the locked storage shed attached to our garage where Morris stored antiques in transit. I shifted aside some furniture, tacked up photos of what the finished motorcycle should look like, and resolved to make it run.

Six months of hunting parts at flea markets, bike shops, and specialty speed shops commenced where I haunted motorcycle dealers, traded correspondence with AJS fans two or three times my age in Europe and the States, poring over an increasingly grease-stained and tattered shop manual (ordered by mail from England) until I finally cracked whatever problem befuddled me in the moment.

I pursued my goal day by day, one problem at a time, borrowing and learning to use torque wrenches, micrometers, and valve-spring compressors until I had reassembled the engine. A few days after that, the entire motorcycle was freestanding on its own wheels and kickstand, a flagrant invitation to trouble.

My hands were trembling with excitement as I poured gas into the tank for the first time. An older pal named Randy Woodward came to my house to help me. A year older than me, he had actually ridden motorcycles in his native Canada, so I delivered pride of place to him and we rolled it out of the shed and onto the steep hill in front of my house.

Randy aimed the bike downhill, and clicked it into second gear while I pushed him off. When the requisite speed had been reached, he stood on the foot pegs, dropped his ass hard on the seat and popped the clutch. The rear wheel skidded sickeningly, but then rolled free as the engine burped, coughed, and then caught, emitting a skin-prickling roar as Randy twisted the throttle. I hopped around in circles, pounding my fists into my thighs, dumb with excitement and self-congratulatory pride.

I will never forget the thrill of hearing that engine fire. It was an all-A report card for having accomplished hundreds of precise measurements and tasks correctly. Randy showed me the rudiments of driving it and I snuck the AJS out onto the Englewood streets, imagining myself potent and cool as Marlon Brando in *The Wild One* when the guy asked him, "What are you rebelling against, Johnny?" and he answered, in his sleepy, who-gives-a-fuck way—"Whaddya got?"

I was the star of my own movie.

I had done this with minimal adult instruction or help, and this revelation elevated the needle of my general mood until it quivered near ecstasy. This condition stayed constant until the afternoon several weeks later when I roared into my driveway just as Morris stepped out the rear door of his limo.

When Morris understood that my "whatever-the-hell-you're-doin'-out-there" was a *motorcycle*, that actually *ran*, Marlon was banished to his room. When I returned home from school the next day, the AJS was gone—without explanation, compensation, or apology. It disappeared as if it had been an apparition.

—◄o►—

I'M CERTAIN THAT Morris loved me as much if not more than he loved most people, and I'm also certain that he tried and probably felt that he had often expressed that love to me. There were times certainly when I did receive the message, but they were startling and out-of-character when they occurred and consequently embarrassing. The daily reality of our family life was that Morris coursed in and out of our house like a hand grenade rolled into the room. Upon his arrival, everyone's attention was immediately conscripted to determine whether or not the pin had been pulled. Morris was my first experience of love and power in all its rawness, and he fulfilled my potentials for delight and pain in equal measure. The first time I heard the great Robert Johnson blues song, "Hellhound on my Trail"—"And the days keep on worryin' me, there's a hellhound on my trail"—I assumed he'd had a father like mine.

Memory begets memory and new ones shift the angle of the scales of judgement. A memory of an extraordinary kindness surfaces: Near my fourteenth birthday, I saw an advertisement in an outdoor magazine for a Marlin lever-action .22-caliber rifle. It was a carbon copy of the Winchester .30-30s cowboy movie heroes carried in their saddle scabbards. In the ad, a young boy of my age, in blue jeans and flannel shirt not unlike mine, was sitting on the ground, steadying the weapon, on one knee as he sighted down its barrel.

I was dizzy with longing for that rifle, daydreamed about it, played "air-rifle" the way kids today play air-guitar. I was too afraid of being rebuffed to request it directly so I cut its picture out of the magazine and left it casually on the kitchen table where I hoped Morris might see it. He never mentioned it and the picture disappeared. A month or so later, when I returned from school on my fourteenth birthday, the blued steel and walnut rifle with its thrilling lever-action profile was lying across my bed. Fifty-eight years later I still have it. Morris took and Morris gave, without explanation or apology—like a king.

—◄o►—

THOUGH MORRIS WAS an ardent and self-interested capitalist he was intellectually rigorous and honest enough to have a number of prominent Left-wing friends, including two, Leo Huberman and Paul Sweezy, who published a respected Socialist journal called the *Monthly Review*. Morris enjoyed debating with them, particularly over chess games, and to this company, I would add my mother's first cousin, Irving Adler.

IRVING WAS A mathematician and an active, committed Communist who was not willing to "settle" for the status quo or to ever remain silent about injustice. During my childhood, he was chairman of the Mathematics Department at Straubenmuller Textile High School in Manhattan and also an official in the Communist-led Teachers Union. Unlike most *service unions,* which normally focus on benefits and salaries at the expense of democratic practices, the more radical Teachers Union created an alternative model known as *social movement unionism,* which:

> *. . . focuses on building alliances with grassroots organizations for the purpose of providing resources to the communities and schools in which teachers work. . . . prioritiz[ing] forging partnerships with Black and Latino parents, civil rights*

organizations, unions, community groups, and civic organiza-
tions to improve the lives of the children they taught as well as
the working conditions of their members.[1]

WHEN IRVING RECEIVED a summons from McCarthy's House Un-American Activities Committee he refused to testify and inform on his friends on constitutional grounds. For that effrontery, shortly afterwards he received a note from his principal, while teaching class, terminating his employment at the end of the day.

Irving was an intellectually brilliant, progressive thinker and this "Red menace" at our table was a wry, reserved, handsome man, with fine, chiseled features. His gestures and speech were precise and he spoke softly and logically, in a non-assertive way, laying out orderly building blocks of an argument with the precision of a skilled mason.

When Morris spoke, it was obvious that a formidable mind was claiming the floor, but Morris's exclamations were also accompanied by a sense of restrained physical threat that kept listeners alert. Irving required no such physical amplification; his ideas were impregnably buttressed by logic. The fact that he was able to best or back up Morris in arguments compelled me to understand him, and I attended their debates and conversations closely.

I could not understand what the threat of Communism might be unless it was the theory itself. Irving did not rant or preach revolution. He never urged sedition on our maid and chauffeur. He was neither didactic nor bombastic and I found his arguments compelling. As an added benefit, I understood that Irving's mental organization and meticulous arguments were a force that not even Morris could always brook. In conversation with Irving, Morris would hunch his shoulders or shake his head irritably, sometimes growling as he often did when irked, but his agitation did not faze Irving at all. I believe Morris knew and respected this.

Irving's patient analysis was a like a surgeon's scalpel peeling away layers of strata of skin, fat, muscle, and sheathing to reach the source of the problem. In Irving's case the "problem" was power's hidden tendrils, revealing unseen connections between apparently disparate social and political events. His arguments were nearly as intriguing as music because he offered me hope that if I could arm myself with similar arguments and skills, I would be in possession of formidable weapons. I could see direct parallels between my own life and Irving's dedication of his mental powers to defend the powerless. I anticipated that his tools might become important to me one day.

—◦—

AFTER IRVING ADLER was fired from the New York City school system for being a Communist, my father had tried to convince him to "lay low," and to be less pronounced and forceful in propounding his ideas for "the sake of your children." Irving responded that his "children needed to know who their father was and that there was nothing shameful or illegal in disputing ideas." Perhaps he reminded Morris that it was not illegal to be a Communist and that it was a recognized political philosophy and as such he had a right to espouse it and intended to, despite the bullies in Congress.

Legal or not, during this time Irving and other family friends lost their jobs due to Senator McCarthy's "witch-hunt." Conversations in our living room were now often muted, depressed, or sorrowful as friends recounted tragic experiences of their agency suddenly rendered impotent, denied status, occupation, and income. I witnessed grown men and women crying; saw them frightened, embarrassed, and fractured in invisible dimensions; becoming weak and often intimidated as they were threatened with the full intimidating power of the government. I couldn't comprehend their entire experience, but I certainly understood their powerlessness.

These men and women had been nice to me, had inquired after my interests, listened when I spoke, teased me, and made me think. They were friends: normal people, eating, drinking whiskey, smoking, telling stories, and joking around. They could be as foolish as all adults sometimes appeared to me, but it never occurred to me that they would ever be so cruelly punished for what they *thought!* It was even more disturbing to understand that they were being targeted in assaults directed by the very government to which I was asked to cross my heart and pledge allegiance every day. (A pledge, I later learned, that was written by a Christian Socialist named Francis Bellamy, who believed that greed was a sin.)

-◄o►-

AS I MATURED into my teens, resentments and frustration with Morris's bullying surfaced more openly, and conflict and discord between us made life inside my house claustrophobic. I began spending as much time as I could in the streets, garages, and wild places where I began in earnest the hunt to discover my own power.

My father had met Harry Palmer while they were both circulating through Manhattan's nightlife and the *demi-monde* of boxers, managers, pols, wiseguys, trainers, and gamblers. They met through a mutual friend, Whitey Bimstein, cut-man and trainer to boxing champions like Benny Leonard, Rocky Marciano, and Rocky Graziano. It was a world of tough men, sharp glances, knowing faces; men who were quick to take offense; a world bristling with power and the itch to apply it.

Harry had been a fixture in our home as long as I could remember and though he was not a blood relative, he was always referred to as "Uncle Harry." After Sadie, his wife of many years, died, Harry married my father's sister, Caroline, a tall brassy brunette with a dazzling smile—who bore a marked resemblance to Rita Hayworth. She had enough of Morris's temperament to doom their relationship and they divorced after not too long a time. The fact that he had threatened to murder Caroline if she left him and that she had dismissed his threat by informing him that she "didn't care," created no impediment to Harry's relationship with my dad, who probably preferred Harry's company to his sister's. At any rate, as far as I was concerned, Harry remained "Uncle Harry."

He was a tall, solid man, with a regal reserve. I never saw him lose his temper or his equilibrium. Men I recognized as normally high-status, type-A individuals inevitably deferred to Harry when he arrived. He spoke carefully and appeared unconcerned with what others might think of him, reserving for himself the power to determine how he would be regarded. It was like him to leave nothing that important to chance. Business suits were his preferred uniform and he disciplined his thick, black, wavy hair with pomade, combing it straight back without a part. While his overall affect was sleek, well-groomed, and elegant, his broken nose and impenetrable self-assurance suggested a well-tested past. I asked Uncle Bert once what Harry "did" and his answer was as intriguing as it was mystifying. "Harry's a 'fixer,'" he said, closing the subject down. When I pressed him for more details, he offered vague allusions to his "knowing people" and being "a leverage expert."

Harry's back story was as shadowy as the realms in which he operated. I don't recall anyone ever mentioning where he was born or how he was raised. He spoke fluent Russian, Yiddish, and English and I heard him speak what sounded like Italian on several occasions. What elevated him in my eyes was the obvious respect and deference that he elicited from my father, my uncle Bert, and their friends. Harry was indisputably an alpha male and when Harry was present even Morris was attentive. A kid could perceive how that marked him as special. I was curious to discover what the source of his power might be.

From fragments Morris and Bert revealed to me, Harry's "professional" life began in his teens after a protracted and violent fistfight with two Italian brothers on the beach at Coney Island. The fight continued for so long and with such unremitting determination from the three participants that a crowd gathered. As the sun began to sink, absorbed spectators drew cars together so that their headlights would illuminate a ring in the sand. The three boys fought to collapse, retching, gasping for breath, and unable to raise their arms. They were splayed out and immobilized in the improvised spotlight before the avid and cheering spectators.

After the fight, Harry and the brothers became fast friends. The brothers (I never learned their names) matured and became "made"

Mafia members of high rank. Harry was reputed to be the only man outside their blood-oath confederacy that they trusted completely and he served them as a *consigliere*, or counselor. Because he was considered incorruptible he was employed as a judge in inter-family Mafia disputes. The fact that he was a Jew and could not be a Mafia member made him acceptable as a neutral jurist. "Harry dealt in cases that could have capital implications," Uncle Bert explained to me one night and I understood. Harry had a privileged view of a *very* closed world.

He also understood perfectly how to frighten and manipulate men, and perhaps learned those skills while he was the partner of gangster Frank Costello when both men controlled the lucrative slot machine concessions in Louisiana. It was Harry who was called to intervene when my grandfather was faced with "intractable" unions threatening to close his factory down. I overheard fragments of conversations as I invented numerous reasons for passing through the room—men had been "imported," fights and bloody punch-ups had occurred, and stories about Grandpa Jack and the baseball bat he wielded (in his fifties) were codified into family legend.

◄o►

GRANDPA JACK DIED suddenly in the winter of 1951, when Morris was already preoccupied with his own affairs. That left the responsibilities for the family business (manufacturing relatively inexpensive lamps and shades) to fall on his brother Bert, fifteen years younger and currently teaching English at Columbia and working for his doctorate in classical studies.

Bert had entered the C.N. Burman company when it was reeling from a crisis of sales and the deaths of its two principals—my grandfather Jack, and Caroline's first husband, Clarence "Red" Burman. The company had recently been unionized and its attorney was trying to negotiate the new union contract. By his own admission, Bert was naïve, and despite his good intentions to create pay incentives to increase productivity and reward workers for increased profits, the negotiations were stalemated.

The shop floor was in turmoil and one day, reviewing a union newsletter, Bert discovered that the union's business representative, an aggressive Scotsman with a thick brogue and a brusque manner, was an obdurate Communist who had publicly vowed in print to make an example at C.N. Burman and Company and teach his members how to "control a company."

Bert knew that the next round of negotiations would require someone other than the company lawyers to negotiate for them and he called Morris, who had had extensive experience with unions during his presidency of the Hudson and Manhattan Railroad (currently the PATH Train). Dad had been facilitated in his union relationships by Harry Palmer. Morris feared (as he feared for me) that Bert was not "prepared" for the fractious rough-and-tumble milieu. He feared that Bert was not capable of navigating the complexities of manufacturing, bargaining, union negotiations, and sales; that he did not possess the requisite hardness and because Morris had no intention of running his father's business and supporting the rest of the family, and had no intention of being slowed down by having to train his kid brother to do it, his solution to the dilemma was to ask Harry to prepare Bert for his appointed future.

When the dour Scot appeared for the second round of negotiations, Harry Palmer was waiting for him in Bert's office and Harry instructed Bert to leave the room.

The precise details of what occurred between Harry and the Scotsman will never be known. It *is* known that the Scotsman abandoned the negotiations immediately after his meeting with Harry and was never heard from again save once, when he phoned Bert to inform him that he could no longer negotiate with him because he would be killed.

A mysterious, previously unknown *independent* union appeared in Bert's shop to represent and negotiate for the workers. A contract was signed in short order, retaining Bert's incentive plans but also asserting management's *absolute control* of the shop floor. Harry assumed the newly-created office of Vice President of labor for C.N. Burman and I overheard Bert explaining to Morris how this arrangement "worked for Harry" because it afforded him a legal way to justify troublesome income to the IRS.

When the independent union later merged with the Teamsters, the Scot negotiator's role was occupied by a man named Milton Silverman and later his son Dennis, both notorious for their Mob *bona fides*. Suffice it to say that Harry had done business with Milton in the past and since Harry now handled labor issues for the firm, the two men came to an understanding quite readily and there were never any labor problems at C.N. Burman again. With those difficulties resolved, Morris prevailed on Harry to teach Bert how to "deal with people."

Harry took Bert under his wing and tutored him meticulously in the skills required to bribe, cajole, and threaten others to advance his interests. He taught him to read adversaries accurately and size up competitive situations strategically. He taught him to search for and identify "hinges" and "leverage points" (weakness, fear, greed) where advantages could be exploited. To judge by Bert's success in the world, Harry taught him well. Unlike my father, who would die so far below broke that my mother would be forced to liquidate our three homes (including Turkey Ridge) and most of her possessions and live the remainder of her life in a small apartment in genteel poverty. For his part, Bert left a functioning business and a goodly measure of his wealth to his children.

—◄○►—

TIME I SPENT with Harry was time on high alert. Simply receiving his attention was an honor but the best times were when he invited me to accompany him on his "rounds," in Manhattan. I learned to bird-dog his heels, but maintain strict silence when we were with others. If I became too "present," a glance from him would back me up into invisibility.

After first securing me a hot dog and a Coke, he would cross to a particular corner near the Astor Hotel and we'd stand in Times Square. Crowds flowed around us like water. The neighborhood was exciting: billboards and seedy shops, flea circuses, and variety stores where you could buy switchblade knives, dice, and playing cards with naked women on them. Everything seemed illicit and fascinating. Neon signs flashed ADMIRAL TELEVISION, APPLIANCES, and CHEVROLET, and everywhere bright lights and motion prevailed. One end of the street was dominated by advertisements for whiskey. Movie theaters, whose marquees announced the newest films, offered the promise of endless entertainment, but from my point of view, why would I go to a movie about make-believe tough guys when I could hang out with the actual model? Rough people who looked like they might be the parents of street kids—whose unsupervised freedom I'd once envied from the backseat of our limo—lounged against buildings scanning the streets, as if they had nothing better to do than be alert.

Harry might say, "I got a couple of things I've gotta do," tapping an unfiltered Chesterfield against his silver lighter, and firing it up nonchalantly. "Do you want to stay or look around?" I *did* want to look around at times and occasionally explored the flea circus and curio shops, but usually I preferred to remain close to Harry. The fact that a man of such power chose to spend time with me softened the sting of my father's absence. I was alert but never tense around Harry, never feared frightening outbursts in his presence. If I made a mistake or a breach of protocol, I was corrected quietly and privately, without intimidation, but in a manner against which there was no appeal.

Harry was kind to me and I loved him. I felt safe and important with him, included in the penumbra of his respect and protection. Thus sheltered, I could take in the life of Broadway as if it were playing out on a movie screen, catching fascinating snatches of conversation in the background thrum of the street.

"You can't take that from a woman, Freddie. You *can't.*"

"He says, 'fifteen hunnert dollars and I walk away wid' it.' You want some of that?"

In the blur of sounds and colors, I could distinguish scents of Wildroot Cream-Oil (what my mom now let me use on my hair); recognized Lilac Vegetal, the sweet aftershave that my dad and Grandpa Jack favored. These familiar scents mingled with the aromas of hot dogs, steaming bagels, Juicy Fruit Gum, stale beer, and automobile exhaust. Harry stood in the torrent of passing people, immobile as an eternal principle. Occasionally, individuals surfaced from the flow and presented themselves before "Mr. Palmer." They scanned the street as they talked quietly, rarely making eye contact. It might be a detective from "the safe-and-loft squad" (known as the "real-deal" detectives, usually reserved for the biggest cases), or a fighter with deformed ears, or a uniformed cop. At other times, men dressed in suits with enormous knots fastening their ties stopped to chat. Occasionally Harry would introduce me as his nephew, and he invariably described them to me as "a frienda mine."

At times one of Harry's visitors might glance at me before beginning to speak. Harry's nod, signifying "He's okay," made me as proud as a boy could feel. Harry's interchanges with everyone were invariably respectful and he thanked them courteously for whatever boon or favor they might have done for him. On occasion, he might proffer a few words of the "I'll speak to him" variety, or an envelope, or a package might pass from their hands to his or vice versa. Only rarely did Harry indicate that I should "go get a Coke or something." The first time he suggested it, however, I missed his implied command and said, "I'm fine, thanks."

Harry pressed a five-dollar bill into my hand, enough for a hundred Cokes, and said, in a soft voice of indisputable command, "Get a Coke and come back in ten minutes." While I hated not being privy to what was transpiring, I comforted myself as I left by inventing scenarios where Harry had to threaten someone.

When I returned I had, in addition to the Coke, also bought a pack of gum. I informed Harry of this as I returned his change. "I told you to buy a *Coke*," Harry said, and his face was like stone.

My blood turned thick and cold. Harry's face was pitiless and I was terrified. "I thought it would . . ." I began, about to stammer some excuse, but I stopped myself. "I'm sorry Uncle Harry," I said. "I owe you a nickel. I'll give. . . ."

He reached out and tousled my hair, smiling. "Forget it. You're my boy. But I want you to remember this. You *never* go into a man's pocket without permission. *Never*. Not even for a dime, do you understand? In certain situations that could be a capital offense."

I never did after that. Ever.

When meetings ended and Harry's visitors plunged back into the current of pedestrians, Harry returned to his solitary post, still as a pike in a deep pool. Harry was a man of action, never voluble. He said his piece and gauged the response and then responded appropriately. In my early understanding of power—"Who can make whom do what"—Harry was preeminent. He explained it to me this way one day. "Some people have power and some don't, Pete. The ones who have it, do what they want. The ones without it, do what they're told. If I were you, I'd be thinking about how to *get* it."

This conversation occurred in the context of a conversation in which I was trying to explain my discomfort at having been raised with privileges that others did not have. In the course of elucidating what I meant I referred to them as "unearned." Harry's response to me rang out like a shot:

"They're not unearned," he snapped. "Your father's killing himself for them."

ON ONE OF our forays, I was excited to discover that Harry maintained *two* offices at different Manhattan addresses. I had visited one before, and assumed it must have been a friend's because the licenses and framed documents on the walls were addressed to an unfamiliar name, despite the fact that Harry was in all of the framed photographs on the wall. On this day he took me to a second office with no explanation and let himself in with a key. It took me a moment to realize that it was also his. Like the former, it displayed photos, plaques, honoraria, and credentials but bore a *different* name from the previous one. The photos in the new office were similar to those in the first—Harry shaking hands with distinguished men. Occasionally I recognized a face from the newspapers. When I inquired why he had two offices, Harry chuckled and responded in his gravelly voice: "Macy's doesn't tell Gimbels." This was high entertainment but what transpired next was terrifying.

Normally, when we parked Harry's car in the Manhattan garage he left it and walked away. He did not take a ticket, talk to anyone, or say how long he would be gone. This day, however, he needed to retrieve something from the car so we ambled back to the garage to pick it up on our way to lunch. There was no one in the office when we arrived, so we walked down a ramp to the next level and discovered Harry's car with the hood raised and two men leaning into the engine cavity. An engine was sitting on a little trolley beside Harry's car.

The men looked up as Uncle Harry approached. "Mr. Palmer," one of them began, "this isn't *your* car, is it?" Harry walked over and looked into the engine compartment where hoses and wires, now separated from his big Chrysler engine, were dangling. He never blinked, nothing changed in his face. The man who had first spoken said, "Oh Jesus, I had no . . ." Uncle Harry cut him off.

"I'm taking my nephew to lunch. I'm coming back in one hour. I'll be taking my car. Will there be a problem?"

The man swallowed like he was gulping water after a week in the desert. He became pale and began to tremble. He said, "No sir. No, Mr. Palmer, we don't. This was a *total* misunderstanding." The man's fear was so palpable that *I* became frightened and edged closer to Harry, taking the hem of his jacket between my thumb and first finger. I had never seen a grown man so afraid and I had no idea what might happen next. Harry walked past him without responding, reached into his car for what he needed, and headed up the ramp to the street. I hopped alongside him. "What happened, Uncle Harry? What *was* that? That was really scary."

"Why were you scared?" he asked me calmly. "You were with *me!*"

I had no answer to that, so he continued. "They were gonna change my engine for a little cheap job. It's good we went back."

"People *do* that?" I asked.

"People do *everything*," Harry said as we emerged into the daylight. Then he said, "Did you see that guy's face? He didn't know it was mine."

"What are you gonna do, Uncle Harry?" I asked nervously. "Is something going to happen to him?"

Harry said, "You should worry about lunch."

To see Harry terrify another man was the newest refinement in my understanding of power.

CONVERSATIONS WITH HARRY never wandered into vague ideas and concepts. His speech was concerned with things he knew to be personally true, or that had been relayed to him by men he considered trustworthy. In Harry's world, some men were honorable and some were not. He possessed encyclopedic knowledge about human indulgences, fears, and weaknesses, and the leverage points with which a man could be pried away from his intentions or his own interests. Life confronted some men with problems beyond their control and Harry's occupation was to fix those problems using his knowledge of human weakness as a fulcrum.

I could never determine if Harry disliked any religions or favored any political party. I gathered from his friendship with Susie that he had no negative ideas based on race. I was in our kitchen once when she called him to borrow a thousand dollars to pay the college tuition of a young friend who had been laid off from his summer job. I could hear Harry through the receiver. "A thousand dollars? I'll give you two thousand. Whatever you need, Sue."

"Don't you want to know what it's for?" she asked.

"No," he said. "I know it's for you."

She told him anyway, and I could hear him through the phone repeating over and over again, "That is just so damn nice. That is so damn nice."

If I had ever entertained doubts about Harry's respect for Sue, they would have been resolved at her wedding to Ozzie, which took place in our living room. It was Harry who walked Sue down the aisle and "gave her away" to her future husband. As they walked together, Morris turned to me and whispered, "I know a number of people who would have paid a fortune to have Harry Palmer walk their daughter down the aisle. Sue did it on her own merits."

◄○►

BOTH OF MY parents drank to excess, and my father ended his life addicted to Demerol and morphine. Morris's addiction was a shadow

with its own identifiable presence, always present as a vapor floating about our house, but never acknowledged or named. Its nature
was a veil of glances and illogical behavior and a feeling that there
was always some inexplicable element missing from all explanations
and events, like a jigsaw puzzle whose pieces never quite replicate the
image on the box lid.

Exploring the upstairs linen closet one day, I discovered a zip-
pered leather case tucked away on the very top shelf, containing
several glass syringes and chromed needles. After examining them,
I re-hid them, like a dirty secret, and neither mentioned nor asked
about them. Several weeks after that discovery, I walked into the
kitchen as my mother was administering a shot in my father's arm.
The oddness of it froze the moment, and I could tell by the height-
ened casualness of her response that she was embarrassed and worried. "Oh darling, I'm just giving your father his medicine," she said
with inappropriate brightness.

Today my anger towards Morris has evaporated—most of it
anyway—and I regard him with much pity and tenderness. No matter
what he ever did to me (or himself), he could not lie to himself. He
understood precisely how conflicted he was between his ambitions for
elegance, power, and high social status, and his simultaneous impulse
to honor the high ethical standards he expected of himself. In *Sleeping
Where I Fall*, I recounted the story of my grandmother's rescue of him
from his father's attempt to push him through a small third-story attic
window in a murderous rage. However much that incident ravaged
Morris's psyche and inoculated him with permanent feelings of worth-
lessness, they were triggered in later life through the negative judgments he received from American culture for being a Jew.

-<o>-

AMERICA IN THE Twenties, Thirties, and Forties was less receptive to Jews than it is today. Quotas limiting their enrollment existed in the best schools and clubs, and anti-Semitism was a casual affair in many of the boardrooms and wealthy homes Morris had access to. Today, I can appreciate how he struggled to deal with his received ideas of what "success" and being "the best" required, but he had his own junkyard dog to placate, and as I would follow his lead ten years later, he pacified his with narcotics. Each of our interior dogs had two masters that hated one another and fought bitterly. He had no more idea how to make peace between them than I did and consequently, he could never instruct me and I could never help him.

BY 1957 I was sixteen. Morris's various endeavors were minting money. As Muff and I entered our teens, he built a summer house in the "up-island" wilds of Martha's Vineyard. The folk music movement was beginning to bloom when our family first visited a year earlier and the Vineyard was an epicenter for the best players from the Boston–Cambridge–New York axis. My sister was soon seeing one of its stars, a lanky, handsome New Englander named Tom Rush, with a wry wit and a clean, funky guitar style. His attraction to her must have been powerful because he was extremely patient about suffering my relentless requests to teach me guitar licks and abet my proficiency on the guitar. By chance or fortune of geography, the friends she and I made on the Vineyard that first summer and the next were early first-magnitude stars in that emerging folk galaxy: Tom Rush, Geoff and Maria Muldaur, Bill Keith, Fritz Richmond, Tom West (whom my sister would later marry), and Davey Gude. The ravishing queen of the Vineyard's up-island folk scene was a dazzling woman named Jessie Benton. She was the daughter of American painter Thomas Hart Benton, a proud, sophisticated beauty who had already graduated from Radcliffe and lived in Italy. She had an intimidating watchfulness and offered the impression that she often struggled to hold boredom at bay and sought amusement and diversion. Her thrilling laugh drove men to compete for her favor. When we met, famous pols from New York were calling to entreat her to meet them in rooms they'd reserved at expensive hotels for the weekend. I remember her hanging up on one such fellow and saying to me as if he had told her an amusing story, "He carries Bobby Kennedy's shirts."

Fate and my good fortune brought us together as a couple a few years later during the summer I graduated college. When I left for graduate school in San Francisco, she and her young son Anthony came with me, and readers who would like further details are referred to my first book.

On the Vineyard, I buttonholed everyone I knew to teach me picks and licks and songs and it is a wonder that my sister was not shunned by the players who were interested in her, because I seized upon all of them for lessons whenever they were in proximity. Davey Gude, the father of Jessie Benton's son and one of the Vineyard's musical stars, taught me to diagram fingerpicking patterns and I began practicing them with manic enthusiasm. By the end of that summer, Muff and I had become Vineyard regulars and I continued to return there for some part of the year for the next six or seven years.

Aware of Morris's respect for musical talent, late one summer afternoon I brought a group of five or six friends home with me. According to custom, a spontaneous jam session broke out. Tom Rush was there, Geoff Muldaur, Bill Keith—the acclaimed banjo innovator who went on to play with bluegrass pioneer Bill Monroe—and several others. Morris was as entranced with their music as I was and it satisfied me to know that I had introduced him to something he found worthwhile.

During an interlude between musical sets, Morris produced a celebratory bottle of Jack Daniel's and poured drinks all around, ignoring the fact that nearly everyone was under the legal drinking age. We were clustered around our dining room table and his acknowledgement made me proud. When Morris raised his glass, I raised mine, joining the toast to my peers. Morris appeared to notice me then for the first time. He growled, as if affronted, "Not you! You're not old enough to drink!" With his free hand he snatched my glass away without lowering his own raised to the others. My embarrassed friends, of course, drank with him.

—◄○►—

IN 1958, I was seventeen and in my junior year of high school. I had been driving for a year, having been eligible in Pennsylvania a year earlier. In addition to auto mechanics, I had become obsessed with the Beats and the social and artistic freedom they represented. I let my hair grow, favored turtleneck sweaters, and began smoking Camel cigarettes (outside my house). I was already conversant with their spectrum of radical politics and social alternatives to the status quo from dinner table conversations and trips to Greenwich Village and never discovered one that I was not willing to explore. There was simply not enough time to attend to my education *and* school.

In my junior year, my tony private school lost patience with me. I had been avoiding my homework and the debilitating tutoring sessions with Morris, which inevitably ended with him screaming "You can't *be* this fucking stupid" until my mother rushed in, screaming at him to stop screaming.

"Morrie, you're making him crazy. Stop it!" Small wonder that I preferred my time in our impromptu garage sessions with my friends. My junior year failures were disastrous and beyond the capacity of Morris's tuition check or largesse to repair. When my final report card arrived, evenly divided between D's and F's, the headmaster, Mr. Umpleby (a Dickensian name and personality), insisted that I leave. I can't say it bothered me very much.

In the previous six months, between spring and fall, I had grown nearly four inches and after spending the first part of my summer doing farmwork and the second on a milkshake-like diet regimen called Metrecal, determined to lose my baby fat, I returned to school at summer's end, six feet tall and nearly thirty pounds lighter. I had edged into the normal spectrum of high school physiological acceptability. I was also shaving, both of which seemed to crank up the gain on Morris's irritability. It appeared to my aggrieved adolescent self that his attentions were even more persistently critical than the year before when I was fat and depressed. I set my mental sights on getting away from home. I wanted my own adventures; wanted to escape the cowardice I'd always demonstrated in his presence and make of myself someone I could respect. "I'll show him," I thought, and I certainly did. I showed myself too.

I begged off farmwork to dedicate the summer to a cross-country trip with my pal, fellow Beat aficionado David Levine. Our plan was to drive to San Francisco and see the Beats, who by this time had been written up in *Life* magazine. Their reputed San Francisco headquarters at the Co-Existence Bagel Shop signaled us like a lighthouse indicating the beckoning wild waters frothing outside the placid bays of suburbia. On our way home we intended to pass through Mexico, to visit an old family friend. He would turn out to be the guide for a much more tumultuous journey than I could have anticipated.

DAVID CAMPBELL WAS a dancer in Martha Graham's famous modern dance company in New York when he entered my parents' circle of friends. He was the first overtly gay man I had ever met, as well as the cultural scout who ushered Buddy Jones into our camp. In retrospect it seems probable that several bachelor friends who sometimes joined him when he came to dinner were gay as well, but they were decorous and dignified while David was camp, mercurial, and outrageous; a being who threw off sparks. He and Buddy became perfect resources for questions too sensitive to ask my parents. David's outsider status as a gay man *and* an artist had sensitized him to the plight of other outsiders—blacks, artists, jazz-folk, and hipsters—and his shimmering wit and personal authenticity granted him privileged admission into an extensive spectrum of society.

Born to a wealthy banking family in Hawaii and "turned out" (his term) by a black convict working in the family yard, when he arrived in New York, David supported himself as a bellhop working at the Hotel Theresa in Harlem, where, for whatever personal reason, he passed himself off as black. He shared a room there with Billie Holiday and they remained friends until she died.

Buddy Jones introduced me to jazz nightlife, taking me with him to hear friends playing at the Village Vanguard or the Half Note at Spring and Hudson streets in deep downtown New York. I was perhaps fifteen when he took me to hear Billie Holiday's last concert at Carnegie Hall. She had been arrested for drugs some years earlier and lost the cabaret card that allowed her to work in any venues where liquor was sold. Concert halls were her last available option in New York. After her set we stopped backstage to chat with her and as if being in her presence were not enough, when Buddy informed her that I knew David Campbell, she turned her watery eyes on me and smiled. "Go *on*," she said, and her speaking voice inflected the word "on" with same timbre and twist she'd have used singing it. "*You* know David. Well, you hug his crazy ass for Billie, huh. . . ." And then as an afterthought, like a drummer's rim-shot punctuating a burlesque gag, she said, "But don' get too close, child," and she and Buddy fell out laughing.

I was in seventh heaven. Billie Holiday knew Buddy Jones, and because of that she had *talked* to me! I was bulletproof for days after that meeting, peppering conversations with my jazz buddies with "Billie" this and "Billie" that until Buddy drawled, only half in jest, "Hey man, you want to pick up that name you just dropped?"

When I relayed Billie's message to David he twinkled for an instant, but asked in all seriousness, "How does she look?"

David appeared to know everyone, from DuPonts (and I would later learn why), street hustlers, and Harvard professors to Dizzy Gillespie. He fostered introductions and cross-pollinations between social sets as if he were a thread stitching disparate patches into a coherent quilt. For a while, Morris secured him employment with John Walton and Sons, the antiques firm he bankrolled. David must have been quite an asset there, because he breezed into the Englewood house one day, threw me a "signifying" look over his shoulder as he sashayed past, informing me archly, "A DuPont grabbed this ass today."

I had never met anyone quite like David. His personal freedom and social courage were compelling. He doubled the number of colors in my Crayola box of personal expression. I did not have to be black to incorporate the melodic scale, pitches, and vocabulary of black speech into my own and I did not have to be a homosexual to take advantage of David's expressive communication. David was so "out there" he gave implicit permission to others to "be themselves" and I seized on the opportunity.

He was neither shy nor conflicted about his sexuality and took delight in educating me about 1950s gay culture, amazing me by identifying one or another famous person as "queer." When we first met, I wasn't altogether sure what "queer" meant until I reached puberty, but I shoved it into my mental satchel for later review.

◄○►

MY PARENTS WERE uneasy about my pending travel plans and particularly the journey's Mexican portion. They relaxed when I promised them that we would stay with David Campbell in Mexico. He had moved by then to Manzanillo some years earlier and now worked for Bellas Artes, the government art agency, teaching dance and Michael Chekhov acting exercises in Indian villages (a gig he must have invented for himself). Ruth and Morris appeared calmed by the fact that I would be under David's supervision and we departed in high, adventurous spirits.

The San Francisco portion was interesting but not what we expected. At a Beat party we found our way to, poet Bob Kaufman seized David Levine and pretended to inject drugs into him with a ballpoint pen while he recited a strange poem over him. It was unnerving and not fun. We had come looking for Gary Snyder, Jack Kerouac, and Allen Ginsberg and found Bob Kaufman. We decided to head for Mexico.

"Under David's supervision" is an oxymoron of such tension between its parts that I can only wonder a) how the sentence can stand unsupported, and b) *what were my parents thinking?* To travel with David in Mexico was to be stunned and overwhelmed on a daily basis. I was no longer a fly on the wall drinking in the distilled wisdom of elders. I was a testosterone-fueled seventeen-year-old with a double-digit IQ in life experience, unfettered and unsupervised in the steaming, spawning, procreating, and rotting fertility of Mexico—with a practiced libertine for a guide.

David led us on a sleepless parade as if he were the Pied Piper of ecstasy. The three *caballeros* (David, I, and my traveling buddy we nicknamed "Little David" to avoid confusion) caroused through bars, slapping piles of salt into our mouths from the backs of our hands before downing shots of tequila and biting tart wedges of lime. (It takes many shots to accomplish that skillfully.) We sang, drunk in the streets, serenaded whores on their balconies, traipsed through brothels, ate *tortillas de maiz* dripping *carnitas* and pungent sauces of smoky *chipotles* cooked on the curb by vendors glazed with sweat.

Life in Mexico for *los gringo*s was cheap in 1958. There were twelve pesos to the dollar and a peso in Mexico was worth something. In the mornings we'd breakfast on fresh orange or melon juice and *huevos* *rancheros* covered with salsa so hot it made my nose run, accompanied by sides of fried red bananas. We chased breakfast with scalding coffee mixed with sweetened condensed milk. Everything smelled of limes, flour, diesel oil, rotting fruit, cheap pomade, jungle flowers, lard, and seared cooking oil. The colors were improbably bright—even the staid ochre-colored Cathedral of the Immaculate Conception glowed in the baking light. The name of that church passed over my lips like the invocation of a Beat anthem. I was in *Mexico*, man, and I was uttering words and phrases that might have been written by Jack Kerouac; living a free and exciting life far from the debilitating conflicts of home.

Houses painted purple, turquoise, canary yellow, and green, vivid as jungle birds, climbed the forested slopes of Mazatlán where the relentless Mexican sun tamed their fluorescent glare to dulcet hues. Taxis, trucks, and busses buzzed and roared, belching clouds of sooty fumes. Artisans clinked hammers in the doorways of closet-sized shops; shirtless men rebuilt car batteries and disassembled engines on the curbs. The winds were balmy. There was no law. We had no homework and nowhere we had to be. Being alive could not have been more fun.

◄○►

I CANNOT RECALL today *how* the subject surfaced, but one day we began to discuss marijuana. Perhaps David could no longer tolerate *not* being high, or, with the refined instincts of a hustler, he might have concluded that some of Little David and my travel money could be liberated towards the end of altering his consciousness.

David's marijuana curriculum was very detailed and knowledgeable. He explained that marijuana was neither addictive nor harmful to the body; that it had been in use for centuries in the Middle East and Africa, and in North and South America by Native Americans, blacks, and Mexicans with no harm done. Memories of Sue's stories about picking and drying fig leaves to mix with her grandfather's "rabbit tobacco" came back to me then, confirming David's assertions.

He explained how, after Prohibition ended, federal and local police departments desperate to retain their inflated agency budgets joined forces with election-hungry politicians seeking campaign issues. They created a *new* scourge that would justify extravagant (and virtually endless) flows of tax dollars, by identifying marijuana and then cocaine as new and previously unknown threats to American sanity and racial purity. August newspapers featured tabloid stories of "niggers" (the word the papers used) raping white women under the influence of pot and cocaine and whipped the white electorate into a panicked froth.

David's explanation was on a parallel track with what I had learned in watching Buddy Jones and listening to the bohemians in Greenwich Village, so I accepted what he said. In the spirit of selfless scientific inquiry, Little David and I decided that we should assess the experience for ourselves. We understood that "weed" was a staple of jazz and Beat-life, and so it appeared to be the next step on our 'stations of the cross' pilgrimage from suburban marshmallows to initiated hipsters.

Big David scored some weed the next day and rolled a joint as we drove around the countryside at dusk. Sucking down the smoke, holding my breath, coughing it up, hacking and wheezing, wiping the tears from my eyes with my forearm, I noticed no difference between my pre- and post-inhale reality. Big David surmised that perhaps we needed more, so he rolled and we smoked another joint. Nothing.

David rolled another and we smoked that as well. Somewhere during that third joint, as I was wondering what all the fuss was about, I spooked and shrieked, jerking the wheel to avoid a phantom dog in my headlights. The car lurched off the road, bouncing across the sand ruts and through the mesquite and sage, with the three of us laughing and weeping like crazy people. I was *high* and boy, was it *fun!*

Our first experiment was a complete success, but intellectual rigor demanded practice if Little David and I were to become thoroughly knowledgeable! We returned to the subject multiple times a day, smoking ourselves into a red-eyed, cotton-mouthed, sugar-sucking delirium. Under the influence of the sticky, pollen-rich leaves, Mexico was transformed. Oil-sheen rainbows glowed on shimmering quicksilver puddles. The interlocking patterns of a Huichol Indian's shirt signaled wisdom just beyond the grasp of language's greedy fingers. The glistening piles of *habanero*, *ancho*, and *pasilla* chiles glowed with inner fire in the market stalls, and the amber-colored faces passing in the street might have been Aztecs or Mayans in possession of ancient mysteries. Mexico's imponderables were far more interesting than my math book's vexing word problems, demanding to know when trains A and B, leaving different stations at different speeds, would intersect. Absent Morris's prosecutorial inquisitions I was free to express my real feelings on the subject, which were "Who gives a fuck?"

My emotions flowed like conversation responding to previously unperceived signals from the universe. Finally, I *knew* in my innermost being how jazzmen *felt*: how a sound, a smell, a phrase could trigger cascading associations and release creative responses that bypassed thought—prompting singing, random poetic phrases and associations, or simply dancing in place if I felt like it. Weed exposed and cracked codes from a parallel reality that I had received intimations of but now, the final keystone had been dropped in place, and the high and open arch of my mind was free-standing and self-supporting.

If I had stopped there, everything might have been all right.

—◦—

AS THE TIME approached for us to leave Mexico, I became convinced that marijuana was a healthier, saner social lubricant than alcohol. I resolved to bring some home, rescue my friends from growing up like our parents and claim my due measure of notoriety as Johnny Weed-seed. Because we had no idea if we might ever return to Mexico, we thought it prudent to lay in an ample supply. Big David made some inquiries and we took an evening's drive ten or fifteen miles outside of Mazatlán, following a simple map his informant had scrawled on a brown paper bag. We ended up traversing a long, sandy wash that only an optimist could consider a road. Creatures skittered into and out of the beams of the headlights, starkly illuminated one moment and the next absorbed by darkness like spooks in a funhouse ride. Owls cried among the darkening silhouettes of *ocotillo* cactus, and the dense brush along the edges of the track obscured what lay beyond in the gathering dark.

The journey ended at an impoverished structure of obviously salvaged, multicolored boards topped by a low flat roof. Several blue tin kerosene lamps of the highway construction site variety dangled from the porch beams, their pallid glow claiming a meager radius of only several feet against the night. A chicken clucked pacifically in the yard, pecking around a dog lying on the porch who leveled a hoarse croak in our direction, without deigning to rise.

Big David dickered in Spanish with a young *campesino* in filthy white pants and shirt, settling on a $60 (720 pesos) price that Little David counted carefully in the headlights. For this modest amount of 1958 dollars, we received *eight kilos*—more than sixteen *pounds*—of uncleaned marijuana overflowing the edges of a coarsely woven bushel basket, which we shoehorned into the backseat and covered with a serape.

The three of us passed the next two days in a motel room with the blinds drawn, and towels stuffed around the bottom edge of the door, smoking ourselves into a numb-nuts stupor. Under Big David's tutelage we stripped the leaves from the woody stems, bundling them into packages roughly half the size of Manhattan phone books. We wrapped them tightly in newspaper and plastic bags, and sealed them with tape. For all our shrewd precautions, had the police actually been looking for us, they could have followed the scent trail leaking out of our room, from a block away. Failing that, they could have selected the one motel room whose window screen was virtually obliterated by narcotized house flies.

"Wow, mom, just like professional smugglers! Who could possibly be better at this than two whacked-out teenagers and their stoned gay accomplice?" After everything was cleaned and wrapped, we secured the bricks in the well under the rear seat of my car. How devious—pull up seat, throw in weed, drop seat! Fiendishly clever. The plan required only three stoned people each contributing a single digit of IQ. All was ready, and on departure day Big David sat us down for detailed Chekhovian instructions designed to help us cross the border safely.

"It's important to *be* innocent," he said seriously. "Acting is not *pretending*. If you pretend, people will see you pretending. You must find something that you actually believe, search your imagination—you're carrying medicine for your friends. Make them specific. Who? What is their illness? You have to *believe* it, and then you'll be bulletproof. You will leak no guilt."

This conversation was invaluable to me twenty years later when I became a professional actor, but to judge by what transpired, either we were not impeccable with our execution of his lesson or David's knowledge of smuggling equaled his knowledge of vaginas.

Big David waved us bravely off, his tiny figure diminishing in the rearview mirror, clutching the generous bundle of weed we had left him as a thank-you. My last vision of him for fifty years was his slender body in a bold Hawaiian shirt and sarong, assuming clownish Martha Graham dance postures against the background of the wild wiggy jungle behind him.

Little David and I smoked our way through the multiday journey north to the border. I had chosen to wear a tie for the crossing, disguising myself as an innocent young man returning from a summer's jaunt (think Newport). In my own mind, I *was* bearing lifesaving medicine for imperiled friends, who might die without it. I was considering turning on Ruth and Morris in the hopes of weaning them from alcohol, and in Morris' case, Demerol. That was a worthy purpose and I did not harbor the slightest shadow of self-doubt as we entered the line of idling cars at Matamoros waiting to pass through Customs.

Leaving the Mexican side with little more than a wave, we pulled into the long line of stalled traffic, oozing towards the international border of the United States, manned by heavily armed and unnervingly alert officials of the U.S. Customs service. The first shadow that dulled the glare of my sunny confidence occurred when our car was signaled out of line by two chesty, unsmiling fellows in uniform wearing identical sunglasses that blocked any view of their eyes. We were directed to an isolated area under a tin roof where we were greeted by more unsmiling armed officers carrying flashlights the length of police batons. They asked us to "step outside," surrounded our car, and began combing through our stuff with the concentration of a mother searching her child's hair for nits. When they began unrolling the balls of newspaper stuffed into a pair of boots I'd bought in the Mazatlán *mercado*, an insistent, queasy flutter began pulsing in my stomach.

Moments later, an agent flipped the driver's seat forward, bent into the rear of the car, yanked up the backseat and demanded to know what was in those taped bundles lying (*glowing* from my point of view) in the seat-well. (How could he have known?) I became light-headed and disoriented. My confidence evaporated. I was instantly his prey.

"What packages?" I responded stupidly. "I don't know."

They seized us roughly by the shoulders and frog-marched us towards the border station, which I remember as a squat, cinder-block affair with opaque windows and bright aluminum trim. Light-headed, off balance, and dazed, imagining the consequences that lay ahead, I staggered as my captor jerked me along. When he splashed me through a deep puddle, I was still so high that I protested his rudeness, turning indignantly and exclaiming, "Easy man, I'm not a *criminal*."

The agent laughed like he was coughing, shook his head incredulously, and released his grip. Instead of pulling me, he now propelled me with repeated shoves. All my research about bohemian life—about political resistance, about being an artist—in this moment felt like being informed that I had contracted a terminal disease.

A series of interviews with stern interrogators followed, and queries on the order of "Suppose someone gave this stuff to your sister?" were hurled at us. Some residual reservoir of sanity checked my impulse to respond—"My sister'd *love* it"—or I might still be in Texas. Little David and I spent six or seven stultifying, boring days (the days it required for me to summon my courage to call Morris) as the only prisoners in a cinder-block drunk tank in Brownsville, Texas. Our twin bunk beds had no mattresses, only wire-mesh supports that transferred their grid-patterns into your flesh after ten minutes of lying on them. The far quarter of the room was divided by a four-foot-high concrete wall behind which was a shower capable of delivering only an impoverished drizzle. A Mexican guard took the $5.00 I gave him "for something to read" and returned with a handful of free Jehovah's Witness pamphlets, which he flung through the bars and left, ignoring my indignation.

During the first disoriented days in our overheated green and grey sauna, it became apparent that we were not going to be released "after a good scare" or some other fervently wished for alternative to prison. David's mother was a single working woman and realizing that our only source of aid would be my father, I began rehearsing opening gambits for the inevitable conversation I would have to have with him:

"Golly Dad, someone must've hidden drugs in our car and when we tried to cross the border. . . ."

"Hey Dad, got *kind of a* problem here. We left the car *unlocked* one night and went camping and when we reached the border. . . ."

"Dad, I have good news and I have bad news . . . well, actually I don't have any good news, except that we're alive. I *do* have a little *bad* news. . . ."

Morris confounded my every expectation as if he had planned his response to keep me off balance by normally bending, bruising, and stretching the love I had for him to the breaking point and then reversing himself in a startling and remarkable manner. Contrary to my gut-cramping fears, Morris behaved impeccably. He did not, on the phone, or *ever* afterward, not *once*, mention my stupidity. He never once lectured or judged me. Instead he sheltered me under the umbrella of his power, moving his knights and pawns to protect David and me (and assuming all of David's legal bills) as a man of power could. I was completely at his mercy, and for the first time (perhaps because I had no other option), I could clearly observe how his power was focused solely on my benefit. I was simultaneously mortified and gratified, and once again in the palm of Morris's hand, which was, this time, mercifully open.

Morris's partner in the Charolais cattle business was a tall slender hickory-peg of a Texan named Harl Thomas, from a town named Harlingen, close to Brownsville where we were being held. According to Morris, Harl was a member of the 100-family oligarchy that still rules Texas. Like Bostonian and Philadelphian aristocrats, these voluble and easygoing Southerners keep track of their lineage and pedigree to the same exacting standard as their Boston Brahmin peers, but do so with a Southern lilt of the "Oh yes, his momma was a Bass outta Corpus, and she married a Kleberg, bless her heart" variety. In describing their power, Morris once observed, "They are never audited by the IRS and their children are never drafted in the Armed Forces."

Harl had married a Mexican woman of reputedly fabulous wealth whose family owned (according to Morris) a *million* acres in Mexico, including miles of pristine beach-front, flanked on either boundary by tourist kitsch and *sobaco barrios* (armpit neighborhoods) whose development screeched to a halt at her property lines. Power and wealth of that order ensured us bail and we were flown home to await trial.

While at home, Uncle Harry came by one morning and ordered me into his car. We had an uncharacteristically silent drive to Manhattan, where Harry ushered me into a downtown police station and into an office with a fogged glass door. A short, muscular man with an extremely broken nose and face that appeared to enjoy meanness as a natural condition entered the room and began an address to me about narcotics and their perils. At a certain point, Harry rose and unceremoniously left the room. That was startling. More surprising was the fact that the man now emerged from behind his desk and sat on the corner poised above me. He offered a mirthless smile with a curious glitter in his eyes. "I'm the man that busted Billie Holiday in her hospital room," he said. I was breathless. Did he know that I had met her? Did he know everything about my life? I remained silent while he continued his tale about a nurse discovering some white powder on Billie's upper lip and calling the police. "That was me," he said proudly, "and I handcuffed her to the goddamn bed. You're lucky you know Mr. Palmer," he said, ". . . and you're fucking lucky you don't know me. But keep it up, you will."

Harry re-entered the room at that moment. The two men exchanged a casual good-bye, and Harry led me towards the elevator. "Sorry I had to leave," Harry said, "but he might've wanted to slap you around a little and he wouldn't have if I was there."

I never understood what that man could possibly have to do with my case in Texas. Morris probably wanted Harry to give me a good scare. He did, and if it would keep me out of prison, I was okay with it.

Six months later, Morris, David Levine, and I returned to Texas for sentencing. I was very apprehensive and so was Morris, perhaps more than I was because he understood what the consequences of a conviction could be. We were going to *Texas*, one of the most reactionary law-and-order states in the Union. Even today Texas routinely executes 200 people a year. It's legal to drink, drive, *and* carry a pistol in your car there and it was certainly not *less* raw in the Fifties.

It was clear to me that I could be going to jail for a very long time. We were facing sentencing in the same state and year where only months before a stripper and porn star named Juanita Dale Slusher, aka Candy Barr, had been sentenced to fifteen years *for possessing four-fifths of an ounce of weed*. We had sixteen pounds! Stating that I was "nervous" would be like comparing a grand mal seizure to hiccups. I was seventeen, how would I survive in a tooth and claw Texas prison with no Morris or Harry Palmer protecting my back? What had I been thinking? Oh, that's right, I *wasn't* thinking. I was *stoned!*

Harl Thomas's personal attorney represented us in court. He was a polished old warhorse with the unlikely name of Ransom Crook. (I'd have liked to have asked his parents what they were thinking when they named him.) As the hearing began, my tongue was stuck to the roof of my mouth. Morris sat just behind me, in obvious discomfort.

Ransom unfurled himself and his chocolate brown suit and rose to his full height of well over six feet. On hearing his first utterance I had a sudden intimation that we were in extremely competent hands. Projected in a gravelly and confident voice, he gargled some turgid sentiment like, "Your honor, these are *good* boys!" (Wrong there, Ransom!) I saw my father visibly relax as the judge smiled, shook his head incredulously, and settled in for an entertaining morning. Apparently some of the players (save for Little David, Morris, and me) knew that the outcome had been arranged. By the time Ransom was done, due to our being seventeen, David and I were "adjudged delinquent" and not remanded as felons. When we turned twenty-one, our crimes would be expunged, our records sealed and returned to us.[2] The judge sentenced us to probation until our majority and ordered us to "go home, go to school (which at that moment, appeared attractive) and keep your noses clean." Technically, I did just that; however, the judge failed to specify for how long.

—◦—

PARTLY OUT OF gratitude to Morris and partly because I wanted nothing further to do with jail, I buckled down and graduated from Dwight Morrow High School, the public school in Englewood. I had to repeat my previously failed junior year, but I did well there and I was happy and comfortable in a school that was 50 percent black and made many friends there.

When the time came to prepare my college applications, the schools guidance counselor informed me bluntly that I was going to attend Grinnell College in Iowa. I informed her equally bluntly that I was not. "I already know everything about farms and farmers," I told her and informed her that I was going to apply to Reed, which Beat poets Gary Snyder and Philip Whalen had attended; or failing that would go to Harvard, thank-you-very-much, where Tom Rush and other friends from the Vineyard and the Cambridge folk music scene were in attendance.

I may have been an A-student, but I was an A-student who had gone to jail for drug smuggling. I never learned exactly what the astringent counselor with bobbed hair and a mouth that appeared to have just sucked a lemon told the other eight colleges I applied to about me, but I was rejected from every school *except* Grinnell.

"You'll like it there," she said. "Trust me."

She was correct.

I entered Grinnell in September of 1960, and learned it was the first year that the college had increased their quota of students from the East Coast. I traveled west on the overnight train from New York with two suitcases—one filled with long-playing records and my portable record player fastened to it by a rope. The second held some clothes. My only other piece of luggage was my guitar.

—◄o►—

GRINNELL WAS A blank canvas and I was an unknown quantity and color, ripe for improvising an identity. College was a heavenly reprieve from the ordinary. Freed from Morris's judgments and criticism and my mother's fretful hypervigilance, liberated from family history and expectations, in short order I became part of a small community of friends with similar interests who offered me the opportunity to experiment and push my boundaries to discover my inherent gifts.

The friends I made at Grinnell were as smart and sophisticated as the kids I'd admired on the Vineyard. We shared affection for the same books and music and they were serious about the same issues I was. My closest circle of friends—four of us in particular who had announced ourselves to one another as writers—met every evening at the student union to smoke cigarettes and share and discuss our "bible"—an anthology named *The New American Poetry 1945–1960,* edited by Donald Allen. We'd read poems that excited us, discuss the authors, and then segue seamlessly into how the others might calculate someone's chances with this or that girl—rehearsing the people we hoped to become. I had no idea that in the not-too-distant future, I would become friends with a number of the poets we discussed over coffee and cigarettes. Of our original group, three of us have published books.

MY PROFESSORS WERE sharp and interesting and several had published in reputable literary quarterlies. Having no graduate school, Grinnell students had access to the best professors as undergraduates, and classes were generally stimulating. Perhaps by being older than my classmates, by my sophomore year I was being called on to bartend for faculty parties by friendly professors who trusted me to keep my mouth shut about what might occur inside their homes. These same professors came to my aid at the end of my freshman when I announced year that I would not live in the dorms the following year. With their help I became the first undergraduate allowed to live off campus before senior year.

At Grinnell I met a coterie of young folk musicians and we formed a bluegrass band—the Kittatinny Mountain Boys—named after the mountains near Turkey Ridge. I met a rangy slender girl named Gretchen who was a long way ahead of the coming sexual liberation movement and college was fun now in every dimension.

NOT EVERYONE IN the student body appreciated our East Coast coterie. Those who did not referred to us as "The New Yorkers," "beatniks," or—because we were considered artsy—"fairies." I wore my hair over my ears and favored blue jeans, sandals, and denim shirts over the khakis and untucked dress shirts that were *de rigueur* for most students. By virtue of our cultural foreignness and lack of interest in traditional campus culture we offended a number of the more conservative Midwesterners, especially the big, cocky, buzz-cut athletes we referred to as "the Jocks."

One night, a number of them jumped my writer pal Terry Bisson, a slight blond with a razor wit who hailed from Owensboro, Kentucky. They jumped Terry and shaved his hair off. It was a shocking and cruel act that could only be considered "fun" if you were not the victim or Mitt Romney. To this day, I am disappointed that, as Terry's pals, our group did not think to cut off our hair in solidarity with him.

FREED OF THE pressures of home, I blossomed at Grinnell. I had energy and found the time to get my required reading and work done every day and still carve out the evenings to meet my pals every night in the Student Union from 9 PM until closing time. None of my friends knew Morris; none knew my previous failures or if I was privileged or poor. I had attracted this circle of young men and women on my own merits, and by becoming my friends, they objectified my worth to myself.

Growing up in a culturally sophisticated family conferred advantages on me because I arrived on campus already conversant in politics, Beat culture, jazz, folk music, blues, and gospel—which were just beginning to emerge on college campuses.

I convinced the Grinnell College concert booking agent to hire the Staple Singers, a black gospel group that was virtually unknown in 1961, and she did, blindly gambling on my opinion. Famous today, the Staple Singers' first college booking was at Grinnell and they were stunned to find themselves in the middle of Iowa performing for an all-white audience. During the concert, Roebuck, the father of Mavis, Cleotha, Yvonne, and Pervis Staples, asked the audience incredulously, "How'd y'all know about us?" Students began to shout out my name and the Staple Singers invited me onstage to sing a number with them. Fifty-four years later, it remains a point of pride to be able to claim that I once performed onstage with Mavis Staples and her family. It was an especially sweet recognition because my personal relationship to music had endured a heavy blow earlier that year, reminding me that one's journey to knowledge is never guaranteed to be successful or easy.

At the end of the previous summer, preparing to return to Grinnell for the fall term, I was relaxing playing a blues in the Booth Avenue kitchen when Buddy Jones strolled in. I was conscious of him listening and could not resist showing off, working in some of the best licks I had lifted off records of blues greats. It was a silly, vain, thing to do in front of a musician of Buddy's caliber, but he was such an important figure in my life that I wanted him to see how diligently I had been working on my music. Life is hard for the stupid.

"Whaddya think, Buddy?" I asked in an offhand manner, when the tune was done.

Buddy was dressed for his gig on the Jack Sterling radio show, wearing his black-rimmed glasses and a suit and tie, which lent him a professorial air. He tried to evade the hook of my question, by retrieving his pipe and filling it. "Hey man, I'm an old bebopper," he said deferentially. "That's all I know, man."

I felt something evasive behind his reticence, and probed more deeply. (I wish I had not.) Finally, uncomfortable at the prospect of hurting my feelings, Buddy shared something of his standards with me.

"You know, Pete," he said, "those old-timers were playing *every-thing* they knew. That's they whole world. But that ain't *your* whole world, man. *You've* heard Forty-Second Street and Broadway, man. *You've* heard Bartok and Beethoven; you've heard the whole twentieth century. You're cutting yourself down to fit *yesterday*. You cain't *ever* be those old-timers, baby, not if you could play 'em note for note. They from a different world man, a different sense of time even. But they being *everything* they are. You got to play who *you* are."

I was crushed, but I knew that he was right. I was sitting in the warm, well-lit kitchen of a suburban house, comfortable, and nourished by every material advantage. Suffering is not a competitive sport of course and I had experienced my share and even some portion of hopelessness. The blues offered me a vocabulary for expressing those feelings, however, mine were not and never would be the hopeless, unrelieved suffering of racism; the constant underestimation and oppression to the point of murder for struggling to maintain one's personal authority before white people. This reality coupled with a forced exodus from native lands and the suppression of familiar language, culture, and religion had produced the marrow-deep, aching beauty of blues—America's first indigenous music (after Native American). I was borrowing someone else's expression as my own; picking and choosing between the beautiful sounds I heard to cobble together a self-expression. The musicians I was imitating possessed nothing *but* their culture and expressed it as if their sanity depended on it. And it did. They were playing to make themselves feel better and I was playing to demonstrate how badly I felt—there's an unbridgeable world of difference.

In that moment I understood the inflexible standards that ruled Buddy and his musical peers. Jazz players on a bandstand who couldn't cut it were played off, without pity. Every kid who showed up for the team was *not* given a prize, and self-esteem had to be earned by real accomplishments. It was a tough lesson but Buddy was a jazzman, and had nothing but the truth and his fidelity to offer me. He would not compromise that—not even for a boy he loved. The lesson stung, but I respected him for refusing to lie to me, and (though I was not conscious of it in the moment) for presuming me serious enough to *want* the truth.

College life fertilized sprouts of agency that were emerging within me as if they had been germinating below just-thawed soil. I recalled a powerful dream from the year before I left home to attend college. I was in the attic of the Booth Avenue house, in a sizeable storage area under unfinished attic rafters and cross-beams. The room was dusty and uncared for, and as my eyes adjusted to the light, I noticed that it was filled with aquariums, stacked in tiers on long tables. The glass in each was overgrown and nearly obscured by algae. Each had little bubbles emerging from hidden pumps keeping a curious entity within each tank alive. The entity was an ovoid object the size of a large egg and bisected in half along its length. The top half was transparent like the clear white of an egg while the bottom half appeared to have the density of a hardboiled egg yolk with a greenish tinge. In the dream I was transfixed by these tanks and their obviously alive inhabitants, trying to work out how I could never have noticed them in my own attic before. As I considered this, I had a revelation in the dream that these "yolks" were parts of myself preparing to hatch in some way. I did not know when they might be fully formed, but I understood that I would have to wait for them to mature. When they were ready, they would emerge, and, in some manner, help me.

The rapid surge of maturity and confidence I was experiencing at Grinnell was what had recalled that dream. Pondering its meaning and reviewing my last several years, it became clear that some combination of natural curiosity, predilections, intuitions, and luck had consistently propelled me, without planning or too much thought, into situations that, after the fact, felt inevitable; delivering me without premeditation or striving, into the orbits of people and events which enhanced my growth, skills, and agency.

I never had a conscious plan for my life. Impulses arrived over my spinal telephone, without purpose or design, and I gave them fealty. In this manner, I met the people I was interested in, and what we collaborated to do appeared to be the leading edge of the *zeitgeist*. An example will suffice:

DURING OUR NIGHTLY *soirées* in the student union, a primary topic of conversation was politics. The Cold War was a gelid reality and nuclear weapons were being tested aboveground and in the atmosphere, spewing radioactivity into the stratospheric winds and ocean currents. The Soviets had recently exploded a fifty-megaton hydrogen bomb that the press identified as the largest man-made explosion in history. Scientists described these new weapons as possessing the potential to obliterate all life on earth. Try as one might to ignore the subject with studies, sex, booze, and incandescent conversations, it was difficult not to feel some anxiety. The United States had broken off diplomatic relations with Cuba the prior January, and belligerence and aggression between nation-states seemed to be the organizing principle of international affairs. What was *new* in those affairs was that for the first time in history belligerents (whose psychology had barely evolved in

100,000 years despite their technological cleverness) now possessed weapons that a quarrel (or an accident) could loose to end civilization and scramble the ancient, genetic codes for every species with replicating cells.

I took these threats personally and seriously as did many of my peers. We were just beginning to enjoy our autonomy, our new skills, and the imagined delights of a self-invented future. The bellicosity of world leaders was placing our future in peril.

Team loyalties and the belief that our government could always be depended on to act the part of "the good guys" had never been my default settings. These ideas had been shredded by witnessing the effects of McCarthyism and anti-Leftist persecutions of relatives and friends. They had been blasted apart from the tales of Susie, Ozzie, and black friends, and the TV revelations of southern cops releasing of dogs on black people trying to exercise their legal franchise. I had witnessed the costs of bullying paid by innocents during these purges and it did not require any Red or Socialist relatives to achieve my level of skepticism about the status quo. Many of my peers felt betrayed by our leaders in Washington. The ideological mania of the Cold War and the manipulative, foot-in-the-small-of-your-back, overly simplistic media framing of every issue instructing us how "our side" was to consider world events dismissed others much like ourselves labelled "enemies," while ignoring the beauty and joy of life, all the while herding the world's citizens, like lemmings, towards a looming precipice.

These concerns reached a climax in 1961, and led fourteen of my classmates and me to abandon our classes to plan and execute a protest in Washington, DC. Our idea was to register our disapproval of nuclear policies by fasting outside the White House for three days to make our perspectives heard. Because this adventure has been explicated in depth in *Sleeping Where I Fall*, I'll be brief in describing the moment here.

In outline, the facts were these: After days of planning and discussion we scrounged the money to buy and prepare two old cars and were given a third (and three two-way radios) by a progressive executive of an insurance company in Des Moines. We drove nonstop from Grinnell to Washington and set up shop in an old rooming house, with the ironic name of Gaunt House. During the day we paraded on the sidewalk carrying signs that read, WE SUPPORT KENNEDY'S PEACE RACE and NO MORE NUCLEAR TESTING.

This was the second year of the new decade. John Kennedy, our dashing and glamorous president, was in power and the counterculture of the Sixties had not yet emerged. In fact, we were one of its embryonic cells. Except for the stirring example of the civil rights struggle and the moral challenge it had cast at the feet of white America, there had been few student demonstrations and public protests for us to mimic. We were breaking new ground and had no idea what the consequences might be.

It did not feel to me then (as it does today) that very little of positive consequence to ordinary people gets accomplished in Washington. We were prepared to find the Washington that had been carefully explained to us in civics classes and imagined it through rosy filters— a Washington that represented people like ourselves, serving our interests; a Washington that *wanted* to know what "we the people" thought. Primed by that point of view, we had come to inform them.

On the day we arrived in DC, Sam Rayburn, the legendary ex-speaker of the House of Representatives, had just died and the city was deserted. Mike Horwatt, our group's elected leader, had the presence of mind (or the effrontery) to call a press conference. We had low expectations for its success and were therefore surprised when two reporters arrived. (We dubbed them "UPI" and "AP" for their respective news services.) They liked us and appeared to appreciate our efforts. Because Washington was a news black hole at the moment, they offered us extensive coverage of our views and plans. The doughty little female reporter we had nicknamed "UPI" turned out to be named Helen Thomas. In the years that followed, she became the outspoken dean of White House reporters, revered by many for consistently speaking truth to power at presidential press conferences.

We paced the sidewalk outside the White House fence, bearing our placards patiently and politely, explaining our purpose to reporters and curious citizens. By common agreement, we were well-dressed, groomed, and dignified, doing our best to not alienate anyone. Our intention was to control the agenda and concentrate solely on the issues that had compelled us to be there.

The Gods of Comedy (who never sleep) ensured that we were hounded by a coterie of zealous right-wingers, the Sixties forebears of the angry dimwits who appear at presidential rallies with placards of President Obama tricked out like Hitler. (I'll take wagers that there are few Jews in those crowds.) Our members remain divided today on just *which* right-wingnuts they were—the John Birch Society or the Young Republicans. Identity aside *some* noisy gaggle of mouth-breathers hounded our steps taunting us, ridiculing our fast by ostentatiously gorging themselves on boxes of fried chicken, expressing democracy in all its battered pungency.

The president had recently been through an unpleasant encounter with John Birchers (prototypical Tea-Partiers) and decided to favor our form of protest over theirs. He read about us en route to Arizona and sent an emissary named Marcus Raskin to Gaunt House to extend his invitation to the White House. Raskin was an assistant to the president's national security advisor, McGeorge Bundy,[3] and because the president was out of state, he had arranged for us to speak with Mr. Bundy.

On November 16, 1961, a photograph of us appeared on the front page of *The New York Times,* and our private concerns were catapulted into a *very* public light.[4] I called home to see if Morris had seen it and his gruff "I'm proud of you son" was worth more to me than any aid the photo might have offered our cause.

We were informed that we were the first protesters to ever be honored with such an invitation and consequently our invitation made national news that we capitalized on by reaching out to other colleges around the country, organizing them to follow us to Washington and sustain the protest. These efforts eventually culminated in a gathering of 25,000 students in Washington in early 1963, prompting Tom Hayden to later credit the Grinnell Fourteen as "the beginning of the student peace movement."

We had been so preoccupied with the technical details of our trip that even though we had *debated* our positions on peace and nuclear issues, even after releasing our statement we had never *rehearsed* an integrated public presentation. The concern that our untested unity might unravel in an embarrassing manner was front and center in my mind as we passed the guardhouse and began the short march to the White House the next day. I was hoping that no one would speak

▶ Morris Cohon

▼ Ruth, Muffet, and me in 1950
(PHOTO BY ROY ROSELIEV)

◀ Jack Cohon

▼ Sue Howard Nelson in 1950
(PHOTO BY ROY ROSELIEV)

◀ Jim Clancy
(PHOTO BY ARTHUR SCHWARTZ)

▼ Ellie Clancy
(PHOTO BY ARTHUR SCHWARTZ)

◀ Bill Jelinek

▾ Walt Poliski

◄ Buddy Jones

▼ Bert Cohon

▲ Harry Palmer

▲ Irving Adler

▲ A perfect AJS 500 Single

▲ Muff and me in the Martha's Vineyard years

▲ The Grinnell Fourteen from the front page of *The New York Times* (*left to right*: Bennett Bean, Ruth Gruenwald, Larry Smucker, Jack Chapman, Kurt Lamb, me)

▲ Meeting McGeorge Bundy (*left to right*: Mike Horwatt, Mike Montross, Curt Lamb, Bundy, Bennett Bean)

▲ Sam and Ariel around 1970

▲ The inimitable Sandy Archer on the Mime Troupe Stage

▲ Gary Snyder

▲ Karney Hodge

▲ The Turkey Ridge family (Nicole and Jeramiah, Kent Minault, Samurai Bob Callow (standing) Peggy "Sigh" Darm, Eileen "Sam" Ewing in red sweater with Ariel, me (in tye-died shirt), Paul "Owl" pickens (barechested), to his left, Nina Blasenheim and Angeline; above Paul, Sigh's sister, and Phyllis Wilner (visiting) and Chris Christianson and his son (visiting) (Vinnie and Joanna Rinaldi, Malcolm, and Nicky had not yet arrived)

▲ Nino Cerruti and me, Café de Flore, circa 1990

▲ My Zen Buddhist priest ordination, 2011 (*left to right*, Peter Schireson, Karen Geiger, Chikudo Lewis Richmond-rōshi [my teacher], me, Al Trive, and Ed Sattizahn)

▲ The Great Vehicle

▲ The end

intemperately or embarrass us by revealing what political greenhorns we actually were, thereby discrediting the issues we had worked so hard to represent. This was the big-time, and though none of us expressed it directly, I'm certain that I was not the only one with adrenaline and alarm coursing through my body as we entered the White House.

We were ushered into a white room whose walls were curiously decorated with mounted fish—the eponymous Fish Room—where Mr. Bundy had chosen to meet us. The decor suited his personality, which exuded the empathy of a mackerel. Comfortable Colonial style chairs with padded seats had been set out for each of us facing Mr. Bundy's desk; the arrangement not circular, but oppositional.

Our first test occurred when Mr. Bundy, courteously (or condescendingly—impressions differed) indicated a frosted pitcher filled with fresh orange juice, resting alongside fourteen sparkling glasses, and offered us refreshments. We had neither anticipated nor discussed such an eventuality, and—hungry as we were—we sat silently for a moment until a group feeling wordlessly presented itself, and we politely declined his offer. After the briefest pause, Mr. Bundy—not a man accustomed to being refused—reminded us that Mahatma Gandhi had imbibed orange juice during *his* fasts.

That collective moment of silence had grounded us, and whether or not his offer was a test or a subtle status play, we declined again, politely but firmly. We were operating with one another intuitively now, honed in on a common wavelength, and confident that we were perceiving events from a common point of view.

I was caught cross-footed when Mike Horwatt, our extremely able leader, inexplicably tapped me on the shoulder and indicated that *I* should be the one to speak for the group. I had assumed that *he* would naturally be in that position and had made no preparations. There was no time to dither however, so I accepted the challenge as if it had been previously agreed upon.

I tried to express the spectrum of group consensus fairly, sharing our concerns about the administration's current policy and strategies. We feared they were leading the world towards an inevitable conflagration before we and the rest of the planet's youth had been offered the opportunity of experience our maturity and autonomy. We wanted to fulfill our potentials and afford others the same opportunity. Stepping flat-footed into a "no shit, Sherlock" moment, I pointed out that these goals would require an undestroyed world. If Mr. Bundy considered me an overly literal idiot, his face never betrayed it (nor any other sign of life, during our visit, including blinking).

Before our meeting, I had naïvely assumed that we young people were in touch with realities on the ground that our leaders might have lost touch with in their rarefied retreats; that we *possessed* information about the hinterlands that they might not. I assumed that we were delivering *intelligence* to them that could be useful in governing and establishing wise policy. Their actions appeared to be so overconfident, so dismissive of unintended consequences and every consideration except for immediate needs of the Empire, we had difficulty believing that they had thought things through from the broadest, interdependent point of view. (I remember this every time I learn of another consequence from the blowback of our ill-considered invasion of Iraq and our failure to ensure that civil society there remained intact.)

We felt they were placing the entire world at risk for ideological and material concerns, privileging concepts, political postures, and "sending signals" more highly than life itself. Based on these perceptions, we might be forgiven for concluding that they were not thinking clearly (or, depending on your perspective, congratulated for being so prescient). In this regard, my opinions of our political "leaders" have changed very little since the death of President Kennedy.

I no longer remember my or anyone else's precise words during the rest of our meeting. However, in the midst of the polite, ritualized parley, observing Mr. Bundy's concentrated attention and sensing his glacial emotional temperature, an epiphany organized itself within me. I understood in a shocking instant that from Mr. Bundy's perspective we were *not* messengers from any public *he* was interested in. We were a *problem* to be *managed* for his president and their common agenda. Leadership had already determined its course and was not soliciting the input of anyone who did not matter in their equations of power (which included us). Commands had been sent down from the wheelroom to the engine room; the compass of national policy had been set and fixed to a destination we passengers were not privy to. All our high-minded idealism and effort was, for Bundy (if not the president), a photo op, perhaps useful as a recruiting tool for an emerging constituency that might prove to be of later value. Bundy was not remotely interested in considering a *reassessment* of his policy. He was THE MAN's Man and their ship had sailed. We were no more important to them than bystanders on the pier waving at the ass-end of a departing boat.

In that moment, I understood that McGeorge Bundy, like Morris, Bert, or Harry Palmer, was a man of power; a man with intentions and concerns so different from my own as that we might as well have been alien species. Everything about him exuded command-presence and unalterable commitment. I understood in that momentary insight, that despite our speaking truth to power that day (and I am still proud that we did), our concerns were inconsequential to its architects.

That insight provoked subsequent revelations and I understood that Bundy's intentions would never be altered by fourteen or 14,000 students waving signs at him. Any effective appeal to this man would require power sufficient to *command* his attention. It would require an army.

Besides realizing that we had accidentally tapped into a tributary of an emerging culture, I learned something of value from observing Mr. Bundy. I learned that he belonged to a category of being with whom I was already very familiar. I left that room with a deeper understanding of how politics operated. What's more, I left it with the intention to help assemble the army that might be required to communicate as equals with men like Bundy. I had no idea at the time how this task might be accomplished, but the eggs percolating in my dream aquariums were beginning to stir. An intention had been planted, and it would send its first sprouts into the light that would gather only a few years away. I never foresaw that its growth would require a fertilizer composed of the murders of millions in Cambodia and Vietnam, an ecological catastrophe of defoliation imposed of the Southeast Asian jungles and ruined genes of millions more humans. I might have faltered had I foreseen that the army I and millions like me were dreaming into existence would require 50,000 dead Americans and thousands more maimed and wounded to become fully formed. I had only an intuition that it was coming but I knew I was going to be a part of it.

-◄o►-

OUR WASHINGTON EXPERIENCE had convinced me that what spoke to my deepest instincts spoke to others as well. In that same year, a number of my pals and I sent to Moore's Orchid Farm in Texas and for a nominal sum received a long box filled with peyote, the psychedelic cactus taken by numerous Native Americans as a deep and stabilizing religious practice. On the night we took it, Terry Bisson and I walked out into the starlit Iowa night, I turned to him and said, "Hey man, I feel like some kind of little wolf or something" and I took off dog-trotting into the night. He reminded me of that remark four years later after I had taken the name Coyote, an event that occurs later in this tale.

ONE EVENING IN the Student Union, a stubborn and insistent drama teacher named Ned Donahoe, half-lit and half-belligerent, dropped into our "writer's table" in the grille and challenged me to consider theater, as "an argument of great moment, danced before the public." He dared me to join his theater troupe, which he had formed as a small repertory company. ("No one asks the basketball coach to use second-string players on *his* team," he said, by way of explanation.) I joined and discovered that I had some knack for it. I greatly enjoyed rehearsing and the camaraderie of collective problem-solving. Furthermore the work was a balm. My girlfriend Gretchen had run off with my close friend Terry Bisson and I was wringing every bit of self-pity possible out of the event.

Working with Donahoe was a revelation. His parents had been the warders of an asylum and he had grown up with the inmates as playmates. Perhaps that accounted for the fluidity of his inner life (and his problems with alcohol). Standing behind him in the wings, watching him observe actors onstage, I could read every beat and thought of every player onstage through his body movements. It was a singular education and reinforced by the fact that our performances were extremely well-received.

I was energized by the approbation I received for a number of productions I appeared in, especially in my senior year after my last performance as James Jr. in Eugene O'Neill's *Long Day's Journey Into Night*. I was flummoxed when my three favorite professors came backstage to offer their congratulations. That had never occurred before so I felt confident that our performance might have been special. I had no idea (or desire) then that acting would become the basis of my livelihood. I was, in my own mind, a poet, but as luck would have it I took the lessons of Washington and Ned Donahoe to San Francisco at precisely the right moment.

—◄◦►—

AFTER GRADUATION FROM Grinnell, I pursued a Master's Degree in Creative Writing at San Francisco State University, choosing it over other schools to work with Robert Duncan, a favorite poet. In San Francisco, I also joined the remnants of a once-famous theater company called the Actor's Workshop. It had recently been gutted of its best and brightest when the company founders, Herb Blau and Jules Irving (who had introduced American audiences to avant-garde theater there—staging works by Beckett, Genet, and Harold Pinter), were hired away to New York to create a theater at Lincoln Center, taking the core of the company with them.

Within my first year in San Francisco I had quit the Creative Writing Program, thoroughly intimidated by the range of Robert

Duncan's extraordinary mind. His IQ has never been charted, I'm told, and floats beyond all scales. Every day I sat stupefied by the range of his mind, which brought Ancient Mythology, Anthropology, the world history of poetry, and poetics into the room. Students on either side of me were nodding sagely while I was completely befuddled and in the dark. Deciding I was not bright enough for Poetry, and increasingly drawn to life outside of academia, I left the MA program after a year.[5]

I also left the moribund Actor's Workshop and joined forces with a vibrant little street troupe that had been renting a small theater from the Workshop. Their lobby was decorated with wonderful photos of their outdoor performances, and everything about them seemed energetic, good-humored, and politically on point. It did not hinder my decision either to notice that two of the most beautiful women I had ever seen in person were members of the company, which called itself the San Francisco Mime Troupe.

A darling of the Left, the Troupe created plays based on 17th-century Italian *commedia dell'arte* street theater, employing stock masked characters and rewriting the original scripts to address topical issues. True to Left-wing principles, performances were "taken to the people" in parks and other popular venues and offered for free, passing the hat afterwards, beguiling, ridiculing, and teasing audiences to increase their donations. The shows were ribald and fun, full of sharp wit, deep cleavage, and heaving bosoms. Story lines skewered the rich and powerful, exposed hypocrisy and championed the oppressed, the underprivileged, and exploited labor.

I THRIVED AT the Troupe, as I did at college, making fast friends, learning new physical skills, soaking up knowledge and a practical political perspective, surprising myself by an unanticipated ability to master whatever external challenges came at me. I was less distracted and depressed and felt alive, full of potential, and lucky.

The most provocative show in the Mime Troupe's repertoire was called *The Minstrel Show: Civil Rights in a Cracker Barrel*. Based on extensive research into early twentieth-century traditional "minstrel shows," a once popular form of entertainment in America, normally such shows featured white performers performing in blackface as "darkies," but the Mime Troupe's show stood that convention on its head. Our show featured three white and three black performers, identically dressed in sky blue tuxedos, blackface makeup, wigs, and white gloves. The show featured a white interlocutor, played to perfection by Marlboro-man-handsome Bob Slattery, who appeared to be the straightest white man on the planet, but in actuality was a dedicated Socialist who lived his beliefs until he died. The show opened with traditional tambourines, songs, high-stepping dances, and jokes from old minstrel show archives on the order of:

> *Interlocuter: Bones, are you a Republican or a Democrat?*
> *Bones: I's a Baptist*

Ten minutes into the show, tired of their demeaning stereotyping, the minstrels "took over," ousting the interlocutor, and proceeded to enlighten the audience with acute renditions of "Ne-go history"—their own stories performed from a revolutionary black perspective. All cast members had been required to read *The Autobiography of Malcolm X* and the minstrels' more accurate historical accounting began with the story of Crispus Attucks, a black man who was the first person killed in the American Revolutionary War, performed by Willie B. Hart—a one-eyed, cock-eyed black man with a genius for comedy. As the story was recounted, Willie shuffled across the stage, sweeping it mindlessly until a shot rang out and he fell over. The show proceeded comically through various historical events culminating in a skit where a white cop shoots a black kid for fooling around and pulling a harmonica out of his pocket too quickly.

The show was a storied local success, and wildly popular. One night at run-through in the Mime Troupe workshop, we were surprised to see Harry Belafonte and the brilliant black comic Nipsy Russell in the audience. They were knocked out by the show's radical politics and energy and convinced their equally famous colleague, comedian Dick Gregory, to sponsor the Troupe in New York.

Ronnie (R.G.) Davis, the Troupe's leader, chose me to assemble, direct, and perform in our road company. The tour was a triumph despite the fact that the show was closed by the authorities in several schools when they discovered that it was not the "traditional" minstrel show they had hoped for. We were also arrested on charges of "performing a lewd act in public" in Denver and held over for ten days of trial where we were acquitted. Otherwise, the Troupe garnered reviews our mothers might have written, and as a consequence, our notoriety was expanded to national dimensions.

The next year, I directed one of the shows in the company's first cross-country commedia tour, which won us more accolades from the eastern press, and students at Bennington, Brandeis, Harvard, and Yale. Several Harvard and Brandeis students actually ran away with us and joined our company. On that tour, a short second play, *Olive Pits*, an adaptation of an old Goldoni commedia (which accompanied our major production, and won an OBIE award from New York's *Village*

Voice newspaper.) I cowrote that play with fellow Troupe performer, writer, and company theorist Peter Berg, and directed and acted in it as well. I was a busy boy.

Having said this, I would have to mark this spot and wonder why, if everything was so wonderful, I had begun chipping heroin? I remember clearly what the initiating impulse was—the fear that perhaps my imagination had been colonized by the majority culture and that instead of dreaming our way to liberation we might just be running around in the playpen the Establishment was allowing us to use. That was an unnerving thought, and a number of us sought refuge in drugs that were so definitely "off-limits" that we could lull ourselves into confidence that whatever sprung from their use might be truly liberated. Sounded good at the time. . . .

Membership in the Troupe appeared to be another unexpected trail—like folk music, like work skills, like the Beats—leading me serendipitously to the right place at the right time. Though the people in the Mime Troupe were initially several steps ahead of me in street smarts and survival skills, I was a quick study and soon an integral member of that family, holding my own in every dimension.

I remember sitting at my crowded and rowdy first Troupe Thanksgiving, feeling flooded with gratitude to be counted among such an open-hearted family that accepted me without fear or criticism. As I gazed around the table at the ebullient talented men and women laughing and teasing one another, I could hardly be blamed for feeling that my life was on the best possible path and that from there on out, it would be clear sailing. The eggs in those attic aquariums were definitely stirring, but if I'd considered them a little more deeply, I would have been forced to admit that I still did not know precisely *what* was hatching in there.

-<o>-

AT THE MIME Troupe, a girl I was keeping casual company with showed up at rehearsal one day to surprise me. I looked up from my work when she hailed me, and over her shoulder I saw her tall blonde girlfriend sizzling like a Fourth of July sparkler. I was gob-smacked and mentally trading in my friend as I kissed her hello. The blonde's name was Sam and she was from Bossier City, Louisiana. She had swamp-bitch magic written all over her and the attraction between us was so intense that the next evening, responding to her invitation to "try my Southern-fried chicken," I appeared at a friend's door where she was trading room and board for housekeeping duties. I laugh today at the baldness of her invitation, but hey, it was the Sixties and she sure as hell had Southern-fried chicken worth sampling.

There was nothing wrong with Sam that was not also wrong with me, but neither of us was able to read the signs of damage in the other. As for *repairing* the damage we had each brought to the party or caused one another, that would have been like asking a man without hands to perform brain surgery. A friend once observed, "Coyote, if she had high cheekbones and long legs, you'd follow an axe murderess into an abbatoir." Sam was not an axe murderess, but we chopped one another up pretty badly.

Two years later, a core group of us left the Troupe (Sam among them), impelled to push our radical politics beyond the safe boundaries of the stage. As in other periods of my life, mentors appropriate to the task appeared. Emmett Grogan was a charismatic Irishman from Brooklyn, and an intuitive genius at reading the *zeitgeist*. He and his reclusive and brilliant friend, Bill Murcott, convinced a number of us that delivering messages from a stage we "owned" was simply too safe and would never create truly revolutionary change. That insight and our commitment to honor it led to the founding of the Diggers.

—◦—

THIS PART OF my education was extensively chronicled in *Sleeping Where I Fall*, so, in the interests of chronology I'll offer the speed-read version. The original Diggers were named after a 17th-century group who lived in England during the protectorate of Oliver Cromwell. They protested the king's seizure of public lands (to raise his sheep for his new wool mills) and stood against private property. Taking back their commons, they were nicknamed the Diggers because the king sent troops against them and every morning they were seen burying their dead.

As their contemporary heirs, we challenged ourselves to imagine a culture we wanted to live in and then to make it real, by acting it out. We did not want to be conscripted as Socialist-realist, Left-wing artists, doing plays about heroic bus drivers and factory workers, any more than we wanted to become "employees" or "consumers," fulfilling culturally generated desires implanted into our psyches like microchips in a pet. The best option available to us was to employ our skills and imaginations to create more compelling and engaging options and demonstrate their feasibility by acting them out. We felt that Americans were never going to throw themselves on the barricades to become part of a Marxist-Leninist *lumpen proletariat,* but if on the other hand they were engaged in meaningful, enjoyable lives, they might step up to defend them. The added benefit to me was that this also appeared to be a way to find the like-minded souls who might dedicate themselves to nullify the plans of men like McGeorge Bundy.

THERE WERE NO leaders or hierarchy in the Diggers. Each person was responsible for actualizing their own vision; for enlisting the allies and finding the requisite matériel to bring their idea to life. The Diggers eschewed money and performed anonymously, believing that men and women who pursued activities dedicated to neither wealth nor fame, were sincere and "meant it." Our highest value was *authenticity*—being true to one's deepest inner directives—which boiled down to doing what mattered to yourself. We shared a common feeling that it was too easy and essentially uninteresting to look after only oneself, so we invented new institutions and forms to aid others as well—our first concern, the influx of runaways and thrill-seekers pouring into the Haight-Ashbury in response to ubiquitous media hype about "hippies."

To this end, we created free stores, free medical clinics, offered free food and free sleeping spaces. Our free store offered perfectly adequate clothes, tools, televisions, radios, bicycles—whatever one might need—retrofitted, repaired, and placed on display in a handsome retail space. The only difference between it and a conventional store was that everything in our store (including the roles of officials—manager, clerk, etc.) was literally "free" for the taking. Furthermore, we challenged people to consider what designated roles like "employee," "boss," and "consumer" might mean in a free economy. Why dedicate your time and labor for the money to "consume" if you can get what you need for nothing? We joked about it as "Love in the Dump."

The Diggers' kitchens (overloaded apartment stoves) offered free food, sometimes five and six hundred hot meals a day, the food scrounged from ripe-that-day cast-offs at farmer's markets and discards from the supermarkets. We enlisted medical student volunteers from the nearby University of California and opened free medical clinics at the free store on Wednesday nights. We also opened free crash pads, communal apartments for people to live or simply "crash" for the night. We utilized these free institutions as street-theater "life-events" and also as a way of manipulating the media to spread information about what was being done "in the Haight" because we understood that visually compelling events—with "messages" designed into them—would be self-evident to people who were awake. They would also attract the media who would (and did) unknowingly serve our agenda by transmitting our messages to America simply by *describing* the events we had created. Fellow Digger and ex-Mime Trouper Peter Berg (our hipster Lenin) called this "creating the message you describe." Judging from the numbers of people who arrived in the Haight-Ashbury, our transmissions were very successful.

◄○►

AFTER SEVERAL YEARS of exhausting and exhilarating work,[6] many of us tired of the endless onslaught of visitors, tourists, and runaways in the Haight-Ashbury, feeling as if we'd enlisted ourselves as counterculture social workers ministering to an endless onslaught of new arrivals rather than serving as exemplars of the lives we actually wanted. Those of us who sought to place our lives on a more stable and sustainable footing created alliances with other like-minded groups and the Diggers evolved into a large confederation of autonomous communities that became known as the Free Family. We established rural land-based communes and began the process of pursuing what Peter Berg called "Re-inhabitation"—learning to live in continuity with and to care for the plant, animal, and human populations of specific places. We were anxious to learn the place-based knowledge of the best sources of such information, namely those Native American cultures whose survival skills and cultural practices had been ignored by our European forebears and I among others began to forge relationships in those communities. For economic and political reasons, we lived communally in cooperative houses and truck caravans, attempting to stitch together an alternate economy with other groups established farther afield, even as we were being forced to learn the hardscrabble realities of living with insufficient money and too many men, women, and children in too little space.

◄○►

IN 1968, I turned twenty-seven around the same time I left the City. A number of important transformations occurred when I took up residence at an isolated 19th-century farmhouse at the end of a mile-long dirt road in a town that was little more than a crossroads named Olema, California. The four-bedroom, one-level farm had no electricity, a five-gallon hot water heater powered by kerosene, a barn, an old horse-shed (where I eventually established my quarters), and an eight-by-twelve-foot shed that also became living quarters for a peripatetic population that eventually swelled to between sixteen and twenty people.

The Olema ranch was southeast of Tomales Bay in western Marin County, separated by one ridge from Lagunitas Creek, where wild salmon still spawned, and about a thirty-minute drive south of the long hill separating the San Francisco Bay watershed from its neighboring watershed, the Russian River drainage. It was to be a staging ground for the next vision of our Digger evolution (to put it grandly).

A year after moving to Olema, I was visiting Carlin, Nevada, at the home of a Paiute-Shoshone shaman named Rolling Thunder, doing chores and fixing his cars and toilets as my admission ticket to hang around, observe him, and ask questions. RT, as friends referred to him, had shown up in the Haight-Ashbury one day inquiring about the Diggers saying he had dreamt that we were the reincarnated souls of Indians killed at the Battle of Little Big Horn. I didn't believe that, but it was a pretty imaginative calling card, and he *had* looked us up. Rolling Thunder was a complicated and sometimes wacky guy, but as the stories about him in my previous book demonstrated, he also possessed irrefutable shamanic power and thus my interest in staying on his good side (and his pupil) by being his handyman.

During this stay with Rolling Thunder, I recounted the story of my college peyote experience to him. He listened, rolling a smoke of his native tobacco, concentrating intently. "The Indian way is to do one thing at a time," he'd told me once. He licked the glued paper, lit the smoke, exhaled, and mumbled a little prayer. Then he turned his attention on me.

"You have two choices," he said. "You can consider that you had a hallucination and go on about your business. You'll be okay. No harm done, but ordinary, you know? You'll remain a 'white man', or . . ." he continued, ". . . you could consider that a Coyote-spirit touched you. You could accept it as a mysterious gesture and try to figure out how to serve it. If you do that, you might just become a human being.'"

"Human beings" in Rolling Thunder's iconography were men and women who had fully realized their natures, which obviously contained powerful connections to the natural world. It was his honorific for "spiritually evolved."

At Olema one day while I was still considering the import of his remarks, a poet friend named Jim Koller stopped by to give me an issue of his poetry magazine called *Coyote's Journal*. The logo was a black coyote track, and I recognized it with shock as the duplicate of those I had seen at my feet in the Iowa cornfield mud when I "came to" after the peyote had worn off. So that *was* "the little wolf." Now I was certain.

About a month later, I adopted the name Coyote as the first step in coming to terms with what I had experienced—an accidentally propitious decision.

Without anticipating it, my new name became the basis of a radical internal shift that allowed me to slip free of the strictures, inherited assumptions, expectations, and conclusions passed down from my family about who I was and was not. Without forethought I had evaded the limitations of (much of) my personal history. "Stupid," "loser," "timid," "rich," and "second-rate" were left behind me in the dust along with my old name and the shards of my history. For the first time I was ". . . a complete unknown. With no direction home . . ." tracking whatever trail in the cosmos caught my fancy. I was finally free. I thought.

I COULD NEVER suggest that everything in my new "post-Cohon," post-urban existence as Coyote was euphoric. Even absent Morris and the perturbations of home, the mangy junkyard bitch I had packed in my psyche became increasingly restless and assertive. I had been "chip-ping" heroin too frequently to be safe and using speed to support the enormous demands on personal energy and imagination required by Digger life. My relationships with women were opportunistic and rarely intimate, unless you consider charm and amusement viable substitutes.

Unresolved issues about violence had led me to befriend San Francisco Hell's Angels I had met on Haight Street and I lived for months with Pete Knell, the San Francisco chapter president, helping him in his garage while I assembled a Harley chopper under his tute-lage; buying a brand new crated engine, and an old 1938 rigid frame and requisite parts with a $3,000 inheritance from my grandmother. By the time the bike was done he had invited me to "prospect" as a member, but I had too many black friends to feel comfortable doing that, and had seen a bit too much behavior during their visits to Olema that didn't sit right with me.

Once the bike was running and I had driven it back to Olema, the Angels visited often (and sometimes unnervingly) until some years later a sufficient number of members (it only takes two votes to deny someone admission to the club) became uncomfortable at the privi-leged access I had been allowed and decided to do something about it. They engineered a long, terrifying, weekend occupation of Olema by a chapter of Angels I had never met, arriving under the guise of throwing a party for a Digger friend who had become an Angel and had been shot in the head during a drug deal gone bad. He had been paralyzed in one arm and one leg and the party was ostensibly to celebrate his relief from the hospital. He never arrived, but those that did made it very clear that my relationship with the club was over.

SAM AND I had split up again and she had moved into the city to have our baby. My life had become rootless and chaotic. I had developed hepatitis from shooting drugs and a number of unsettling physical events occurred due to being weak and ill. One day, visiting Sam at a friend's house, I passed out due to poor health and nourishment, and tumbled down an entire flight of stairs. Some part of me knew that I was heading for real trouble. Drug use was keeping the dog at bay, but when it wasn't fed there was hell to pay and my behavior was becoming increasingly erratic. I knew I needed help but knew no one who could provide it; certainly not Morris. I felt that I would have to parent myself, but had no idea how. It was clear to me that I would need a mentor appropriate to my new free life and intentions.

By luck, a frequent visitor to Olema was the poet Lew Welch, a true member of the Beat inner circle and an old friend of Gary Snyder's. When he suggested introducing me to Gary one day, the nascent healthy part of me leapt at his offer. By grace, that introduction turned out to be to the person who initiated my next important development.

-◄○►-

I HAD READ Gary Snyder's poems since my mid-teens, when curiosity about bohemians brought me into contact with Jack Kerouac and the Beat writers. Snyder, the Beat poet and ordained Zen priest, was legendary in those circles. He had lived in a Japanese monastery for ten years; had introduced Jack Kerouac to Zen and been the model for Kerouac's protagonist, Japhy Ryder, in the novel *The Dharma Bums*. Gary had a reputation as a sage and had been shaped in my imagination as a highly evolved human being. By this time too, his essays on politics, environmental sanity, and wilderness were being reprinted and widely distributed in the counterculture, granting him iconic stature.

A number of Gary's contemporaries had disappeared or died early but Gary's duration and successes on many levels inspired me to hope that if I could meet him I might be able to absorb a working model that balanced the competing rigors of sobriety and ecstasy in a healthier manner than I was managing.

The meeting Lew arranged turned out to be nothing like the event I had anticipated. Gary and I ate peanut butter on crackers in the back of his new (and in my eyes, bourgeois) VW camper chatting blandly. The meeting was insignificant, except just before leaving, Gary regarded me with such undisguised directness as if he were making up his mind about who I really was. His perusal was so penetrating and transparent as to its intention that the moment became unsettling, like being called upon to speak in class when you were unprepared.

After Gary drove off, I had to admit to myself that I had been insecure in his presence and that my characteristic fluency (or glibness) had deserted me. He had managed to deflect every opportunity I attempted to wax philosophical and had edged me out onto the thin ice of being unable to define myself. This had always been potentially dangerous terrain for me because my parents habitually informed me as to what kind of person I was or what my motives must have been for doing something, citing my unconscious as evidence—an entity I could not understand but they could. It was crazy-making, but now, subtle wisps of my own competitiveness, jealousy, curiosity, and personal doubts began to tint my impressions of our meeting, making me unable to decide what had actually transpired.

—◄o►—

I HAD ATTENDED the birth of my daughter Ariel in San Francisco in a room filled with fellow communards, and Pete Knell and Sweet William from the Hell's Angels. Bottles of wine were being passed around and the normal bedlam was underway at a respectful muting of volume. I went out on the stoop of Sam's flat on 17th Street and looked out over the winking lights of the City and the Bay while I rolled a smoke. I had the sense that my life was going to be very different from now on, but I did not know how.

I was not wrong. About two months later, Sam showed up at Olema with our daughter, Ariel, at her breast. She said she was there to stay. "It's free land isn't it?" she demanded. She moved into my cabin and we took up once again, only this time the air between us was lightened by a lovely, blue-eyed little sprite that had me entranced from first looks. My life *had* changed, irrevocably.

IN THE SPRING of 1971 our experiment at Olema came to an end when we were evicted from the ranch by the cowboys who leased the grazing rights from the owner. They had never been too happy about thirty people, dogs, motorcycles, and visitors in such close proximity to their livestock. They had dropped by one day while we were roasting a poached deer, and fifteen naked people were bathing in one of their cattle troughs we had dragged over a long ditch in which we had built a fire. We might have finessed that incident but when word got out that the Hell's Angels often came by, their discontent morphed into dread, and we were sent packing.

With common geography no longer binding us together, many members of Olema headed off for parts unknown and personal destinies. Word had arrived via traveler's gossip of a Summer Solstice celebration at a famous commune in Colorado called Libre, and a core of Olema regulars began to prepare our vehicles for the long trip there, setting up shop at a nearby communal house belonging to Ron Thelin, co-proprietor of the Psychedelic Shop in the Haight, and filling up the street with our old trucks. An opportunity appeared to have been delivered to us that might allow us to fashion a semi-permanent life-on-the-road caravan. We believed that we could visit various communes, paying our way by creating a trade route and employing our skills as good mechanics, musicians, and seasoned communards to be of service. The details were sketchy, but a sketchy plan was better than no plan.

I was, by this time, virtually out of touch with Morris and Ruth. There were no phones or electricity at Olema and life was too challenging, chaotic, and demanding, framed by arcane Digger philosophies that made explanations incomprehensible to those who were not initiates. (An uncharitable observer might liken this state to membership in a cult.) We corresponded sporadically by mail, but months often went by with little or no communication.

In the dead of our last winter at Olema, amidst roaring winds and pelting rain, Morris and Ruth unexpectedly pulled up in a rental car in front of the ranch house for a surprise visit. This story is recounted in all its nuttiness in *Sleeping Where I Fall*, but by the time they left, Morris and I had a breakthrough. He had seen through the chaos and poverty of our physical life and decoded and applauded our true intentions. We parted on excellent terms, after a chilling pronouncement from him on the fate of the capitalist economy that we thought might

fall imminently, but that Morris assured us would take fifty years—
"There are huge historical forces at work. Keep your head down, take
care of your family, and hang in for the long haul." Despite that clo-
sure, there had been few opportunities to speak with them afterwards.
The bluntest explanation would be to admit that I was simply too full
of myself and my plans to unseat McGeorge Bundy and his minions to
stay in close touch.

On the positive side, our absence from Olema created a de facto
separation between me and some regular visitors to Olema like Doc
Holiday, the birdlike, dapper, and delicate smack dealer who kept me
supplied with quality heroin in return for allowing him to crash at the
ranch.

Furthermore, the ensuing several months of diligent effort preparing our trucks for the road and the relatively clean living at the Thelins'
more spiritually-oriented Red House restored my health and good spirits. Most of the Red House people were "original" Diggers, close and
old friends and/or lovers. The nights were filled with music, and the
Red House, perhaps because it was built around a core of the extended
Thelin family, seemed to operate more harmoniously and with less
chaos than Olema.

I remember this as a good time that provided me with the next
opportunity to meet Gary Snyder. The uneasiness that had attended
our initial meeting continued to orbit my awareness, disappearing into
the dark shadow side of my unconscious before cycling back into the
light as a barbed memory. I was anxious for an opportunity to modify
or erase what I imagined his impression of me might have been.

The opportunity arose when four of us who would be a core of the
pending caravan decided to make a shakedown run to the Sierras to

visit Snyder and his community, to sell them on the idea of participating in our proposed trade route. Despite the cover of "Digger business," I was also proceeding for my own purposes.

<o>

OUR SMALL CONVOY of four old Chevys and GMCs cruised east on
Highway 80, past Sacramento into Gold Country, gaining altitude in
the foothills. Pine and fir trees rooted in rust-red soil there replaced the
sere khaki grasslands and the contorted live oaks of lower elevations,
and the air became sweeter. The last hour of our journey traversed
progressively smaller and more remote county and finally dirt roads,
until we nosed down a dim parallel track in the woods, terminating at
a small gravel clearing, parking before an open shed sheltering a battered old Jeep wagon. We located the footpath through the woods to
Snyder's house and entered the forest.

The skinny trail along the flank of a moderate slope was cooled
and shaded by second-growth pines, occasional live oaks, and sensu-
ous smooth-skinned madrones. The air was thick with the scent of
witch hazel from the small native *kitkitdizze* shrubs for which Gary's
homestead had been named. Except for our feet rustling the leaves
underfoot, and the chitter and whistle of small birds, the day was
totally silent.

By the time we reached the clearing containing Gary's house and
outbuildings, the nervous acceleration of our trip had dissipated and I
was actually and undistractedly *there*. Perhaps it was the silent interlude of the quarter-mile between the car-park and the house, but I

arrived with an internal stillness that allowed me to "see" Gary's house clearly. What I saw made a deep impression on me.

From the vantage point of the hill, his home radiated a sense of order, timeless solidity, and dignity. The clay tiled roof of his house rested on thick hand-hewn lintels and posts. Between these, hand-daubed adobe walls had been fitted with two doors of numerous small-paned windows, lightening the massive feeling of the house's construction. The structure felt fastened in place, as if the trees supporting it had simply been peeled and pressed into service where they stood. It was a house that felt exactly "right"—smaller and less grand than Morris's, more elegant and rustic than Jim Clancy's; no bigger or smaller than necessary, practical, impeccably constructed, and very much better made and finished than any of our overcrowded communal shacks and homes.

Built onto the house's near corner, sheltering the kitchen door and facing the hill, a small, roofed cubicle with an open front offered a convenient, sheltered spot to store boots, firefighting tools, and rain gear out of the weather. A sink for washing up was built into the shared wall next to a sliding door, which, I soon learned, opened wide enough to admit a wheelbarrow load of firewood into the kitchen.

Parallel to the house and separated by a narrow gravel corridor, a slender rectangular structure had been divided into a toolshed and a wood-fired sauna. Built in board-and-batten style, the general impression was of simplicity, durability, and fitness. An upright red hand-cranked water pump stood beside the sauna. Each guest to Kitkitdizze was tithed 100 strokes on it, the energy required to send their daily ration of water uphill to the holding tank from which it would return to the house by gravity.

Gary's house intrigued me because its form and function were so married and well thought through. It appeared to be comfortable and sufficient for his needs, but did not appear to have required much wealth to construct. If it was a statement of Gary's "philosophy," it was well-said and without an excess syllable. I could imagine myself content in such a house and owning it without internal conflicts about it being too "rich" or showy.

I continued my scrutiny after we were invited in. The flagstone-floored kitchen was cool and shaded. It contained a large wood-fired range and a glass-fronted cabinet stocked with simple black ceramic Japanese dishes and cups; a well-crafted oak table with two benches sat before the windowed doors I'd noticed from the hill. Everything seemed poised in its task, floating in the limpid interior, as tranquil as sleeping cats.

Adjacent to the kitchen, a single step admitted me to a wood-floored living room. In the center, four massive posts surrounded an octagonal fire pit edged in stone and supported a log rectangle upon which *vegas* (slender timber rafters) rested. They, by radiating out to the house's perimeter and resting on its walls, supported the roof. The spaces between the walls defining the living room and the house's outside walls were organized as a pantry, a children's room, a library, and a master bedroom—900 square feet in all. In that space Gary and his wife Masa raised two children and arranged their full and productive life.

Over the fire pit a small hanging log was suspended threaded through parallel loops suspended from a roof beam. Anchored to that floating log was an adjustable iron device of obvious Japanese origin, which allowed one to adjust a large iron water kettle over the flames. Above the pit, a small windowed cupola completed the roof

and (theoretically) served as a vent for the smoke. The logs were black-
ened by pitch and might as easily have been the interior of a Japanese
farm or an Indian longhouse. The interior smelled of smoke, leather,
juniper, incense, tobacco, whiskey, and oiled wood. It felt timeless.

These elements—stone, wood, iron, and fire—had been melded
and elegantly integrated by an observant, pragmatic, and sophisticated eye; fashioned with obvious respect for the various traditions
the house had borrowed from. This was what I *imagined* "reinhabita-
tion" might look like—only Gary's expression of it was more refined
and meticulously organized then anything I had conceived. The house
easily contained contradictions—a small ghetto blaster sound system,
a Winchester rifle, a banjo, Japanese pillows, a Buddhist altar, and
a bottle of Jack Daniel's resting on the kitchen table. It was not the
product of theories, but of a *life*; of thoughtful, patient work that made
even my meander through it feel frivolous.

My reaction to his house forced me to reevaluate Gary, who at the
moment of our arrival was stark naked, save for cheap plastic thong
sandals, throwing a boomerang with his young children. At his feet lay
a small pile of yokes cut from forked madrone branches and used to
hang pots over the outdoor fire pit that served as their summer kitchen.
Gary's Japanese wife, Masa, was squatting on her haunches before the
fire, wearing only a skirt, looking as if she might have evolved there.
Next to the fire pit was a modest, pole-framed ramada roofed with
bamboo matting, which sheltered shelves, counters, and a refrigerator
that I later learned ran on kerosene.

I spent the better part of that day trying to untangle what it was
about Gary's home that was simultaneously moving and challenging. Every time I asked myself what Gary was "about," the answer

appeared self-evident—he was *about* his life and everything this house implied: a civilized, practical, elegant, comfortable, and efficient space, meticulously designed and carefully constructed as a canvas on which to express his family's existence. Its design and construction had been tumbled smooth in Gary's mind over years of meditation until each detail had rubbed every other into a smooth, nearly seamless fit like those stone foundations in Peru that will not admit a knife blade between the carefully hewn blocks.

I liked being there. There was no city filth and roil to contend with, no revolutionary posturing or ideological justifications required; no weak joint into which I could insert a wedge of radical-chic criticism. His family was joyful and healthy, having a good time in the sun in a manner that implied minimal reliance on late 20th-century capitalism. Their skin was sun-browned and squeaky clean—hair, eyes, teeth, bright and shiny—(in unavoidable contrast to my own grimy, hepatic pallor.) The house and grounds were shipshape. Gary laughed easily, and he and Masa teased one another affectionately.

It was an unexpected shock when, later that day, what had been scratching insistently passed through the door of my consciousness and I realized that I was *challenged* by Gary's house. It was a more concrete, beautiful, and practical imagining of the future the Diggers sought, a superior work, and it exposed a seam of laziness, a lack of commitment, and a measure of indulgence in our shacks, overcrowded communal homes, feverish conversations, drug binges, and endlessly rebuilt trucks. Gary's house *began* with a healthy self-respect at its core and established a standard of living for himself and his family based on that respect.

From that revelation onwards, my glorious visions of free food, expanding communal networks, national trade routes, and depots of junkyards to service our fleets of pre-1950 vehicles palled. I had excused many of my own and our collective failures of execution, shoddy work and making-do (along with my use of methedrine and heroin) as necessary for mocking up a pre-rehearsal prototype of our imagined future. It would be the "set" as we do in the theater: taping out the dimensions of structures not yet built upon the stage floor so that rehearsals could begin with a sense of how the finished reality would operate. Now, I was no longer certain that the temporary would not be forever. A clearing had opened in my mind, and a path was visible leading somewhere unknown that I definitely wanted to explore.

That first night we camped near Gary's on the stone flats above the Yuba River, under stars winking in a black sky. I tried to order my thoughts. What would it mean to my Digger relationships and community, what strains would it impart on our collective life if I respected my personal standards and fashioned a life that reflected them? What would it do to our communal structures and harmony if I insisted on order, beauty, and utility in my environment? Would I be perceived as a snob? Would my friends condemn me as bourgeois? Would I be rejected from this new and precious family?

The fresh air, the soughing whispers of trees and breeze made me too drowsy to answer my own questions. My last thought as I surrendered to sleep was resolving to answer them and to one day live as I had imagined men might the day I first met Buddy Jones, Al Cohn, Zoot Sims, and Dave McKenna—the jazzmen. I wanted some feeling of freedom and joy like that in my life but to craft that life without requiring wealth or power over others to support it. It occurred to me that Gary might be an appropriate guide to help me on that quest, but would he be interested in that?

—‹o›—

IN THE MORNING, I rose early and alone and slipped down the trail to Kitkitdizze. En route, it occurred to me that I had, by now, run as far from Morris's home and influence as I possibly could. Finally established (sort of) at the antipodes of the continent, I was forced to admit that there were aspects of Morris's civilized life and high standards that were worth imitating and preserving. Compared to Gary's deeply rooted Ridge community, the Diggers were gypsies. Consequently, we inherited the ancient suspicions that all landed people hold for the rootless.

The morning was clear and bracing, and the air tangy with autumn. At the far end of Gary's pond two deer were drinking placidly, undisturbed by my presence or the mist rising around their slender hooves. The house engaged my attention again, as if I were obliged to consider it so that I would not forget it. The tool shop and sauna, the outdoor kitchen and laundry room were all in good order. The rustic architecture was elegant in an unaffected way, and other than a child's pink sandal, nothing was out of place. The trunks of the fruit trees were painted white to repel pests, and each tree was carefully surrounded by wire fencing to deter the deer. The portable fire extinguishers, shovels, and hoe-dads for clearing fire-lines were in place on their racks and ready for work, each handle stenciled with the word *Kitkitdizze*. The aesthetic was strictly utilitarian and more pleasant for that.

By the end of my morning's review I had concluded that only a fool would ignore the opportunity to study a man who could and would build such a house. While I may have been a fool the first time we met, I resolved that I was not going to remain one.

The San Juan Ridge community (of which Gary and Masa were high-status members) was not keen on our trade-route idea because they feared an influx of travelers. They were nice enough, warm even, but they had their own work—thank you very much—and their own work involved assuming responsibility for the place where they lived and the health of their community. They had little time or inclination to spare time for ours.

I could not argue with their reticence. I had my own complaints and reservations about our Digger life. For all its celebration and festivity, the incandescent visions of what-could-be and the wild comedy of courageous, indulgent, and imaginative people compressed into overcrowded, emotionally pressurized spaces. The truth was that we were always contending with insufficient space and insufficient resources for our numbers. The shadow side of our leaderless anarchy was often chaos and usually marked by a lack of aesthetic finish and beauty.

Next to the stolid, skilled and practical Ridge people, the Free Family members appeared wild and raw—with all the attendant virtues and faults of those qualities. To imagine living at fifty as I currently lived at 28 invoked exhaustion.

—◦—

OUR EXPLORATORY CARAVAN returned to base at the Red House for the final preparations to leave for Libre. Everything was set for our departure, when we received word from Libre that we were definitely not to come—a minor setback we decided to ignore. Too much momentum and kinetic energy had been expended to cancel our plans now, and there were plenty of other places in Colorado to visit. Besides, the

Thelin household was groaning at the seams, swollen from our presence. It was becoming obvious that the permanent inhabitants needed us to be gone. Shortly after the Vernal Equinox, when the last vehicle was shipshape, the caravan finally pulled away heading east—nine trucks, nineteen adults, and eleven children.

IN MID-JULY WE rolled into Boulder, Colorado, and convened at a motorcycle shop on Pearl Street where we had friends. As the trucks pulled in, Julie Boone, our bike-riding Digger sister from San Francisco, emerged from inside. Uncharacteristically, she did not stop and clutch the other women in greeting. She walked directly through everyone, and before I could register the anomaly of her behavior, she was standing directly before me, looking deeply into my eyes. Smiling sadly, she said, "Ahhh, Peter. Morris is dead!"

My first thought was, "How did she know Morris's name?" Then a rushing in my ears obliterated most other sound. The air around me solidified and closed in. I was shocked but felt nothing. Word spread through our group, and people hugged and tried to comfort me, but I was too numb to be suffering. How could *Morris* have died? It was like saying Manhattan was missing.

I called my mother from the pay phone on the wall of the motorcycle shop. She was relieved to hear from me for about nine seconds and then became furious. "Where *were* you?" she demanded. "We've tried for *weeks* to find you. We called the *police* in several states, *no one* knew where you *were!*" The accents in her speech were like slaps.

I explained that we were traveling on back roads and camping without electricity, phones, or money. I could not explain how the police could have overlooked this mélange of decorated 1950s-era Chevy and

GMC trucks. I ascertained that she was all right; that people were with her and that there was nothing to do for her in the moment. Morris had already been buried.

Then she dropped the second bombshell.

"Morris died broke," she said. "I had no idea. My God, Peter, they were tugging me over his coffin. All these people saying, 'Ruthie, we want our money.'"

I could hear her stop and light a cigarette. "He's been broke for years," she said bitterly. "Somehow he managed to keep everything cobbled together. I had no idea. I'll have to sell *everything*, even the farms."

She waited. A pause like a chasm into which I threw a tiny pebble—"I'll come as soon as I can, Mom." I declared this with the best of intentions but hip time is not civilian time. "I have a few things to clean up here first," I explained.

It would take me another two months to reach Englewood.

I had not seen my parents, except for one weekend, in nearly five years and could not remember when I had seen my sister last. Now, I would never see my father again. I would never have the opportunity to capitalize on the intimate moments we had shared during his last visit to Olema. He had finally understood and appreciated something fundamental about me, only it was too late now for me to exploit his knowledge and guidance.

I spoke to him once after that Olema weekend. The caravan was camped on a high plateau in Utah called Strawberry Flats. Morris came to mind, so I drove down the highway and called him from a payphone we had passed earlier. We had a simple, warm conversation and he signed off by saying, "Take care of yourself, son." I drove off, anticipating a happy future with him. I had no intimation they would be the last words of his I would ever hear.

—◦—

TWO MONTHS AFTER leaving Boulder, my truck rolled into the driveway at 90 Booth Avenue. Ruth, older, greyer, and startlingly frail, crossed the front porch to greet us. She was wrapped in a thin housedress and smiling broadly. She lifted her nearly two-year-old grandchild from Sam beaming with delight, cooing over Ariel, and clutching her tightly. She kissed me perfunctorily on the cheek and then spat out a greeting "I'm so angry at you I could kill you," she said and turned on her heel and entered the house. My spirits sagged. I turned to Sam, who responded archly, "Nice." I followed Ruth indoors filled with apprehension.

The house appeared unchanged—still cool and stable, still emanating elegance of a high order, only now, every single item—tables, rugs, silver, books, mirrors, paintings, chairs, clocks, and end tables were tagged with white labels listing an item number for a pending auction. It was early afternoon and Ruth was already drinking.

"It was the attack on Cuba," she said as if it was obvious what she was speaking about. "It wiped out the American bond market."

A memory surfaced when she said that, and I understood that she was describing an event that had transpired years earlier. In the spring of 1961, Morris walked into the house and nearly filled an Old Fashioned glass with Scotch. He downed it violently as he stood alone gazing out through the picture window. He was so unnervingly distant and still that I dared not interrupt him with any questions and left him there gazing into the middle distance. Listening to Ruth, I realized that must have been near the time his losses occurred. My cousin Arthur, son of Aunt Ruth who brought us Susie, told me he ran into my father one day and found him distraught. He looked at Artie and said, "I lost fifteen million dollars today," and walked away.

"Moish was such a fucking egoist," Ruth continued, smoking and gazing into the emptiness of her future as if she were considering a thought she disliked. "If Aunt Frieda gave him five thousand dollars to invest, your father would give her five thousand dollars every year and they'd all say, 'Oh Morrie's a *genius*.' The truth was that he couldn't be fucking *bothered!* He could make money so fast he just took care of everybody. Everybody but *me!*" She stubbed the cigarette out with evident bitterness and her lips worked a few times, as if she were sucking a flake of tobacco from her teeth. "He had all our safekeeping money in government bonds. What could be safer, right?" she demanded.

She looked at me directly and answered her own question. "But your father bought them on *margin!*" emphasizing *margin* as if the stupidity of that decision were self-evident. "He didn't want to tie up his money," she continued as an afterthought.

I had the good sense not to mention that neither she nor I knew anything about money. That we had always left all decisions about it to Morris, and now she was paying for that unfounded trust. There was nothing I could say, and I suspect Ruth had already flagellated herself with that exact observation.

"Goddamnit," she snarled, and finished off her Scotch and soda. She handed me the glass, "Make me another."

"Are you sure, Mom?" I asked, even as I rose to do her bidding.

"Oh, look who's concerned about health," she said, giving me a visual once-over that suggested that I was in far worse shape than she was. I had made this drink hundreds of times—Cutty Sark or J&B over ice, with seltzer. I had been doing it since I was ten, and I made it again. Nothing had changed except that Morris was dead. That meant everything had changed.

THAT NIGHT, WHILE Sam and Ariel rested in my sister's old bedroom, I wandered through the Englewood house as if I were exploring Morris's mind. All the familiar books and furniture, the rugs, photos of the cattle, paintings, even his shoes, lined up and so meticulously cared for in his closet, summoned his ghost. Each object had been selected by him and represented some image he once had of how he had wanted his life to be. Now it was all going or gone.

I didn't mind the physical loss of the houses and the material wealth. They had never been mine. Since childhood, I had filled the emotional void between Morris and me with surrogate fathers—Jim Clancy had been my kinder, more moderate model in childhood, Buddy Jones as I grew older. I culled spare parts for a self from mechanics and grease monkeys, and mentors and models of every stripe were wedged into empty psychic spaces where positive images and memories of a father (or a self) should have been. Each important male adult in my life was an attempt to find the loving, nurturing father I needed. Except Gary Snyder.

Gary was a mystery and it was unclear how our relationship would develop. He was cool and a tad distant. He moved through the world in a unique way. He was famous and lauded but he somehow did not leave footprints as he passed. He offered nothing to grab onto. Any relationship with him would be an uncharacteristic one for me. Besides, none of my paternal surrogates were ever adequate substitutes for Morris. They were never the flesh of which I was made. None had inspired or deformed me to the degree he had. The dominant shaping force of my existence was dead and we had never healed the wounds between us.

Morris was dead. I was free at last . . . and heartbroken.

—◄o►—

I WAS THE man of the family now but too unprepared and untrained in the skills my parents' life required to be of any help to my mother. I was not the man my father was, which I confirmed to myself by sneaking off to New York a number of times to score heroin—my reliable champion of unresolvable conflicts, doubts, and tensions. One of those trips was extended by the request of a famous singer friend from California for a three-way with her girlfriend. This started well, but was interrupted by the guy we'd sent to score for us returning to the Chelsea hotel room, having been stabbed in the leg by the dealer. The singer tried to pull her girlfriend off me to tend to him and when the girlfriend preferred concentrating on a possible orgasm, the singer grabbed her hair and pulled her off, initiating a screaming catfight between the naked women on the linoleum floor. Having nothing better to do, I cleaned and bandaged our friend's leg and we watched the girls fighting together while I pondered what my life had become. Events like this tended to "come up" when drugs were involved.

Even without drugs blowing my life apart, I had no idea what to do as I watched the vultures descend on Booth Avenue to pick over our home, making lowball offers for the widow's treasure. Adding insult to injury, Sam and Ruth were a flammable mix in the house. Sam was lonely and bored and the friends' daughter she had impulsively brought east with us as a nanny was not working out and had to be sent home. Sam was not used to civilian routines and unintentionally created chaos by cooking at odd hours or just for herself and the baby. Ruth was not amenable to communal life or life with Sam (I was not sure which), and the atmosphere was degenerating quickly. I needed to do something.

I had driven east without a plan, buoyed by a poorly thought-out impulse to help my mom. My communal brothers and sisters were now scattered across the continent, and I was alone with my nuclear family and it did not feel good. I felt as exposed as a leper, walking through Englewood in my coveralls, filthy fedora, and long tangled hair. My mode of dress made no sense outside my counterculture community. Tensions between Sam and Ruth continued to escalate; Ruth was stressed from dealing with creditors, lawyers, merchants, and close friends who had lost their money to Morris. My few attempts to intervene and bargain on her behalf had threatened the sales of books or cameras that she felt she needed to unload. I was bored and restless (and only twenty-five minutes from New York and its promises of easy distractions). I was certain that we were becoming a burden and the only helpful thing I could think of was to remove ourselves from cohabitating under Ruth's roof.

Consequently, after several weeks of low-level unease, guerrilla warfare in the kitchen, and complaints in the bedroom, I arranged to move Sam, Ariel, and myself to Turkey Ridge. Buddy and Betty Jones would be nearby there, and I craved their company and support. Furthermore, Turkey Ridge was a power place for me. All my memories of it were, enabling, and positive. From the moment the idea occurred to me, I could not wait to leave.

We packed and loaded the truck. Ruth wished us well, kissed me with real warmth (and perhaps relief), and sent us off with the following admonition: "The farm is no longer mine. It needs to stay in tip-top shape for sale. Don't hurt it." She might as well have been explaining the issue to a cat.

After the rough-and-tumble, motherly clutter of communal life, living with just Sam and Ariel was debilitating and lonely. Sam was starved for female company and I was starved for any company. Jim Clancy, my childhood mentor, had hired on to work for the Park Service. Bill Jelinek had found employment elsewhere and Walt Poliski was leasing some of our fields and working the land for himself and his brothers.

I remember the autumn light that year as persistently grey, and the stone house as barren, quiet, and cold. My friends were far away and the worlds on the East Coast that had once comforted me were now unraveling and unrecognizable.

Buddy and Betty Jones had recently gone through a bitter divorce during which Buddy had a breakdown of sorts, and ran around his yard firing his shotgun into the air and screaming, while Betty and the kids cowered inside. Betty had grown weary of the uncertainties of jazz life and become a realtor, but after that night, she grabbed the kids and moved out. Buddy had taken up with a *much* younger woman (eighteen when they'd met) named Lynn, a trainer of dressage horses. He was happy when I saw him again and Lynn was easy, smart, and fun, but as a couple they were unfamiliar. I missed Betty's cooing and mothering. I had lost another important pillar of support.

Turkey Ridge—the farm I was "never to sell" (I cannot type the words without recalling Morris's precise inflection)—was left without funds to care for it and I had no idea how to earn anything. I could not even afford pre-rolled cigarettes, and rolled mine from a big yellow tin of Top tobacco. I generated onerous comparisons between my abilities and Morris's and they richocheted around my inner life like the hardball in a Jai Alai game. Morris had been "the boss" because he had been *capable* of being the boss. My skill sets qualified me to be a hired hand (if the place was small) and not much more. My previous fantasies of altering the culture of the United States to create more compassionate possibilities of livelihood and social interaction now appeared as delusional as Tinkerbell. My life felt like acid reflux.

I WALKED DOWN the road to visit Jim and Ellie one day, but things were no longer the same. Jim was working for the Park Service, wearing a uniform, a badge, and carrying a gun. He was charged with watching (and eventually evicting) the hippie squatters—people like me—who had lawfully rented homes from the Park Service after it had evicted the legitimate farmers under eminent domain to build a dam creating a reservoir of cooling water for a nuclear power plant to be built at nearby Tocks Island. When those plans met resistance and slowed down, instead of leasing the land back to original farmers, the Park Service put an ad in the New York papers, offering the farmhouses for cheap rent and New York hippies flooded in, establishing a community at Shawnee-on-Delaware amidst much justified local anger. Later, after the Squatters (as they were referred to by locals) had established gardens, workshops, and animals and had been living in place for over a year, the government ordered them off the land. It was a mess perpetuated by tone-deaf bureaucrats, but the ripples and back-eddies reached into my community and directly into Turkey Ridge. Ellie now regarded me as if I were a stranger. Lines were being drawn everywhere.

It's said that Nature abhors a vacuum and it appears to be true. As the autumn progressed, several friends from California showed up at Turkey Ridge, pulling down the long drive in their old purple moving van. Their arrival was like sunshine and fresh air to a convict and I invited them to stay. In short order others followed and before three weeks had passed we were filled with the number of souls the farm could possibly bear, which in this case was fifteen including children. We had reconstituted a Digger commune at the opposite end of the continent like a magic act. After the obligatory catching up and gossip, we reactivated our plans to create a counterculture in the slate quarry country of Pennsylvania.

Ruth was nervous when she found out about the "few" new people staying there, but I assured her that we would take good care of the farm. I was nearly happy. I had my brothers and sisters around me again. Ariel had playmates, and it was lovely to hear children's laughter. I was an "Uncle" to these Digger kids, and Sam had the support of other women when she needed to nap or take a break from parenting. At night we played music and board games, and in the daytime, returning to our practiced patterns of group work. Aided by a tractor-mounted large circular saw we cut and stacked five cords of wood for the coming winter in a week. Life was good, except for the fact that my relationship with Sam was coagulating like the blood on an old wound.

AS IF THE gods had decided to generate invidious comparisons, Gary Snyder came to visit us. He had had a speaking engagement somewhere on the East Coast and dropped in to spend the night. We made a sweat in his honor and had a party with lots of drinking and music and went to bed very late. I arose before sunrise to clean up and was startled to see Gary sitting zazen meditation in the living room before the still-red coals in fireplace. He looked as if he were made of stone. His back was erect and a compelling force field of concentration surrounded him. I wish now that I had taken advantage of that moment. He had, once again, without a word indicated a path to me, but I had farther to fall before I would be able to clamber up on it. I wanted to live an exemplary life, but my examples were *political* and not personal. I wanted, no, I *needed* to make my life shine like his appeared to, but that morning at Turkey Ridge, other than rereading his poems after he left, I did not know how to take the first step in that direction.

◄◦►

THE FOLLOWING EVENTS were explored in depth in *Sleeping Where I Fall*, so what follows are simply placeholders for a chronology. Politics infected the estrangement between Jim and Ellie Clancy and Turkey Ridge. One morning before dawn, federal marshals rolled into the squatter community at Shawnee-on-Delaware, gave the inhabitants fifteen minutes to gather what they could, and then restrained them at gunpoint as huge Caterpillar bulldozers flattened their homes. Their animals were cut loose to roam, their gardens plowed under, and the Squatters were sent packing. As a Park Service employee Jim Clancy was expected to help his cohorts with the eviction and that fact rendered communication between us impossible. In fairness, Jim and Ellie both felt that their beloved Turkey Ridge was going to the dogs and with some reason. We were not a neat and tidy group, but neither did we have Morris's capital and three full-time employees to keep the place in its previous shipshape order.

My father's old business partner, Joe Konwiser, drove down the long gravel driveway of Turkey Ridge in a cream-colored Cadillac. Many years ago, Morris had hired Joe after he had done a short stint in prison, having something to do with the failure of the brokerage firm where he'd worked. Joe had been a pariah on Wall Street and remained steadfastly grateful to my dad for the second chance that had rewarded him generously. Joe was an old-school hustler, a salesman to his marrow, with a large square face fixed on a fire-plug body, eyes that had seen it all, indescribably pale and diffuse as if disappointment had scrubbed them of expectation. He once told me that "Morris was the most self-destructive son-of-a-bitch I ever met," and in the next breath that "Your mother was a class act who deserved better." He was here on her behalf this day.

"Your mother's drowning," he said, "and you're standing on her shoulders."

"Jesus, Joe," I was crushed. "What can *I* do. We're barely hanging on here."

"I'm glad you asked," he answered steadily, undeflected by my disclaimer. "I'll tell you. You can put her on *your* shoulders."

That simple sentence condemned me to the worst year of my life when Joe conscripted me to go to Wall Street and enter my father's firm, convinced that he could use that announcement to gain a year's holiday from debt interest due to the firm's creditors. He failed, I failed, and the year is too miserable to recount. For those with a penchant for unrelieved misery, I commend them to my earlier book.

EVERYTHING DISINTEGRATED COMPLETELY due to a phone call Ellie Clancy made. She heard of a plan I had developed to try to sell off fifty-acre lots to high-end bidders and in that way be able to preserve the original 150-acre homestead and bury Morris there. When I placed an ad in the local paper, Ellie called one of the major creditors for whom she had been spying and informed him that I was planning to sell Turkey Ridge and run off with the money. That malicious whisper caused several creditors to collaborate and sue my mother for fraud. Fraud is a criminal charge and therefore is not protected by bankruptcy. Consequently the farm had to be put up for immediate sale and we would be forced to leave.

A particular irony of this situation was that years earlier Morris had gifted Jim seventy acres of land and the deed to his cabin. He had helped my cousin Arthur to sell land he had bought with a bequest from his grandfather (Morris's dad), and Arthur built himself a lovely home in the midst of a large field not too far away. Buddy sold his land and moved to California. When all was said and done, everyone but Ruth was cared for, and me, who was "never to sell the farm," who received as an inheritance only Morris's Montblanc pen and his belt with an old Zuni turquoise buckle.

Morris was dead. His brother Bert was dead. Harry Palmer was dead. The men of power who might have intervened on my behalf were gone. I had lost all credibility with Jim and Ellie and never bothered to call and complain about how wrong they were about my intentions. I could see things from their point of view: the golden days of Morris and little Petey Rabbit were over. Petey the Pet Bunny had returned as Pete the Predator, a member of the hippie scourge that was ruining the country and the Delaware Water Gap in particular—promoting promiscuity, resistance to authority, indulgence, and an end to civility.

I'm certain that Ellie felt she was doing her civic and religious duty by trying to ensure the farm's being passed on to people who would care for it as Morris would have wanted. Whatever her reasons, it was done and the fine-grinding millstones of the law had been set in motion, reducing our community to powder.

◄○►

MY RELATIONSHIP WITH Sam foundered permanently when she conceived the bizarre strategy to save our relationship by inviting one of my lovers from California to come and stay. Nichole arrived from California with her young son and that *pas de trois* was described in *Sleeping Where I Fall*. It amounted to several weeks' ecstatic frolic and then the bitter end of Sam and my relationship. Sam awoke one morning and punctuated a definite and hostile end to the party by demanding, "What is that cunt doing in my bed?"

Nichole moved to a private bedroom in the attic and I spent nights alternating between them until Sam issued an ultimatum to the group one day: either Nichole or she would have to leave.

The rest of the family defended Nichole, feeling that she had been invited, traveled to Pennsylvania with her young son, and then earned her place through sharing the hard field-work and chores. Furthermore, she was popular and no one wanted her to go. So Sam left, leaving my daughter with me. A year and some months later, after the eviction, Nichole and I packed up everything we owned, kids and Josephine, my dog, and stuffed everything into a ruined old wooden house-trailer we'd dragged out of a neighbor's barn and repaired. We left for the West Coast in the beginning of winter, with $70 in our pockets. Ariel needed to see her mother, who was now back in San Francisco, and I needed to find a life.

◄○►

BEFORE NICHOLE, I, and the kids departed for good, I took a long, good-bye walk around Turkey Ridge. Every object my vision touched triggered memories—Morris and me lying in the hay while rain thrummed the roof, learning to drive, exploring the woods with my rifle, riding my horse for hours. Accompanying each memory was a background static of harsh judgments and pitiless self-regard. I had no wiggle room in which to feel better. Turkey Ridge had been lost on my watch.

The barn was nearly 200 years old and still solid. It would be standing after I was dust. All that remained here for me now were memories: the hay mow where my sister and I romped as children, the smell of the alfalfa and grass hay bales sweet and thick with pollens, familiar and deeply comforting. But there were no longer any cattle to be fed, no life rustling, chewing, and steaming in the winter chill.

I said good-bye to the blacksmith's shed and walked through the bays of the shop, fingering tools I could not carry with me, surveying the wealth that had been temporarily mine. Morris coursed back and forth through my mind like a phantom, appearing here and there, confusing present and past, fact and memory. What would he have said? How might he have judged my failure? Perhaps not as savagely as I imagined after his own, but every time his face appeared in my mind, I translated his facial expressions as reproach.

I walked through every room in the house and stood in each a while, thanking it sincerely as I left. Life leaves fingerprints in the places where it has breathed. I could recognize scars and stains of times past on the walls and scuffed baseboards. Occasionally my sister or an old playmate appeared to me in one room or another, but my attachments were already weakening, and the memories were thinning and curiously without luster and power, as if they were exhausted.

I understood that I was bidding farewell to my family as I had always known and remembered it. The life that had once felt so oppressed and tortured to me had been sustained by unremitting effort on my parents' part, acts of love in their own mundane right—Morris's daily treks to work, the labors of my mother, Sue, Jim and Ellie, ranch hands—all cooperating to actualize Morris's vision and keep our family healthy and prosperous. They were all dissipating like smoke. Furthermore, I was losing my Digger family as well and all our dreams of a glorious future lived by heroes. The others had moved on in search of a stable place to live. Everything had failed simultaneously. Our ecstasies and bold imaginings were as cold as the ash in the dead hearths.

My sister Muff was busy with her marriage and child-rearing far away in Boston. Her life had a new center now and Turkey Ridge was no longer a part of it. Ruth's life had shrunk to the dimensions of a small Englewood apartment where she did *The New York Times* crosswords in ink and watched television all day, once again immobilized by depression. My sense of failure was so great I did not know if I would be able to face either of them again. Them? Would I ever be able to face myself? I had never felt so alone. I had never faced the fundamental Buddhist truth that "everything changes" quite so nakedly.

I walked out to the far corner of the big hay-field and stepped over the rock wall and into the woods. Just outside the fence-row claimed by the woods was an old stone burial mound. Four birch trees with startlingly white bark grew out of one end, their leaves bright as jets of burning gas. I had once spent an entire LSD trip on this mound, letting my spirit be washed in the spaces between the jittering leaves. That was when I conceived my plan to bury Morris at the edge of that field from where an unobstructed view of the entire homestead, the lake, and the Delaware Water Gap was possible. I said my good-byes to the ancient spirits of place there, stepped over the rock wall and crossed the thick grass of the hay-field, towards my waiting truck, passing over the spot where I would have buried Morris, without a backward glance. I was crossing the borders of superimposed kingdoms to which I would never be allowed to return, and I understood that my banishment would be permanent and irreversible.

Looking due north, I could see the entire farm and out buildings and from this distance none of the wear and hard use we had caused were visible. Morris had built something beautiful and from this remove it still appeared pristine. I was about to leave it now and pile my family and belongings into a claptrap old house-trailer and cross the country with no money, no plans, and no imagined future. There was no one to blame for this situation but myself.

—◦—

WHEN WE ARRIVED in California, in the winter of 1974, I was as out of synch with my spiritual intuitions as I have ever been. Sick, dispirited, still craving opiates, and attempting to nurture a daughter suffering the trauma of the inexplicable disappearance of her mother even though I could not take care of myself. I dropped Ariel off with her mother and made plans to take her half time as soon as I found a place. The next night, I had gotten high with some dude I met when we were copping dope and we went to his place to get off. When I woke up, he was dead, his upper body and extended arm lying across the table from me, blue as a picture of Krishna. Tiptoeing out of his apartment and closing the door behind me, I was deeply shaken. It could as easily have been me and would be if I continued. If that happened Ariel would have no one but her mother to look after her, and that did not bode well for any future I wished for her. I *had* to clean up my act.

I was thirty-four and living on the unemployment insurance of Danny Rijkin, manager of the Grateful Dead who had learned to live on half his salary so that when work stopped he had no worries. Sam and I were on decent terms, sharing Ariel, who was four, going on five by this time. I found a basement apartment at Holly Park Circle in the southern end of the Mission District, with space to park my truck and trailer at the curb. I didn't plan on doing much there besides sleeping. I was sick of myself. I understood that ending my use of drugs would only be the beginning of reclaiming a life worth preserving, but I had to begin there.

An old friend and Digger doctor named Felix Lenneman gave me enough Dolophine to pass through the physical symptoms of withdrawal with bearable discomfort. Even Felix's drugs could not stave off all the symptoms of kicking, the first of which is a craving of unimaginable intensity for more. Addicts will and have done nearly anything for a fix when they are junksick. That illness is a composite of acute depression, compounded by diarrhea, nausea and vomiting, spiking fevers, and the body's overproduction of fluids—sweat, tears, and a continually runny nose, as if it were attempting to flood the toxins from its tissues. Occasionally, for variety, all the hairs on your arms, legs, and head may rise as if animated by electric currents. You cannot get comfortable, cannot sleep or eat, and these reactions, combined with acute anxiety, continue for a week or so. Dolophine will soften, but not obliterate these symptoms and once you are free of the physical addiction, the real work starts. The feral dog I'd placated by feeding it gobbets of my psyche for years had received no nourishment in a week and was dangerously angry. Every doubt, insecurity, self-accusation, fear, and paranoia I could conceive of was aimed at my tattered psyche like streams of piss from this enraged demon-dog. No longer addicted, but unfit for human company, and intending to get healthy by finally killing off my deranged invisible twin, I took myself off for a ten-day solo wilderness hike through Desolation Valley (appropriate name, Pete) that ended with a visit to Gary Snyder's place in the Sierras.

–◄o►–

DURING THAT VISIT, for the first time I noticed the Buddhist paraphernalia tucked around Gary's house. Every morning Gary disappeared to meditate or run through his Buddhist chants. The connection between the qualities I admired in him and these artifacts and practices finally coalesced as understanding and by the end of that visit I had resolved to learn something about Buddhism.

I began to make the four-hour drive from San Francisco to Gary's home in the Sierra foothills with some regularity. Farmwork had trained me to be useful and Gary readily accepted my company as an able hand. My relationship with Gary was new to me and without anxiety. He was neither a father figure nor would he stand still to be regarded as a teacher. In the absence of such projections I was able to see and hear him without too much psychic interference. It made things easy between us.

It was around this time too, in 1974, that I finally committed to protecting my health and permanently ending my use of drugs. I located a psychiatrist who agreed to work with me on a sliding scale and committed myself to three sessions a week with him. After two years of work together he died, and I began the process again with a new doctor.

Previously, all my attempts at liberation had been sought through altered states of mind, employing, besides heroin and methedrine, LSD, STP, San Pedro cactus, magic mushrooms, peyote, and DMT. Except for the higher Tryptamine series—(DET and DPT)—which made me feel like my retinal cells were crisping, all these experiences reinforced Jim Clancy's early assertions that the entire universe was a single organism. The problem with my experiments was a) that they ended (you "came down" and returned to your habitual "self"), b) they sapped the body's strength and energy, and finally, c) what does one *do* with such experiences? After you "return," a gap remains between the drug-induced insights and the moment-to-moment demands and stressors of daily life. That life is always compounded by one's habits, indulgences, fears, and delusions and I never found find that life *after* a drug trip was easier or more illuminated than it was before. Neither did I ever consider drug highs as the highest possibilities of consciousness. They were certainly not what my readings in Zen Buddhism, shamanic literature, and Carlos Castañeda's books had suggested. So I resolved to discover whatever enlightenment was in a drug-free manner.

◄o►

WHILE GARY AND I cut and piled brush or thinned over-dense stands of timber, we would, in the fashion of men who work together, discuss the day, its attendant issues and ideas. I had never spent as much uninterrupted time with a scholar before and the breadth of Gary's knowledge and recall was impressive. It also gave me a clear idea of how carelessly I had wasted my time at school as boy. He had the broad outlines of global history readily available, detailed and precise knowledge about Asian culture and religions—particularly Buddhism, world poetry, Paleolithic art, indigenous cultures, anthropology, and forestry and wilderness, as well as encyclopedic knowledge of American political history. Our conversations were master-class tutorials in one subject after another and each visit passed too rapidly, leaving me with many more questions to ask and copious notes to organize. Furthermore, because our relationship was not clouded by ghosts of the past, I did not take umbrage at his teaching or resent his authority and expertise. Neither did I expect him to quell my anxieties or pacify my self-doubts. There was definitely something of a master-pupil relationship between us, but a) I was requesting it, and b) Gary was assiduous in his refusal to allow his knowledge to elevate his status. That left only a peer-to-peer model for our relationship despite the doubts I held about our intellectual parity.

Gary and his first wife, Masa, had divorced and Gary's new wife Carol Koda was an easy, fun-loving woman of great acuity. She loved hiking and the outdoors as much as Gary did, and was a dedicated bird-watcher who participated in annual bird counts, and netting, identifying, and tagging local species. What stood out about her from my point of view was that she appeared to like me, and regard me as a peer of Gary's. It was hard for me to accept, but she would say, "Oh God, I told Gary that he should talk to you about that," and absent any irony or pretense, I had to accept that she found some value for her husband in our friendship.

One day as we worked together, Gary's conversation had touched on eleven centuries of Buddhist history, across India, China, Korea, Vietnam, Japan, Tibet, and Thailand, until I dropped my axe in exasperation and demanded, "Gary, how the fuck do you keep track of all this?"

He grinned broadly and said, "I'll show you." Setting aside our tools, we walked into his barn-study and in the center of the room he indicated an industrial-sized wooden card catalog perhaps eight feet square that he had retrieved from an old library. I pulled open a drawer, then another, and another. They were stuffed with meticulously detailed library cards cataloging not only Gary's entire bibliography of reading and research, but also subdividing the subject matters into distinctively refined categories. Buddhism, for instance, was further categorized into Hinayana and Mahayana, and how those divisions played out culturally and practically in India, Indonesia, Japan, China, Korea, Vietnam, etcetera. An equally large number of drawers were dedicated to anthropology, and its own subdivisions: the Paleolithic, Amero-Indian, Okinawans, Ainu, Kan Bushman, and cultures I had never heard of.

Gary pulled out a library card with a series of Roman and cardinal numerals he'd inscribed in black ink, and explained, "These tell me which of my journals elaborate this particular issue." He indicated a high shelf running around three walls of the room, dense with numbered black notebooks, that he had assembled over the preceding fifty years. Putting the card back in its proper place and closing the drawer, he smiled. "You're the first person that ever asked me about this."

◄o►

DESPITE THE SERIOUS intent of our conversations, Gary was quick to laugh, and liked a drink, and (until he developed lung trouble) rolling a smoke at the end of the day. He loved his tools and cared for them well (a characteristic I always mark about workmen).

As I grew more intimate with his life, the connective tissue between his various concerns gradually became visible. One day, we were discussing the notion of the mad and tortured artist and the ways in which even contemporary audiences tend to measure the sincerity of young artists by the degree of self-destruction they're willing to wreak upon themselves. I had been good friends with Janis Joplin and guitarist Mike Bloomfield, both of whom had died of overdoses. Add to that number Jimi Hendrix, and up to the present, Amy Winehouse—they form a lineage of artists who behaved as if self-destruction were the goal of their explorations. In the conversation I referenced Verlaine and Rimbaud as archetypes of such behavior.

Gary's response was illuminating. "When Verlaine and Rimbaud were young," he said, "they were protesting the iron grip that bourgeois rationality had on all aspects of nineteenth-century French culture—the manners, the view of reality, and the exclusion of 'the wild' from public life. Rationality in business and society were dominant values. 'Deranging the senses' was one strategy artists like Verlaine and Rimbaud employed to break free of that.

"Today," he continued, "the bourgeoisie is sociopathic, overindulged, distracted, spoiled beyond measure, and unable to restrain its gluttony, even in the face of pending planetary destruction. In the face of such a threat, it has, by necessity, become the responsibility of the artist to model health and sanity."

Oh.

-◄◦►-

SHORTLY AFTER I returned to San Francisco, I phoned a woman whom I would later marry. Because we're no longer married and she no longer uses my name, I'll call her Jean. She seemed like she might be the ticket for a trip from my old life into something healthier, kinder, and wiser and I went for it.

Jean was quiet and quite shy, but observant as a fox, sometimes sparking off wicked Irish humor. Her people were from the Kentucky River Valley near Columbus, Ohio, and while her speech and manners had a down-home country ring to them, she spoke three languages, had travelled widely, and did not miss a trick. More importantly, she appeared to be as wholesome as homemade bread.

She was beautiful in a sunny, Midwestern way, the kind of girl you would not hesitate to introduce to your mother, and her personality expressed an upbeat, can-do sense of fun. I had met her when her boyfriend and she had stopped at Turkey Ridge for a night, and I remembered her when I returned to San Francisco. The boyfriend was long gone and she was now a formal student of Richard Baker-roshi, the Abbot of the San Francisco Zen Center—the recognized lineage-holder of Shunryu Suzuki, the Japanese Soto Zen Master who had founded San Francisco City Center, Green Gulch, and Tassajara Monasteries. Jean possessed a gravitas and strength that I found appealing, and the fact that she was a serious student of Zen added to her allure. In short order I found myself pulled into her gravitational field and consequently into orbit around the San Francisco Zen Center.

It was with Jean that my tether to the Diggers thinned and snapped. There were numerous small incidents where her insistence on order and calm became increasingly appealing, even when they were at odds with our anarchic Digger practices, but the seminal rupture occurred at a celebration of the midwinter Solstice (December 21) in 1975.

It was the year after I'd returned from Turkey Ridge, and although our various land-bases had failed, the Diggers, despite interpersonal difficulties and geographical separations, were still my community and hope for the future. I joined them in planning one of our annual Solstice celebrations, this one to be held in San Francisco's Glen Park. At those observations of planetary clockwork, we feasted and partied together, made music, and collaborated with the children in inventing ad hoc ceremonies, like tying gold "wish" paper from Chinatown inscribed with the children's wishes and prayers to an old fir tree and burning them in a bonfire. This year was to be no different. Jean, excited by the opportunity of participating with "my people" for the first time, brought her Zen aesthetics to bear on the occasion.

She collected stemmed plastic wineglasses, a tablecloth, metal flatware, and plates for relatively elegant table-settings. She gathered autumn leaves and acorns for thematic table decorations and worked hard to prepare an enormous *Kulebiaka*—an entire salmon shredded then combined with rice and herbs and covered over with a layer of pastry dough, like a pie. She decorated the domed surface of the Kulebiaka with silhouettes cut out of rolled dough—small deer, fir trees, a sun, moon, and birds—glazing the surface with egg whites and baking the entire, nearly yard-long lozenge to an enticing golden brown. It was impressive and beautiful and I was proud to introduce her to my friends through this offering.

We arrived at Glen Park early and set up the table near the fire pit. The Kulebiaka was still warm and fragrant when it was unwrapped.

I was gratified by the "ooh's" and "aah's" as friends approached and commented on Jean's handiwork. Wine was poured, children raced around, shrieking with delight, a few people started to make music— an otherwise normal beginning to one of our recurring holidays.

What was not normal that day was the mood of Samurai Bob, my astringent friend from the Haight-Ashbury and Turkey Ridge. I knew Bob originally from Haight Street, and he used to visit Olema on his rounds delivering Irving Rosenthal's beautiful free *Kaliflower* newspaper. Bob was a tough ex-Marine, simmering with anger. He was a good but not an "easy" friend and he been asked to leave Turkey Ridge by the mothers because of his edgy temper and penchant for drumming and drinking late into the night. ("Do your thing" is a workable philosophy until mothers who have to wake at 5 AM to nurse are kept awake until three by others' partying.) Bob strode up to the table and jammed his hand wrist-deep into the Kulebiaka, remerging with a large clot of rice-salmon-and-pastry dough that he flung onto a plate. The crudity of his gesture had to have been designed to shock, and indicate to me that he regarded Jean's refinements as a bourgeois cancer introduced to the body of Digger culture.

Others followed Bob's example and in short order the table was reduced to a stained and filthy disaster, smeared with wine and food until it resembled a public toilet after a political rally. The Kulebiaka looked like a carcass gutted by wolves, and shortly after Bob's initial violation, another pedal-to-the-metal Digger party was accelerating like a dragster at the track.

Jean was mortified and angry, and so was I. I remember thinking, "There is nothing here that reflects my sense of the order and beauty of the Universe." It was a far cry from the aesthetics of Snyder's house and a sobering wake-up moment for me. It marked a distinct break with my unequivocal acceptance of Digger values. Nothing would alter my individual friendships certainly, but our laissez-faire, "everything's-free" ethos had revealed itself as impossibly flawed and always inclining towards the lowest common denominator.

In that moment I realized that we were living an *idea* and not actually building *lives*. No "pre-civilized" tribe would ever have behaved with such rudeness and disregard in a ceremonial context. Perhaps Bob's act was releasing steam about having been evicted from Turkey Ridge but I knew that Jean would never participate again and that she had not missed the intention of Bob's gesture as excluding her. At that moment the Digger lifestyle ceased to interest me. I remain bound to this day with many Digger brothers and sisters, but I am no longer bound by unquestioning loyalty. That insight freed me to claim something that Jean and Gary had in common. I mark that day as the commencement of my Buddhist practice.

—◦—

LIFE BEGAN IMPROVING on a number of fronts. Jean returned from a three-month sojourn at Tassajara monastery in the winter of 1975. She had asked me to mind her apartment while she was gone, and to care for her plants. When she returned, the interior of her apartment resembled a jungle. I was relieved that everything had not died and she was pleased. I had no place to live and stayed, and we were now living together.

My relationship with Jean was new, driven by equal parts attraction, affection, and respect. The latter two categories appeared as surprising interlopers in a psyche normally flooded by impulses aggregated on the goat end of the spectrum. Meditation seemed to have opened up a more spacious interior in me, but I felt unsure in it. Unlike myself who was often in an emotional fog, not knowing exactly what I was feeling at a given moment, Jean knew her own feelings with certainty. Given the history of my past decade, I concluded that her instincts were probably better than my own, and began deferring to them uncritically as a kind of training. (Always a bad idea.)

Life with Jean was calm and good. Ariel was with us for long periods of time and comforted by Jean's attentiveness to her. I was timidly beginning to feel that I might be on the verge of creating a happy home environment. Despite being thirty-five, with no money and a child, I had been drug-free for over a year, and was beginning to experience glimmers of confidence about my future.

Jean was a serious and dedicated Zen student and I had been joining her in daily meditation, and taking my cues from the way she operated in her life. Like Gary, she pursued whatever she was involved with thoroughly, with a focused attention on detail. Unlike Snyder, however, she was rarely calm. She suffered crippling bouts of anxiety and apprehension about tasks demanded of her, despite being enough of an expert in the rigor of formal Japanese tea ceremony that her teacher, the Zen master's widow, often chose her to perform for visiting Japanese dignitaries. Crippled by the pain in my knees from sitting on my haunches during the interminable tea ceremony, I marveled at how poised and accomplished Jean was, displaying no impatience or pain as she went through the intricate choreography involved in boiling water, preparing, and serving a cup of tea. I had high hopes that with her practice as an example and the study of Zen meditation as a base I might master a direct path to qualities I admired in both her and Gary.

—◀◦▶—

THE STATELY JULIA Morgan building that the San Francisco Zen Center occupied was an island of calm in the otherwise turbulent cross-currents of San Francisco's black ghetto, the spine of which was nearby Fillmore Street, colloquially referred to as "the razor." Monks were regularly robbed here and I had previously copped dope in the projects within walking distance on Fillmore Street at the old Eddy Hotel.

Jean and I rose at 5 AM every morning and entered the calm, sweet-smelling, *zendo* (meditation hall) by 5:30. People sat on the fragrant woven grass *tatami* mats, in the entrance corridor, side by side, facing the wall, their backs framing the narrow corridor to the Zen hall. Inside the *zendo*, the floor and raised platforms around the perimeter of the room were covered with similar mats. Each individual place was marked by a flat, black pad about two feet by three feet, called a *zabuton*. On it rested a firm, round black cushion called a *zafu*. The *zafu* raises the buttocks enough so that with crossed legs, the spine can be erect but still maintain its natural curve. Having the pelvis tipped slightly forward makes it easier for the hips to open for cross-legged sitting, with the knees stabilizing the body by acting as the corners of a triangle.

After two forty-minute periods of sitting, separated by slow, meditative walking (called *kinhin*), participants file out in silence and upstairs into the large, *tatami*-floored Buddha Hall for morning service. There, we knelt and chanted expressions of gratitude in Japanese or Japanese iterations of Sanskrit to the rhythm of a hollow wooden drum called a *mokugyo* carved in the likeness of a bull-headed fish. (The fish, which never sleeps, is a symbol of wakefulness). Although the service appears "religious," Zen Buddhists are not worshipping a god and in that sense is not technically a "religion."[7] Buddha was a human man who came to understand the cause of human suffering and devised practices and a way of life to end it. The ritualized bowing and expressions of praise are not entreaties for divine intervention, but expressions of gratitude to a beloved teacher.

When I first began my practice at San Francisco Zen Center I was struck by the self-control and discipline manifested there. I had never before been in a room with five people, let alone forty or fifty, where one could speak without raising one's voice. The self-restraint and lack of competitive clamoring for personal attention were revelatory.

After service, fifteen or twenty minutes were dedicated to *soji*—cleaning the environs: trimming the altar candles and kerosene lamps, and washing the chimneys. We swept the *zendo,* hallways, steps, and sidewalk, dusting and maintaining the bathrooms and public rooms of the entire building in good order. By 7:30, I was free to begin my day.

Life in the counterculture had habituated me to doing exactly what I chose when I wanted to. Because of this Zen Center was a challenge to me. I had always shunned schedules and routines as impediments to freedom and the province and concern of squares, consequently Zen Center's order and observances chafed. I was honest enough to admit that I had nearly killed myself (and others) pursuing my "freedom," and that insight helped me to remain resolved and follow this new path.

Slowly but surely, daily Zen practice wore down my resistance until one day it occurred to me that it didn't matter whether I "liked" or "disliked" the schedule, or preferred some tasks to others. The "self" who selected and chose what it liked and disliked was the habitual, unquestioned identity which had also chosen heroin, numerous inappropriate sexual liaisons, and generally ignored my health and state of mind. "I" was, if I was honest enough to admit it, often angry, anxious, miserable, and insecure, creating back-washes and eddies of disorder wherever I traveled and impulsively seeking facile opportunities to quell those discomfiting feelings with classic addict behavior. I concluded that my newer, healthier dog could benefit from this training.

At some indeterminate point in my second year of practice I accepted by observation that an unstructured, do-your-thing reality does not afford opportunities to "catch" one's habitual patterns. As soon as something chafed or touched a nerve I would (BZ—before Zen) reflexively distract myself by changing my environment or internal chemistry. That was a *kind* of freedom certainly, but it was achieved at the cost of missed opportunities to become intimate with the "self" actually pulling the strings and orchestrating my choices and habits. It might have been freedom, but it did not offer me the opportunity to consider whether my behavior was useful to me or not. Such observation may appear too much extra work for normal people, but I was not "normal" and had a detailed history of self-destructive or counter-productive behavior that I wanted to end. A schedule established boundaries and limits, which proved useful in organizing my time and also highlighting (and thus observing) the complaining, compulsive, lazy guy "I" had always been. *A schedule is just a schedule,* I thought, and if I followed it and didn't think about it there *was* no problem. I would eventually find time to do what I wanted to only not in the instant it first occurred to me.

-◄○►-

THE ENVIRONMENT AT Zen Center was spare and clean and, in the manner of Japanese culture from which it sprang, was aesthetic to a highly refined order. This pacified the hunger for order and beauty I had been missing. Even the garments in which I meditated, designed for comfort and utility, had an elegance I appreciated. Long, black, outer robes with full flowing sleeves (a *koromo*) were worn over a light grey inner robe—a *kimono*. Under both was a half-length white inner garment with a grosgrain silk collar called a *juban*. The white and grey were both visible in the V-neck of the black robe and the the whole was stylish as a tuxedo. Those who did not have robes usually wore "fat pants"—loose trousers or sweats that made crossing one's legs easy, and *hiparis*—loosely-fitting jackets closed by ties. There was no uniform (except for priests, who always wore those three aforementioned garments under their formal priest's robe (an *okesa*). There was nothing precious about costume there. Sweatshirts or sweaters were acceptable as long as they were dark and not distracting to others. I say this easily today, but my first introduction to these clothes caused me difficulty.

While I appreciated Zen Center's cleanliness, and order, it is helpful to know I also considered the inhabitants generally "uptight," preoccupied with "mindfulness" (as they referred to it) and woefully short on spontaneous expression. Furthermore, when my "interest" in Zen evolved into a fledgling "practice," I began to chafe and miss the ecstasies of my hipster life. (Random anonymous fucking and narcotics being numbers one and two on my short list). Furthermore, I was convinced that I had absorbed enough Buddhist texts and lived through enough madness to understand Zen's "Crazy Dog wisdom"— expressed as "eat when you're hungry, sleep when you're tired"—the highest liberated state of a Zen Master. It goes without saying that in my certainty, I overlooked the inconvenient merging of "freedom" and "indulgence" in my psyche, but distinctions like these are usually not understood until practice has brought the unruly self to heel.

In my own mind, Zen Center was a kind of finishing school, to pick up a few tips and help me polish my act. I was convinced that I had already mastered freedom. Besides, by considering my personal interpretation of Crazy Dog wisdom as the apex of Zen practice, I felt justified in picking and choosing *which* rules I would follow and which I could ignore. I was "cool" with the costume so I wore it. I was not so "cool" with observing my moment-to-moment thoughts, impulses, and gestures, and restraining them in consideration of others.

Zen Center behavior, with its dearth of impulse, anger, and joy, drove me up a wall. I was bursting with energy and eager to explore my "new" life. I had landed on my feet, found a pretty girl of good character and, thanks to a public-works government job I had managed to win, I was employed teaching acting in disadvantaged schools—making $600 a *month*—25 percent of any income I had made annually in the previous ten years. I could buy new parts for my truck instead of scavenging them from junkyards, and celebrating this good fortune, had with my first paycheck bought Jean and myself matching down sleeping bags. Life was good.

JEAN WANTED ME to experience Tassajara, Zen Center's traditional Japanese-style monastery in the remote Santa Lucia Mountains, three hours south of the City. It was the only traditional Zen training site in the United States and she and I drove down to stay for several weeks as volunteers helping with their profitable summer guest season which paid for the site to operate as a monastery the rest of the year.

I was chopping vegetables in the kitchen one morning, with a firm grip on my razor-sharp Japanese slice-and-dice knife, reducing a large pile of carrots into orderly ovals. I was content. The kitchen was a hive of concentrated activity and except for the gurgle and tinkle of running water, the *thunk* of cutting, and the dull clunking and scrape of industrial-sized pots, the work environment was silent. In my own mind I had morphed into Han-shan, the ego-less wise man—with his crazy grin and twig broom—working anonymously in a Zen monastery kitchen. I was *doing* it, man! (Shades of Mexico!) *This* was liberation and I was SO down with it. I began humming a celebratory ditty as accompaniment, keeping time with one foot while rhythmically dismembering the carrots . . . just like drumming!

My coiled samurai instincts sensed someone nearby. I looked up and saw Steve Weintraub, an ordained and very senior priest standing next to me. I noticed the pale, milky color of his eyes and how quietly and patiently he appeared to have been waiting for me to sense his presence. It occurred to me that had I *been* the samurai I imagined myself, I would have already been dead because I had no idea how long he had been standing beside me. He smiled in a kindly way and said in a gentle voice, "We don't sing in the kitchen."

"Oh, yeah. I get it," I said and touched my temple respectfully to indicate that his instruction had penetrated my consciousness. "No problem." I returned to my enlightened work wondering how anyone so uptight as to snuff a spontaneous expression of joy could possibly be a Zen adept.

Because my powers of concentration approximated a gerbil's, within five minutes I was humming again, slicing and dicing, enjoying the hell out of Zen. I was immersed in the problem of how I was going to spirit Jean into the woods for a little tantric Zen of my own devising, when I noticed Steve again, by my side—(dead again, Coyote-san). I was startled. I had not been aware that I was making any noise or how long he had been standing there, but in the absolute silence between us now, I did observe that *someone* had been humming. The sound had stopped, but my lips were continuing to vibrate. "Sorry, man," I said, actually contrite this time. He smiled genuinely again and said, "There's a *reason* we don't sing," bowing and turning away to other tasks.

"A *reason* we don't sing?" What could that be? I mused on the possibilities as I continued my chores. I did have to admit that if *everyone* sang, the monastic kitchen could become a cacophony of clashing arias, folk ballads, and Broadway show tunes. Okay Steve, universal singing would radically alter the nature of the kitchen as a meditative space.

"But I was the only one," I complained silently, and satisfied that I was in the right, returned to hacking the limbs off carrots with samurai vigor . . . but silently.

With little else to occupy my mind, my kitchen encounter with Steve Weintraub kept cycling in and out of my consciousness. (If that is what my waking state could be called.) Reviewing it led me to consider what else I might be missing. I was comfortable here. Most people were calm and self-disciplined. They were by and large engaged in practical work that required little conversation, consequently they were free to concentrate on whatever issue was of primary importance to themselves—the common denominator that seemed to draw people to practice.

Conversations at Zen Center had an unsettling quality of simply allowing silence to descend when someone had finished speaking. There appeared to be no compulsion to keep conversations afloat. If you had something to say, you said it, then simply sat with others in silence until someone else chose to speak. That silence was unnerving to me. I found myself rushing in to pick up conversational threads so that the speaker would not be embarrassed. When I observed that I was the only person doing that, it led me to wonder why. What if the conversation *did* die? How did I know that the speaker would be uncomfortable? Was *I* uncomfortable? Suppose they *were* uncomfortable, was that my problem or theirs? Each thought initiated a thread of inquiry and zazen offered the perfect spaciousness in which to track such questions to ground. I mentioned my reaction to the Abbot one day, who asked me innocently, "What's wrong with being uncomfortable?"

What was it with these guys? Isn't it natural to avoid what you don't enjoy, and chase what you do? The teacher's query suggested that living with and *observing* discomfort without reacting to it could be an opportunity to learn more about myself and smothering that opportunity under nervous chatter denied me self-knowledge.

Oh.

BUT I WAS too egocentric to understand that at first. On one occasion, I was "sharing my wisdom" in a coffee klatch (without invitation), when two people rose and left the room without apology or explanation *while I was speaking!* I was shocked at their rudeness. "I was talking!" I screamed to myself in high dudgeon at such insensitivity and rudeness. That evening in zazen, the event arose with its full measure of outrage and hurt. Clearly, "I" had felt insulted, devalued, and judged. In the stillness of sitting, I observed these feelings rising from nowhere and flowing by like stock quotes on an electronic ticker tape.

No matter how diligently I searched, I was unable to locate the "I" who had been so offended earlier in the day.

SEVERAL DAYS LATER another small epiphany fell like a dime into the tin cup that I held begging for knowledge. I had been working on one of the monastery's trucks, and was rushing to my room to wash and change clothes for evening zazen, scurrying down the path in cut-off jeans and grease-stained undershirt, with my hair unbound and splayed out by the wind.

A slight and rather delicate monk I knew from the City was approaching slowly from the opposite direction, already wearing his crisp robes for evening zazen. His name was Arnie Kotler and he ran a small publishing company that had introduced Americans to Thich Nhat Hanh, the great Vietnamese Buddhist teacher. Pleased with my day and Tassajara in general, and supercharged on self-satisfaction, I greeted Arnie by raising an arm over my head and shouting, "Hey Arnie, howya doin', man."

Arnie regarded me tranquilly. He smiled mildly, bowed, and said, "Hello, Peter," in a perfectly conversational and adequate tone. After he passed, I stood on the trail in his ripple-less wake. His sense of calm had retarded my racing motor to idle. Absent internal preoccupations, I was aware of the weight of my body on my feet, the gravel under my shoes, bird songs in the trees, the sounds of bathers splashing in the pool, and the heavy pressure of summer heat on my exposed skin. Which is to say, I became aware of my actual physical life. Without a word and probably without intention, he had illuminated every "extra" element I had brought to our interchange simply by not drifting away from his own center. Buddhist practice seemed to prompt such events.

I WAS A quieter, more attentive person when I returned to San Francisco. Even Jean noted the difference. All my psychotherapy and self-examination seemed less radical (and perhaps effective) than allowing myself to sit still, without distraction, immersed in my *actual* (as opposed to only my mental) life. Sitting is such a simple practice that it was difficult for to me have confidence in it at first. And yet, it was fostering palpable changes in me—little changes to be sure—but they were accumulating and I was beginning to feel something about myself that I was *comfortable* with. It was deeply familiar, and somehow accruing duration. What's more, I was beginning to experience it more frequently.

THIS EARLY PERIOD at Zen Center, late 1974 through 1976, was a period of accelerated learning. It had never occurred to me to question who "I" was (or where "I" was located and might be identified) before; to consider that was not exactly my train of thought and internal dialogue. I had often questioned myself from a political or ethical perspective, and challenged my own conclusions but most of what I had previously considered my "individuality" now appeared to be arbitrary (and unnecessary) "badges" of identity attached to an idea of myself, advertising my concerns and beliefs, my taste, status, values, and politics. Compared to monastic simplicity, the relentless projection of personal identity was exhausting.

After returning to San Francisco from Tassajara, I was amazed by how sexually projective people were in the City, as if they were advertising desire or the need to be found attractive on the surface of their skin. People appeared to be consumed by thoughts and passions and to the degree that they were locked in their own minds, hardly in the world. Observations like these accrued throughout my first years at

Zen Center and I relished them with the enthusiasm of a new convert. One such insight in that period struck directly at my personal concern with "originality" and "authenticity" and made me question the energy I expended trying to distinguish myself from others.

I explained earlier that meditation stations are arranged on either side of the corridor leading into the zendo. Walking between the backs of sitting people on my way to the zendo, looking slightly downward with unfocused eyes, after several months I knew in my peripheral vision exactly whom I was passing, despite the fact that their backs were turned and everyone was dressed virtually identically. Each person was instantly identifiable from their posture or the shape of their head or bare feet. They were *indisputably* who they were, and counter-intuitively, the identical nature of Zen clothing highlighted rather than blurred their uniqueness.

The revelation brought to mind an instance when I was practicing the guitar on Martha's Vineyard, trying to imitate a recording perfectly. I knew the notes and the feeling of the singer, but try as I might I could only get *so* close. Remembering that moment in the *zendo* I concluded that I had been able to imitate up to the mystery separating the guitarist's psyche and organism from mine. Beyond that line he and I were indisputably "other" and try as I might, I could never *express* him perfectly. His spot was already taken . . . by him. I saw clearly that *striving* for originality was gilding a lily. We come into the world physically and mentally unique *and* just like everyone else. If we accept that, there is no need to struggle to distinguish ourselves. Our uniqueness is a given.

◄○►

IN 1975, GARY Snyder won the Pulitzer Prize for poetry, and California Governor Edmund "Jerry" Brown Jr. appointed him to transform the underfunded, and ineffective California State Arts Commission into a new, creative policymaking body renamed the California Arts Council. Gary approached me about joining it, and initially I responded in reflexive Digger-speak, saying that I wasn't too keen about supporting "the government." Knowing me well by that time, Gary suggested that serving might be "a good opportunity to define the state." I took that bait and he set the hook.

Working with Gary challenged me to rethink my habitual attitudes about government and my own relationships to power. I had been invited to help him design and administrate a government bureau that would support values that we both shared. I knew that my decision to join him would vex a number of my old comrades, but I was entirely out of options. Gary's proposal was the most novel and interesting opportunity I had been offered in many years.

I would be shaping government policy, true, but my ideals and imagination were influenced in many ways by counterculture thinking and Digger values even after our Solstice debacle. I was still mourning the loss of Turkey Ridge and the dissolution of communal life; still showing up regularly for therapy, and pursuing the hard work of self-investigation. I was also drug-free. Still, intuition informed me that *all* those efforts were not enough, which kept me wedded to my Zen practice.

From the first day of the new Council's swearing-in, I attempted to imitate Gary's good humor and equanimity. Unfortunately, my efforts were more a veneer of civility sugar-coating a dense core of anger. At meetings and social encounters in Sacramento, Gary addressed each person directly and fully, offering by his consideration and attention the unspoken assurance that he and they were on the same side—even when they disagreed. Regular Zen practice was, if not actually changing me, at least allowing me to perceive my own behavior and compare it more accurately to his. *Imitating* his was another problem.

The politics and successes of the Council were highlighted in *Sleeping Where I Fall*, and I refer readers there for details. What is of narrative importance is how I met my next mentor at the Arts Council.

IN THE FIRST meeting of the Arts Council's second year, my peers elected me to succeed Gary as chairman. My elevation may have been due to the fact that the others were busy with their own art and careers and I had the time and inclination to dedicate myself to Council goals. Furthermore, I had a knack for expressing and clarifying complex issues (even if too acidly). Whatever the reason, I held that post for four years and might have held it for the entire eight years of our existence if the Council (and me in particular) had not angered enough legislators so that they passed a law barring me from any further terms.

IT WAS ONLY after I was elected chairman that I began to pay close attention to the Council's one non-artist member, the enigmatic and politically connected Karney Hodge, a Fresno businessman and chairman of the American Symphony Orchestra League. Among the Council members, he was the most definitely "not-me," different in kind and affinity from virtually every other member as well.

In his position as the chairman of the Orchestra League, Karney hobnobbed with boards of directors, pols, and major patrons—usually the richest and most established people—in any given city. A friendship between us appeared unlikely. I was a long-haired, denim-dressed hipster promulgating political philosophies closer to Malcolm X than Malcolm Forbes, and I had only recently stopped living in a truck and eating roadkill. In the area of social skills, I had not yet mastered the diplomacy required of me as chairman. Still, it was my job to serve the Council's agenda, and if I wanted that agenda to be consonant with my own, I would need to know what made Karney tick.

One of the first acts that the new Council executed, under the guise of clarifying our policy, was to publicly announce that with limited funds we intended to favor the *community* arts—the diversified, low-budget, local cultural expressions that historically received short shrift from funding sources. We believed that rooted community endeavors were the unacknowledged soil from which the state's *actual* culture developed. "You can't grow roses without mulch," I liked to say, but I may have been the only one who enjoyed hearing it.

I was also concerned with rectifying past cultural injustices, and protecting the "weak" from the "bullies" who controlled the lion's share of capital and power ("paging Dr. Freud," as Ruth used to say, maddeningly). Because of our stated bias, and because the Western European "high arts" had been accustomed to running cultural affairs without interference, public meetings were often contentious, sometimes degenerating into shouting matches as one or another side's favorite ox was gored by the implications of our policies. (It had not yet occurred to me that as a state leader my responsibility might be to serve *all* the taxpayers.)

Karney sat through the *Sturm und Drang* of these meetings calmly. I am fairly certain that our discussions about Bioregionalism, "the People," and "Diversity," appeared to him like disputes in a Congress of the Mad. However, he registered no impatience during my hectoring speeches, demands, pronouncements, "appeals to reason" (short for "my point of view"), and occasional spats. The rude boys and girls had seized the levers of power and Karney accepted that as a fact. He did *not* accept that fact as a defeat, however, and had I known him better I might have realized that he had simply hunkered down to wait.

If he was embarrassed about being a member of a Council dominated by the rest of us, he never revealed it. More often than not he appeared amused and unfazed by whatever transpired. In retrospect, I can also understand that he never abandoned his certainty that, come what may, he *would* achieve what he wanted.

At several meetings, I observed legislators normally hostile to the new Council dropping in to monitor our proceedings. When they did, they always stopped to chat with Karney. That attracted my attention and so I doubled down on my efforts to determine what his agenda might be.

CONSISTENT ZEN PRACTICE was beginning to slow my snap judgments and superficial categorizing of others. I could see that behind his Establishment façade that Karney was a complex man, more so than I had previously supposed. It had not (though it should have) occurred to me initially that he must have possessed a great deal of "juice" to be the sole Republican appointed to the Council by a Democratic governor.

I learned from my staff that Karney was "good friends" with State Senators George Zenovich and Al Alquist, and realized that if he chose to utilize connections like those he could become a formidable obstacle to the Council's majority consensus. The possibility of his being a *threat* had not occurred to me before. *We* were in charge now. What could Karney do?

I then learned that another very popular state senator named Ken Maddy had *worked* for Karney while he was in college. Fellow Armenian (and Republican) George Deukmejian, who would soon become state attorney general (and governor after Jerry Brown), was also a Hodge ally. With a growing sense of unease I began to feel surrounded by this one stranger in our midst. Karney *was* the Establishment in all its well-mannered, well-groomed, confident certainty. He believed in it and shared its core American values without irony or cynicism and America had repaid his loyalties. He appeared to be the hub of a substantial network of establishment connections and this thought made me paranoid enough to believe that an Establishment coup might be brewing, intent on taking the Council away from "the crazies."—the consensus about the Council in the State Senate, which had begun to hog-tie and limit us at every opportunity.

—◦—

BECAUSE I WAS working for Jerry Brown and had social responsibilities attendant to that job, and because Richard Baker, the abbot of San Francisco Zen Center, was zealous (and skillful) about integrating Zen Center into the cultural mainstream and had become good friends with Governor Brown, he generously offered Jean and me a three-bedroom apartment directly across the street from Zen Center. (One room was occupied by a Japanese Zen teacher, a quiet and very brilliant long-haired Japanese artist named Kaz Tanahashi). The gift of such space was a rare luxury in our community.

Because of our extra bedroom, I was able to move my daughter Ariel in with us permanently after her mother made another of her impulsive "geographics"—careening four hours north to Humboldt County the dope-growing capital of North America. Jean lavished attention on Ariel, who was now about seven and hungry for stability and order. Jean made curtains for her room, coverlets for her bed, and took her shopping for the kinds of clothes young girls adore. She understood Ariel's needs more intuitively than I did and enrolled her in ballet classes, and an excellent liberal Catholic school with much the same sense of devotion and calm as Zen Center. They offered Ariel a full scholarship because of our Zen Center connection and Jean began teaching Ariel how to dress and behave appropriately.

With such sustained attention Ariel calmed down and began to ameliorate her Digger edges. She blossomed and her gifts became more apparent, not only in our household, but also in the Zen Center community.

I remember speaking with my mother once during this happy time and waxing optimistic, telling her, "Things are great, Mom. I'm in love. I'm happy. I'm beginning a spiritual practice and continuing my therapy. My work is going well. Ariel's in great shape. My health is good and Jean is a great cook and stepmom."

Ruth had been too wounded by life and then death with Morris, and its subsequent upheavals to settle for any premature victory laps. "Oh darling," she said, distractedly, "those things are so superficial."

In the moment, I laughed to myself and thought, "What a Jewish mother!" As things turned out she knew some things I did not.

ZEN LIFE, AS interpreted by Jean, was definitely not "free." She had high standards I found challenging. She would not, for instance, abide my answering the phone during dinner, even for Arts Council business. I had never seen my father ignore a ringing phone and tried to argue for the necessity of emergencies or certain conversations and issues. Her counter was simple and direct.—

"I worked hard to make a dinner for us," she would say. "I put a lot of thought and care and time into it. You have a choice. You can eat attentively and savor your food and *be* with me, or you can answer the phone. You can't do both."

This was a novel way of looking at life. I decided that her clarity might be related to the seniority of her practice compared to mine and resolved to follow her example and see what I learned. It was more difficult to follow her admonition to avoid political discussion in the house. Politics was the center of my endeavors (and remains a preoccupation today). Furthermore, I *enjoyed* discussing issues, enlisting her opinions or those of my guests, hoping that I might gain a fresh purchase on a difficult problem. Jean would not abide it however, and, in my spirit of trying to break old habits and see things anew, I decided, perhaps too easily, that she was creating a refuge for us—a quiet, domestic zone where the world would not be allowed to intervene. I conceived what she was doing as a practice of intimacy and tried to follow her edicts.

JEAN AND I married at Green Gulch Zen Center in 1977. Nearly eighty chanting black-robed monks and priests, virtually the entire *sangha* (followers of the Buddha) attended, along with the senior staff from the California Arts Council and some of my Digger pals. It was an eclectic mix of the religious, the laity, and the louche. (Forty years later, the new abbot confided to me, laughing, that someone had stolen

his brand new Birkenstocks out of his car that day.) The CAC staff had
chipped in and bought "us" a McCulloch chainsaw as a wedding gift.
I threw it in the back of my Power Wagon at day's end as Jean and I
hopped in and departed up the North Coast for a honeymoon. If there
were shadows and clouds ahead I didn't see them. I didn't even dwell
on her father's remarks to me when he shook hands to say good-bye.
"Well buddy . . ." he said, ". . . you got 'er now!"

◄o►

PERHAPS BECAUSE I had less of a professional career than my Council
peers, my communication at meetings played on my strengths, which
was a take-no-prisoners edginess, a good grasp of policy, and the ability to clarify complex issues. Furthermore, I had been appointed by the
governor, which afforded me some political protection. I was resent-
ful about past injustices levied against the SF Mime Troupe, my former theater, which at one time had been featured on the cover of the
Chamber of Commerce's magazine as testimony to the city's joyous
diversity, but had been denied any of the hotel-tax monies distributed
to art and cultural institutions. I was also reflexively opposed to those
in power. (Which never included myself.) I had yet to learn that anger
always blunts skill.

My first lesson in political skill came directly from the governor,
who found it necessary to jerk my chain over my polarizing behavior.
The Council had managed to create an effective stalemate in cultural
politics by antagonizing the state's power structure and bringing it to
loggerheads with our allies in community arts. Explaining politics to
me succinctly, the governor said, "In a democracy all boats rise, or

all boats sink. That's the way it works." He also clarified the obvious implication (which had eluded me) that *every* culture and subculture in California had a legitimate claim on state resources, whether or not *I* approved of them. To Governor Brown's credit, each time the Council messed up in some manner, rather than getting a roasting from him or his *éminence grise*, Jacques Barzagi, a wily ex–film hustler from the South of France who brought bare elbows, knuckles, and street-smarts to the governor's office, they patiently clarified the political realities and sent me back to improve. The governor never once intervened or made any demand of me or the Council to spare himself embarrassment or shelter himself from the line of fire.

It is amazing how different one's attitudes about governance become when one is "in" power and struggling to hold on to it (hopefully, to govern effectively), as opposed to struggling *with it* and trying to crack the cipher as to why a specific decision was taken. It was also shocking to learn that just because I was the titular head of the Arts Council, I had no power to rule by executive fiat. This was made clear to me by Karney Hodge, the first time he revealed the blade normally hidden beneath his velvet exterior.

That revelation was transmitted during Council deliberations in our second year, while deciding which grant applicants would and would not receive funding. Under the sway of bioregional principles, it seemed wasteful (to me) that every county have a symphony orchestra. Perhaps that money could be better spent by having the state's best symphonies tour and teach more often. It appeared that the counties were mimicking the high-status behavior of the major cities, as opposed to developing their own place-appropriate culture. "Why be a second-rate Los Angeles," I queried during deliberation, "when you could be a first-rate Kern or Tulare County and support your own indigenous cultural expression?"

When I suggested rejecting the application of a small local symphony without realizing that it was *Karney's* version of a "community" arts organization, his face flushed. He ducked his head and regarded me directly and coldly from under his thick brow. His face resembled the bust of a Roman wrestler I had once seen in an Italian museum. He never raised his voice when he said, "If you don't *intend* to be fair, Peter, just *say* so. Tell the symphonies not to bother to apply. Tell them you have different policies and concerns and they're not it. You'll save everyone a lot of trouble."

Karney had put his finger on the nub of the issue. Even if he was correct (and he was close) in describing my thinking, if I had stated it aloud it would have brought a shit-storm upon us. Karney had exposed me to myself and because I could not accept the baldness of the prejudice he described, I folded and retracted my motion.

Through this and other events it became apparent that a sizeable share of the Council's political problems stemmed from my intemperate behavior. In my years in the Mime Troupe and the Diggers, I had always operated collaboratively as a point of pride. We had been comrades in arms, equals, and we struggled diligently to erase hierarchical relationships. As a leaderless community, collaboration was a sacred principle. The only plausible explanation for the abrupt change in my behavior was my new political power.

From then on, I regarded Karney with a new respect and understood that there was much that I could learn from him.

◄○►

BECAUSE OF THE Council's insistence on perhaps too-rapid and one-sided political change, the state arts community had become deadlocked. Our Council majority claimed the high ground of numbers and the *hoi polloi*, while the major institutions, elite board members, and patrons had the state legislators in their corner (or pocket). Nothing budged; people were frustrated and disappointed and their dissatisfaction reached me pungently and often. In desperation I approached Karney one day and suggested we grab a coffee. Stirring my sugar, I observed to him that "for all the thunder we've generated, neither of us has made it rain, have we?"

He chuckled. "You could say that," he said good-humoredly, waiting to see where I was going. I analyzed the deadlock to him as I saw it: I made my description evenhandedly comical, parodying my own sense of outrage and the casual, entitled behavior of the wealthy.

"I think that we're blowing a big chance here, Karney," I finally said seriously. "I'll take a big piece of the blame because I know I shoot my mouth off and my anger makes me mean sometimes. But man, I *am* angry," I confessed. "I think you would be too if you were in my shoes. I'll bet that you'd never heard of *any* of these artists on the Council before you were appointed. They're people of real quality and worth like Gary and Luis Valdez and Noah Purifoy. Ruth Asawa is very well known, but if you've never heard of *the others*, you probably have never heard of any of the people we fight for, have you?" I asked, without challenge.

"No, I haven't," he said candidly.

"They're good, Karney. They may not leave big footprints and they don't have buildings or staff, or you may not have heard of them because they're doing something too new to be recognized yet. Even the ones who aren't as good deserve an opportunity. They work and pay taxes like everybody else, and more important, they can make a contribution, but they're continually ignored and shunted aside as if they don't count."

"I can see that," he responded, in a tone of voice that made me believe that he'd heard me. Perhaps, in the rarefied air of the American Symphony Orchestra League, a small-town guy like Karney had suffered his share of snubs and indignities.

I had his attention, so I went for broke. "Look, Karney, the rest of the Council members have their own work and careers to see to. I'm the only one with nothing to do but this and I want to do it. The others are happy to have me step out front, like a Jew with a bell around my neck. . . ." I paused because Karney was laughing so hard that he was forced to wipe tears from his eyes. (With a crisp handkerchief, I noted.)

His laugh was so infectious that I laughed too. "Jesus," I said impulsively, not aware in the moment of the truth I was uttering. "It's pretty tragic to consider that the fate of the arts in California may depend on what you and I can work out."

—◦—

THERE WAS NOTHING extraordinary about our conversation, but it broke the ice and initiated a rapport between us that soon evolved into a real intimacy. I can safely say it would never have occurred had I not been meditating and positively inspired by the patient and kindly monks of the San Francisco Zen Center. I could not explain *how* meditation was working on me, but I could *feel* it rearranging me internally, softening my pride, defensiveness, and aggression, making me more permeable to the feelings of others.

Karney and I continued our conversation over a lunch. I explained that he was my only real adversary on the Council and yet he represented the sector of the state that the rest of my team together could not defeat. If he and I could make some common agreements there would be nothing to impede the Council from operating as a unified body, mitigating resistance from the legislature.

I confessed that my us-versus-them strategies were a failure. "My dad used to call me a stupid son-of-a-bitch," I said, "and I'm starting to feel he might have been right."

"You're not stupid," Karney shot back, with some heat, as if he wanted to derail that train of thought. "You just don't know how power operates. You've been 'out there' a long time, but believe me, if they thought you were stupid, they wouldn't be fighting you so hard."

Few conversational gambits are more relaxing than an unasked-for compliment. Karney's endorsement was pleasing to me and we continued a long, easy talk. He was a good listener (I can be as well, when I remember to keep my mouth shut). What's more, Karney was fair. I could see how his fairness was a significant contribution to why people trusted him. He was not after the entire budget nor was he representing *all* high culture as I had supposed—just a slice of it—the plurality of small, local, symphony orchestras also often snubbed by funding sources. In his duties as president of the Symphony Orchestra's professional organization, he wanted to protect them as fully as I wanted to protect my community constituency.

"It's hard to argue that playing and listening to beautiful music is a bad thing," Karney said. "It's *not* a bad thing and people never like to be painted as the bad guy. When you do that you make one hell of an enemy, because then they're fighting for their self-respect. The fight will *look like* it's about the issues, but it isn't. It's really about—'I'm a good person too.'"

We agreed that the choke-hold for both sides was the paltry $1 million budget allotted for California's population of twenty-three million people. We both agreed that a scarcity of resources would keep the various factions at one another's throats, struggling for paltry grants that would never sustain any of them. "If we want to do something significant, Karney," I said, "We need a larger budget."

Karney looked at me and shrugged. "Why not twenty million?"

That was ludicrous! An outrageous amount. I looked at him incredulously but it was obvious that he wasn't kidding. "Twenty million?" I asked, as if saying, "Are you nuts?" I was prepared to tell him that it was impossible, but I reconsidered. "Wait a minute," I thought. "He's a *businessman*. He's done this stuff before. What the hell do I know about money? I've been a Digger for ten years."

"It starts with the governor's budget," he said. "You and [Gary] Snyder are his people. I'm a Republican . . ." and he laughed again, but his tone, his posture, his relaxation, everything convinced me that a deal was hovering over the table and that if I went for it he and his troops would be behind me. "You and Gary can convince him, Pete. I think you can. Hell," he said and he laughed, "What the hell do we have to lose?"

—◄o►—

OUR SUCCESS AT doing precisely what Karney suggested succeeded in raising the Arts Council budget—first to $5 million and then again each year until with federal money we approached $18 million—transforming the California arts scene. That story has been recounted in *Sleeping Where I Fall*, but the next evolution in my maturity, again due to Karney's influence, was not.

KARNEY AND I worked well and continued working together. Once my paranoia about him was put to rest, I was relaxed with him and began to investigate him the way an actor investigates a new character. Qualities I had noticed but failed to attach importance to—his buoyant optimism and his elegant grooming—which I had once dismissed as the semiotics of social status, I now regarded in a new light.

"It might be something more than class-signaling," I thought. It might be *important* that Karney was consistently well groomed, his shirts crisp and spotless, his clothes beautifully tailored and elegant. Even in the corridors and meeting rooms of the State Capitol, I adhered religiously to my blue jeans and denim shirts. I took pride in my scuffed old work boots, and felt they "expressed" my values. Perhaps Karney felt the same way about his tasseled Gucci loafers. If that was the case, what, exactly, *were* those values he projected?

Council Member Ruth Asawa, perhaps the most renowned and celebrated Council member, usually arrived at our meetings in a faded Japanese *hipari*. Gary came in an open shirt and vest with a patch on it symbolizing Turtle Island—the native name for North America. Sometimes he arrived in an Amish suit he'd bought from a mail order company named Gohn Bros. in Middlebury, Indiana, of which he was inordinately proud. Like soldiers in the uniforms of their particular armies each Council Member's dress signified their social affinities as well as their personal taste.

My clothes were appropriate for the hardscrabble life I'd been living for the last decade, but in the State Capitol sartorial defiance was working against me. I had stepped up to assume a leadership position as a representative of the State of California, and I was still holding fast to my identity as Counterculture Charlie, apparently spurning accoutrements of power or success.

In Zen Center I had by then bought a used set of black robes for the *zendo* as much to express my deepening commitment as for their utility. In that community I had less trouble with elasticity, making it easier to don and shed costumes as circumstances dictated. One day I asked myself, "If style and clothing were as inconsequential as I insisted, why then was I so defensive about changing them?"

Tiptoeing into the subject, a wealthy friend introduced me to his tailor, a Savile Row firm named Anderson & Sheppard, who made regular visits to the Bay Area from London to service their American clients. When they made their next trip through San Francisco, I emptied my savings and ordered two elegant tweed jackets. While I was waiting for my clothes to arrive, I took the cloth samples and matched them to some dress shirts, ties, slacks, and a pair of dress shoes. When the clothes arrived, I left them in the box while a hairdresser friend of my wife's nipped and clipped my shoulder-length hair into a stylish haircut.

I changed into my new duds, looked in the mirror, and liked what I saw!—a new character with my face. I felt comfortable in the clothes and they conformed to the social strata I needed operate from in the big leagues. If the costume was not going to be perceived as lipstick on a pig, I also needed to play the part seriously and well.

There were more than a few jokes at my expense when I returned to Sacramento and my first CAC meeting sporting my new duds. I was nervous only about Karney's reaction. When he entered the room and saw me, he smiled, and drew his head back to get a better look. He scanned me from head to toe, then walked closer and examined the Harris Tweed of my jacket, flicked the "surgeon's cuffs" that actually unbuttoned and tested the little ticket pocket on the left side to ensure that it was real. "Classy," he said, nodding appreciatively. Then he dropped the subject and never mentioned it again.

I had passed his muster.

—◦—

WITHIN A SHORT time, Karney had become an intimate friend. Under his tutelage, I had widened the parameters of my cultural inclusions to embrace the American mainstream—the one that had once supported the persecution of my Left-wing family and friends, and the Susies and Ozzies of the world. However, if black people managed to interact civilly with white people on a daily basis after three centuries of execrable behavior toward them, and if the Vietnamese could move past our murderous assaults on them, I imagined that I could as well.

I would not surrender my values or sacrifice my intentions of living a compassionate life and speaking for those without a voice, but I *could* end my facile prejudgments based on the way people dressed or what I imagined their politics might be. I removed the steam-iron-sized chip from my shoulder and felt lighter and freer for it. I vowed to myself that I would forget the little stuff—personal style, the juvenile team allegiances fostered by mass media and "team" oriented viewpoints on the political spectrum. I would take things on a case-by-case basis, and remain as free to change as the weather.

After our budget successes, the Council's work expanded and as it did Karney and I worked together more often. If the two of us agreed on a tactic or policy, because we represented the poles of opinion on the Council, the rest of the members would likely accept the idea. Karney had a folksy, colloquial manner and made his points like a shrewd country lawyer. Compared to him I was still blunt and impatient, but not nearly as divisive as before.

KARNEY'S AND MY friendship continued after we left the Council, which was virtually beheaded by the new governor when Jerry Brown's second term ended. Practically his first executive action was to return the Arts Council annual budget to $1 million and throw out the bulk of our eight years of work together. It was a chilling lesson in the vagaries of politics—that what can be accomplished politically can be undone the same way. That insight ended whatever fascination I might have maintained for public life.

Though I can't speak to what Karney found attractive in me, I can say without equivocation that he made me feel as if my life was expanding beyond its previous limitations. I had felt frustrated and confined within the counterculture for some time, but hadn't been able to think/feel my way free of what felt like a boa constrictor crushing my imagination. It was directly due to this new sense of expansion and inclusion that I began to consider film acting as a possible livelihood.

Not long after my sixtieth birthday, which Karney drove 200 miles from Fresno to attend, I received a call from him, informing me that he was going into the hospital for "a routine procedure." We chatted amiably for ten minutes or so and when we hung up, I had no idea that it would be the last time I ever spoke with him. On April 15th,

2002, Karney Hodge passed away, but, like the classy friend he was, he would never leave without saying good-bye.

—◦—

THE SIXTIES WERE definitely over. The times were colder and harsher. My daughter was growing and required actual clothes and school books and my income was inadequate to consider ever owning a house or putting her through a good school. My victories on the Arts Council had convinced me that it was no longer necessary to stay confined to the counterculture. I had forged relationships with people of various backgrounds and political beliefs and had discovered a talent for it. Recognizing this gave me the confidence to reflect on my interrupted acting career at the Mime Troupe and I resolved to try to reconstitute it on the largest stage—which is to say, in film. It was the one marketable skill I possessed that I *might* be able to capitalize on. It would involve exploiting no one but myself and I could pursue it in good conscience.

Reasoning that even the best actors could have "a bad year" I decided to allow myself five years before I made my final decision about the viability of acting as a career. If I could not win gainful employment within that time I would still have time to seek employment in another field, and most importantly, I would not die with a case of the "what-if's?"

High on Arts Council energy and reputation, I convinced the premiere San Francisco talent agent, Ann Brebner, to sign me solely on the strength of my political accomplishments, asserting to her that "I'm a man who does what I set out to do."

She believed me.

Shortly thereafter, I was called into Ann's office to audition for a one-line role in a four-hour TV miniseries called *Alcatraz: The Whole Shocking Story,* which was shooting in San Francisco. It was the story of an escape attempt, starring Michael Beck and Art Carney, and the one-line part I was to read for (important because *any* speaking role could qualify me for union membership) was that of a leg-breaking mob enforcer.

I was excited when I entered the office. I had passed the first hurdle of landing an agent, and now I was going to try to put myself in play. My excitement cooled and then chilled when I surveyed the room. Every chair was filled with a guy who could have ripped off one of my legs and beaten me to death with it. I knew immediately that the part of an enforcer was not going to be mine.

Not wanting to waste my time, I thumbed through the available "sides"—pages of script handed out to actors auditioning for various parts. One in particular attracted me, a lovely soliloquy of the reminiscences of a check forger detailing the delights of pre-imprisonment life financed with stolen jewels. The character was described in the script as sixty. I was thirty-seven.

I memorized the speech anyway, deciding that he was telling the story to amuse his pals, putting visions of sugar plums in their heads as a respite from the grim daily life at Alcatraz. When I was ushered into the audition room, the director and producer were younger than I was. Neither man's face appeared to have ever been creased by a distressing thought. Taking the bit in my teeth, I pitched my idea: "Hey, I was called in for the role of a leg-breaker, but you can't tell anything about what I can do with the one line I'm supposed to read. I've waited here for two hours. How about just letting me read this little soliloquy as my audition?" They shrugged and said okay.

When I was done, Tweedledee glanced at Tweedledum and some silent communication passed between them. I left the room with a *very* plum little part that normally would have gone to a Hollywood actor. That role (also a feather in my agent's cap) played on national television and attracted some notice. Shortly after that I won ten weeks' work (at $1,000 a week) in a forgettable confection called *Die Laughing*. My film career had begun with more money than I had ever made in my life.

These successes convinced my agent to arrange a trip to Los Angeles for me to meet casting directors—the people responsible for finding and submitting actors to the director for each role in a film. They are much easier to access than Hollywood agents and voracious in their search for the right "face." Ann Brebner's office felt that they should see mine.

Before meeting with each casting director, I prepared a three-by-five card with their coordinates—phone number, address, and the date of the meeting. As soon as the meeting ended, I jotted down notes of our conversation, the names of any books or articles we'd discussed, and any physical descriptions of them (so that I wouldn't forget). In each meeting I asked them to recommend any talent agents they particularly respected, calculating that if I got a job, I would call one of them, use the casting director's name, and ask them to negotiate my contract for a fee *without* signing me (a process known as "vest-pocketing"). It is found money for the agent and no threat to any of the other actors in their stable. I reasoned that if that happened more than once, I would be in a better position to ask them to sign me as a client.

After our initial meeting, I hand-wrote each casting director a thank-you note and included the book, poem, or article in question. Every eight weeks, I thumbed through my card file and sent each an update on what I was doing (a lot of theater in San Francisco), included reviews and new photos, and anything that I could dream up to keep my name under their nose. I vowed to myself that I would continue working those cards for the next five years. Eight months after beginning this process, I received a call from a Hollywood agent named Andy Freedman. "I've been hearing a lot about you," he said. "You are definitely under-represented."

In 1980 I was cast as one of the two lead roles in the world premiere of *True West* by Sam Shepard, a fellow Northern Californian, Pulitzer prizewinner and Sixties icon. The show was to open at the Magic Theater in San Francisco. Sam had spent an apprenticeship similar to mine in the counterculture, but blessed with extraordinary talent and iconic American looks, he was already a star and a Pulitzer Prize winner. It was a big boost to my confidence when he asked me to be one of his leading men in a production that would undoubtedly attract a great deal of attention.

I invited Andy Freedman to attend the opening as my guest. At the end of the evening he invited me to Los Angeles to meet his partner, Susan Smith, the principal of their very well-regarded agency, Susan Smith and Associates. A week later, I had signed with a first-rate Hollywood agent, and Susan and Andy remained my agents for the next eight years, building my career from nothing to starring roles in major Hollywood and European films.

-◦-

BY 1987, AFTER an apprenticeship of small films and pretty fair movies for television, twenty-two in all, I began to land important commercial roles—*E.T. the Extra-Terrestrial, Outrageous Fortune, Cross Creek, The Legend of Billie Jean,* and a breakthrough film in European markets named *A Man in Love.* I had become a bona fide movie star. I don't mean the third-tier, "old what's-his-name" status my post-sixty American career has settled into. I mean the generally accepted definition of a movie star, with billboards, posters on the street, full-page photos, and my face on the covers of magazines. It's true that the grandest of these stellar victories occurred in Europe and not in my home country, but I did not care. I might not have been the brightest star in the Milky Way, but I *was* a star and definitely sharing the same constellation with the brightest.

On a dazzling afternoon in May of that year, I was being photographed on the red carpet that extended from the very top step of the Palais des Festivals in Cannes, France, where my new French film *A Man in Love (Un homme amoreux)* was chosen as the opening event for the Festival's fortieth anniversary birthday party.[8] The carpet cascaded down broad tiered steps, and along a hundred feet of the generous seaside walkway called la Croisette. The tall glistening palms, the highlights sparkling off the chrome fixtures of luxury yachts, the shimmering ocean, the white plastered buildings and ochre-tiled roofs—all bathed in the vivid Mediterranean light that has attracted *plein air* painters since artists first blinked in it after crawling out from the caves of Lascaux and Chauvet.

Off to one side, starlets were posing, hair-tossing, smiling, and baring their breasts to attract the attention of photographers. This day I didn't have to resort to any of the cheesy numbers all actors must capitulate to at times. I was forty-six years old and appeared to be in my late thirties. I was starring in an "A" film opening the most celebrated film festival in the world. Other than the opportunity to earn a living, acting (and particularly celebrity status) did not compel me overmuch.

It would be an egregious lie to pretend that being "on top," sought out, plied with inordinate attention, gifts, and privileges was not better than a sharp stick in the eye and that I did not appreciate that the alpha wolf never has to roll over, but perhaps because I began acting so late in life, and understood that my shelf-life would be brief, I could never take it all quite as seriously as I should have if I wanted to achieve maximal advantage to my career.

The gyroscope that kept my head level, even then, was that I thought of myself as "a writer who earned his living as an actor." Only a few years after that stellar evening at Cannes, audiences would repay my tepid regard for my livelihood with their own ho-hum estimation, but that day of reckoning was yet to arrive.

I had made it through the portal of movie-land well before my five-year deadline had expired. My luck had been that the crop of leading ladies edging towards "that certain age" had devised a survival strategy to perform alongside older men. Their insecurity (or valid instinct) had allowed me to play opposite interesting and formidable actresses: Tuesday Weld, Ellen Burstyn, Jamie Lee Curtis, Bette Midler, Jean Smart, Sharon Stone, Shelley Long, Greta Scacchi, and Claudia Cardinale—all gifted, attractive women, but all teetering around the chasm into which so many actresses are heartlessly pitched as they age beyond the interest of insecure men.

I had begun my film career seven years earlier and now at forty-six, I was perched on an unimaginable crest. Wherever I looked that evening, I saw deities of cinema ambling by, smiling, saluting well-wishers and friends: Wim Wenders, Robert Altman, Barbet Schroeder, Paul Newman, Nikita Mikhalkov, Stephen Frears, Louis Malle, Lars von Trier, Humberto Solás, Woody Allen, Jonathan Demme, and many others who had films in competition or on display that year. They made up the crowd that I stood among, and that night I dared to think of them as peers. Perhaps I could be forgiven the effrontery of believing that I had entered the pantheon of the gods if I had known then that I had only been granted a day pass.

Standing atop those steps, looking down at the world from my temporary elevation above the ordinary, I felt a pang that Morris had not lived to see me sober, healthy, and successful. I missed his laugh, I missed his worldly wisdom and needed his guidance. His (and my mother's) losses are abiding sorrows that visit from time to time, compounded by the bitter knowledge that the consequences of errors can be irremediable.

I had doubled-down on my life by then, sliding all my chips forward to bet on normalcy: a wife and family and the sanity of Zen practice. I had radically curtailed my indulgent, self-destructive behaviors, but I was not yet certain that they were firmly cast in the stone of habit. Ten or fifteen years earlier, acting on impulse was simultaneous with the first blush of that impulse. Reflection or hesitation was never considered. On this magical Cannes night, however, I knew that I no longer possessed the emotional reserves to overspend my energy as I once had, or could guarantee the time to rebuild what I would lose by surrendering to the wrong desires. I was clinging to an idea of sanity as my only refuge from chaos and death—both of which felt as if they were biding their time, waiting for my first false step.

—◄○►—

BY 1985 JEAN and I had produced a son, Nick, a normally merry and gig-
gling little package except at bedtime, when the idea of being separated
from his parents could make getting him into his own bed a stressful,
heart-rending affair. I could relate to his anxiety. My wife and son
and mother-in-law had visited me in Rome during filming of *A Man in
Love* and things had not gone well. I was away from the house many
hours each day and evening and Jean was left with her mother and our
son all day long; forty minutes outside Rome in a lovely *castello* we
had rented, but far from the shops, the sights, the high life and diversions of that romantic city. The success that the world offered me as
an actor was not being mirrored at home. Things had become tense
between Jean and my daughter and consequently between Jean and
me. By 1989 my home environment was becoming toxic.

We had moved from the city to nearby Marin County in 1984 or
1985; bought a house and all that entails. Ariel had been sent to a
boarding school not far away because Jean wanted to travel with me.
"I didn't marry you to stay home and take care of your child," was the
way she put it, on the worst day I could have imagined, when I had to
tell Ariel that she would have to go away.

She returned home for some weekends and the holidays, but things
remained grim in every dimension. My career opportunities seemed
to improve as home life was faltering, and taking advantage of work
opportunities became a respite from tensions in the house. As a consequence, our life became comfortable economically. *A Man in Love* had
done well at Cannes and become a major European hit. (Both people
who saw it in America spoke highly of it.) My face was all over the

Parisian magazine stands and walking through Paris, people stopped and addressed me often, "Monsieur Coy-oat?" which was as close to pronouncing "Coyote" as the French could manage.

My European career was burgeoning and Jean was not shy about expressing her appreciation of the perks, travel, raised standards of living, and privileges that success afforded. She appeared to have a grander idea of who I was than I did, however, and plans of her own for my future, telling me once that "being an actor is so low-rent. You should become a producer." The luxuries that we began to accrue often made this Digger as uncomfortable as my status as a "low-rent" actor apparently made her.

Filming took me away more often and the money and distance functioned as a safety valve for unresolved issues between Jean and me. Towards the end of our marriage I did not go back to narcotics, but from the safe remove of the road I began to seek the comfort of my second favorite drug, available women. Shrouding my life in secrecy and lies, tattering my self-respect, and wondering where my joy and carefree days had disappeared to, I somehow managed to keep working, and more miraculously adhering to my meditation.

Jean and I persevered for nearly fifteen years, often distracted, absorbed, or consoled by the realities of child-rearing and daily life, in some way replicating the unhappy lives of both of our families. I grew increasingly disconsolate and neither of us possessed the requisite skills to work things out. One day we simply fell apart. I had told her that we needed to talk and she interrupted me by saying that she "couldn't take it anymore," and that was the end of our story as a couple, but as anyone who has ever left a marriage with children knows, that is never the end of the story.

I left our house, carrying an armload of books and clothes to my car. Sitting there, with the motor running, about to back out of the driveway (and my marriage) the revelation struck me as claustrophobically as if a wet towel had been pressed against my face. It was no fault of Jean's, but I understood with horrifying certainty that I had, in some way, married Morris.

—◦—

MY FILM CAREER continued, but waned as I aged. Having started at forty, it seemed like a short run until I was fifty and poised at the border beyond which consideration for leading roles becomes problematic. I appeared to have won the respect of other actors, and consequently if a producer signed me for a role, it upped his chances of signing other respected actors he wanted. I traded on that reputation for a number of years, until the terms of my divorce settlement with Jean and the responsibility for two children eradicated my ability to say "no" to virtually any work for the next five or six years. I refer to that period when I took every job offered as my "Wash-the-donkey-I'm-coming-to-Tijuana" period. By the time my obligations had ended, I had aged out of the demographic most valuable to the film industry and was firmly replanted amongst the much larger field of players known as "character actors." Combined with the string of turkeys I'd made, all of which I referred to as either "Mortgage" or "Rent," my luster as an actor appeared to be permanently dimmed.

These are facts, not sniveling. Movies afforded me a grand and fair run at modest fame, a stable, nearly-forty-year career, and on balance more fun than distress. I was able to send my children through college and have them graduate debt-free, buy two houses and a few nifty cars. I was famous enough to meet whomever I chose and to gain admittance to any restaurant I wanted to try. I was able to employ the dim bulb of my celebrity to illuminate issues and causes that I believed worthy of public attention, and compared to the remuneration offered to nurses, day-care workers, janitors, teachers, and farmers, I had been vastly overpaid.

At this moment, my career had a brief resurrection that produced my last secular mentor, a formidable teacher who polished my secular education to its highest sheen.

◄○►

BY 1990, MY fiftieth year, I was dispirited. My marriage was done. A post-marriage love affair with a beautiful and brilliant woman uncomfortably close to my daughter's age was stressful and teetering. Since I did not know any 100-year-old people, I was forced to admit that middle age was definitely finished. I had managed only one film that year, and that for a good friend who habitually hired me for everything he did. My career now resembled those plastic window displays of sushi and tempura in pedestrian Japanese restaurants—bright, without nutrition, and totally lacking in heat.

I was in that state of mind when the president of an agency I had left Susan Smith for, hoping that their size and stature would help me (it did not), called one afternoon. After six years there I had never met the man, but he called me at home and we exchanged the casual pleasantries that maintain the fiction that everyone in Hollywood is friends. He had called to ask if he could give Roman Polanski my phone number. He knew as well as I did that any actor worth an *empty* salt cellar would salivate to talk to Roman Polanski, so I restrained myself from cracking wise—"Hmmm, not my home number. Have him call my assistant," and said, "Sure."

Roman called shortly afterwards and the following brief conversation ensued: (Imagine *his* dialogue in a purring Eastern European accent, freighted with irony.)

Roman: "Peeteh, do you know ze dif-fer-ence between eroticism and pornography?"

Me: "Well, it's kind of a floating decimal point isn't it?"

Roman: "No, I have a very *pree-cize* definition. With eroticism you use a feather. . . . With pornography you use ze whole chicken."

WITH THAT DISTINCTION clear, he asked if I would be interested in reading the script of his new film, to be called *Bitter Moon*. Derived from an extremely dark French novel called *Lune de Fiel* by Pascal Bruckner; Roman, screenwriter Gérard Brach, and a very snooty Englishman (who once described an excellent English actress as having "bad vowels") had created a script about a twisted, sadomasochistic relationship so graphic, sexual, and violent that after I read it, I faxed Roman my first impression:

> *"Roman, what do they call it when you use the whole ostrich?"*

Roman's call had arrived at the perfect moment, and offered me an opportunity to "do a geographic," to leave America and the sorrow, shame, and failure clinging to me about my failed marriage. There was blame enough to go around, but none of it applied any balm to my sense of being in free fall returned to a life stripped of boundaries. I no longer went home, discussed my day with my wife, or played with my son and read to him at bedtime. My daughter did not live nearby.

It occurred to me that the graphic nature of Roman's script might be career suicide, and I considered that perhaps it came to me because no other actor would consider it. I could not blame them. In the first draft he sent me, there was an explicit scene where my lover peed on my character's head for sexual thrills. Reading that I laughed aloud and thought, "Of course, no actor with *anything* to lose would consider this." However, I was not in that category, and with no career to speak of to protect I decided that if I was going to jump off a cliff, why not jump with one of the world's great directors?

---◄○►---

THAT IS HOW I came to be sitting in Roman Polanski's Paris apartment with Roman's wife, actress and model Emmanuelle Seigner, and their friend, the iconic fashion designer, Nino Cerruti, the teacher of Giorgio Armani. He was to be my costumer for the film.

Roman was already a complicated legend. A Holocaust survivor, he had made excellent films in a number of countries, any one of which might be a source text for aspiring directors: *Knife in the Water* (nominated for an Oscar), *Repulsion, Rosemary's Baby, Cul-de-Sac, Chinatown,* and *The Tenant*. In 1969, his pregnant wife Sharon Tate had been brutally murdered in Los Angeles by Charles Manson's deranged hippie gang, and America's shameless press was febrile in its insinuations that her death had been somehow incited by the mordant subject matter of Roman's films. Eight years later he fled America when he learned that a judge was about to make an example of him for having had sex with an underage girl during a nude photo shoot. Consequently, he now lived full-time in Europe.

On the afternoon in question, we were perched in his living room over the Avenue Montaigne, where the great fashion houses—Dior, Chanel, Valentino, et al display their wares on a generous, tree-lined side street radiating from the Roosevelt Metro station on the Champs-Elysées. We were ensconced in front of a gargantuan rear-projection television, watching the final moments of the Tour de France as the three top finishers raced across the finish line in a virtual dead heat.

Roman turned to me:

"Peeteh, can you eemagine? The three *top* cyclists in the world, cross ze finish line vithin four one-hundreths of a second of one another. And *one*, by some superhuman dedication (which sounded like '*dead-é-cay-shun*) and effort, by *struggle* against inconceivable exhaustion, by enduring *unimaginable* pain, this one beats *the two best riders in the world* by one one-hundreth of a second. Can you imagine . . .?"

Roman took a breath, and in that pause, I tried to consider what it must have cost those three men. Roman allowed me about three seconds to muddle around in my imagination before he finished his, thought, adding: ". . . *That* is what I want from *you*." Having delivered his message, he turned his attention back to the race, leaving me to wonder exactly what the hell he had in store for me.

To forestall any possibility of further elaborations from Roman, I crossed the room to chat with Nino Cerruti. He was comfortably dressed in a casual suit of nubbly black-and-white wool that softened the edges of his lanky frame. His blue and white checked gingham shirt and solid black knit tie "dressed down" the suit, making the overall effect casual but very chic. His long legs were crossed, and by his amused expression I surmised that he had overheard Roman's exhortation.

After *A Man in Love* had been released in France, *Vogue Hommes International*, the French *Vogue* for men, had asked me to write a major article about fashion reviewing the season's *prêt-à-porter* (ready-to-wear) offerings. I wrote a sizeable piece reviewing every presentation of the 1989 season. At Nino's show, which I had included in my article, I had not been close enough to the stage to see the merriment that glinted in his eyes, a quality I came to recognize as characteristic, but I had loved the casual elegance of clothing and said so in print. Studying him at Roman's, the deep creases in his face suggested a life passionately lived, what the French call *les nuits blanches*—sleepless nights—with no intimation of insomnia intended.

His salt-and-pepper hair was short, brushed back, and out of the way. There was about him (unusual in the fashion industry) a pronounced masculinity and unstudied ruggedness. Distracted by cataloging my first impressions, I was unprepared for his first question. "Perhaps you could illuminate for me whether actors perform more ably if they are inspired by terror." (I learned later that Nino's formal and slightly eccentric English was due to his translating perfect Italian into English rather literally.) He was teasing me in such a good-natured way that I could only smile and shake my head to indicate that my response was inexpressible. Having established that point of contact, he asked, with genuine curiosity, "If I may ask you Peter, what is it that you intend for your life?"

His opening gambit was so removed from the normal froth of social banter that I did not know how to respond. It was indisputably the first time in my life a new acquaintance had leapt so directly into the deep water of my personal affairs. Nino gave the impression that he was not given to unkind judgments. Perhaps that's why I surprised myself by answering him more nakedly than I had intended.

The preceding months of separation and divorce had been so unsettling and my isolation from friends and family so complete that I must have needed an understanding person to talk with. I startled myself by responding, "You know, the ruin of my marriage was the greatest single failure of my life, Nino. I have no anchor anymore, no tethers, and the feeling of floating is unnerving and disorienting. It's as if I've lost all the meaning in my life."

Once over the edge, I continued my free fall, compulsively: "I took vows, deep serious vows. I was married in a Buddhist monastery, and the ceremony is like a priest's ordination. All my friends, many of them monks and priests, were witnesses that day. Breaking vows made in such high seriousness costs you. Really. I feel damaged. As if I've lost my power.

"I used to feel 'lucky,'" I continued, "as if things would always break in my favor, or that I would always float into the part of the pool with the most interesting people. Now, I don't trust myself. Don't trust my intuitions because they seem to lead directly to catastrophe. Nothing is easy or automatic anymore." If a stranger had made a confession of similar intensity shortly after meeting, I would have bolted the room.

Nino was monk-like in his imperturbability. He listened deeply, nodding occasionally, his gaze averted like a confessor's. Occasionally he said, "That is very interesting." At one point, he laughed at a horrific recitative of mine concerning a ghastly day at home, but he did it with such merriment and understanding that he made me smile.

"Marriage," he said, shaking his head in wonder and chuckling as if pondering an unsolvable puzzle he found amusing. "Time will propel you beyond this moment," he said. "The trick is to be ready."

"Time will propel you. . . .?" Who *speaks* like that, I wondered? What I said aloud was, "From your lips to God's ear," and I meant it.

As the evening was ending, Nino thanked me graciously for my previous "kind words" about him in my *Vogue Hommes* piece, and invited me to his *atelier* to see where his clothes were conceived and designed.

"Perhaps this film will afford us the opportunity of more pleasant meetings," he said in his elegant English, bowing slightly as we shook hands and parted. Either I had just been hustled by a master of Old World charm, or I had been fortunate enough to meet the real thing. As our relationship evolved, it turned out that I was not as unlucky as I felt in that moment.

—◦►—

I REMAINED IN Paris for a number of months filming *Bitter Moon*, a dark and cruelly funny film that (prompted by Roman) pushed me to the extremities of my abilities. Roman is nothing if not thorough. On our soundstage at the Boulogne-Billancourt studios in Paris, he had constructed an enormous set replicating the interior hallways, stateroom, and ballroom of the third-rate Greek gambling liner where the exterior shots of the film would later take place. The entire set was constructed on a platform that was rocked from side to side by hydraulic pistons. The front-to-rear motion of a ship was replicated by having wheels on the bottom of the set following large steel tracks with crests and dips built into them, so that the set was always moving in two directions—heightening the reality of being on board a ship—water would tip back and forth in glasses, and open doors would swing on their hinges.

Many nights I stumbled out of the Boulogne-Billancourt studio after an eighteen-hour day half seasick and with only fumes left in my emotional tank. On several nights, when I was not too exhausted, I met Nino for drinks and a friendship gradually developed between us. I learned that his family was from the Piedmont area in the north of Italy, between Milan and Turin. Nino's grandfather founded Lanificio Fratelli Cerruti in the town of Biella, in 1881. The date is important enough that the family integrated it into their brand. "Cerruti 1881" became recognized the world over as a guarantee of unaffected elegance, the highest quality cloth, and the durable and impeccable construction of their clothing.

When he was nineteen, Nino's plans to be a journalist were derailed by the death of his father. Like my uncle Bert, Nino was not ready to shoulder the responsibilities of a family enterprise but had no choice, and was forced to make his way as best he could. He told me that the shaky period when he was forced to rely on members of his family and his father's most trusted advisors, was responsible for establishing the manner in which he did business from that time on.

"This created for me a condition of importance of human relations with people I work with. I need to feel they are friendly. Human relations have always been a crucial point through all my career."

Trailing Nino through his flagship boutique and his office in the Place de la Madeleine was like hunting new fields behind a great bird-dog. Nino's long legs, and his characteristic walk—head thrust forward as if sniffing out opportunities for enjoyment—reminded me of an eager hound. Smiling, walking with a slight stoop in his frame, as if it were his intention to bring his face closer to the level of others, I sensed no anxiety among his employees and salespeople. People seemed to be enjoying themselves at their work in what, I would come to experience in other fashion houses, was often a pitiless, stressful business. Employees and tradesmen approached Nino without undue deference or timidity, confident in his good manners.

The office interiors were painted in cool greys and not unduly decorated. A display cabinet in the entranceway showcased belts, wallets, gloves, and other accessories. The design rooms were dominated by enormous windows and tables where quick, annotated sketches on scraps of paper—often accompanied by smears of color in the margins—were strewn alongside cloth samples, buttons, and fasteners, as the next season's collection slowly emerged from the recesses of Nino's and the other designers' imaginations. The organized chaos reminded me of film sets, where various departments and functions collaborate to produce the final product.

Nino's love of beauty and design is visceral. He said that he believes beauty to be the critical ingredient of his intention to humanize an overly materialistic world. "If I can contribute something of beauty and quality, to soften perhaps something of the acquisitive and competitive nature of our time," he shrugs, looking for the words, and the moment I think that he will not to finish his thought, he adds, "I will have accomplished something of which I can be proud."

NINO HANDLES CLOTH as if he receives tactile communications from it. In this regard, he shares with other artists the instinctual ability to instantly and accurately determine the "rightness" or "wrongness" of an object or detail of a design. When Roman was trying to decide on my costume for a particular scene, he would often ask me to leave his sight, to change my clothes, and then return. "Surprise me," he would insist. Re-entering the room, I would hail him. He would turn, and in that instant of seeing me anew, would render a judgment.

Jessie Benton's father, Thomas Hart Benton, was similar in that regard, and told me once that every painter is involved in the act of "waking up his eyes," to see things afresh and as if for the first time. That accounts, he said, for the penetrating expression in many self-portraits.

Nino was equally instinctually certain about the cut, style, pattern, material, and appropriateness of clothing. His designs and cloths from the family mills were engrossing, subtly patterned, and never veered into the showy or vulgar.

Nino is eloquent on the subject of material:

"A fine fabric is the combination of very sophisticated technologies. Like a very fine yarn, which allows you to make a fabric with the highest possible number of crossings per square centimeter between warp and weft. This creates an inevitable super-performance, but can be, as well, as a fabric, very creative, generating a 'surprise look,' color combinations, fancy treatment. Like a cat, fabric has seven souls, so it can be always different, surprising."

I would hazard that the appreciation of beauty is a common denominator for all Nino's pursuits and I was moved by his commitment to it. The quality of that dedication forced me to reconsider dismissive attitudes I had harbored about the *monde* of fashion. Anything to which one dedicates a life is worth a life, and Nino was a man of such qualities that his attention ennobled what it considered.

IN THE *ATELIER* one day, when I was distracted by one of the legion of attractive, long-legged women working there, I made a wry joke about the uniformity of beautiful *objets* in the room and his face creased into a smile. Always ready for play, he riposted, "Peter, if you can discover equal competence and intelligence among women, is there fault to be found in choosing to spend time among those you find most lovely?"

"No argument from me, Nino," I responded.

His remark reminded me of a comment made to me by a senior woman editor of *Vogue Hommes* named Jacqueline Degioanni, with whom I worked closely while preparing my article. Over lunch one day, Nino's name came up, and Jacqueline smiled, shaking her head in wonder as she described his amorous adventures among women in the fashion world—journalists, models, clients, and publicists. When she caught me appraising her for clues to her own relationship with him, she laughed heartily, wagged her index finger at me, and suggested that I sample the *foie gras*.

Even after I could afford to buy excellent clothes, had I been queried about my opinions concerning fashion, I might have been dismissive about those who elevate style to an importance rivaling ethics or the self to deserving of worship. The *demi-monde* of the fashion world can be self-important to a degree that Hollywood certainly equals but cannot surpass. The preeminent value of fashion is "taste"—valued even above style—the intangible refinement of exposure, experience, semiotics, and sensibility that discriminates the real from the fake and the elegant from the *arriviste*. In this milieu, the considered opinion of a few tastemakers can determine a reputation or the fate of a collection to which millions of dollars have been dedicated. In this rarefied atmosphere, taste is often criticized in asides and arch pronouncements, air-kisses and stilettos of dialogue wielded with a chilling absence of empathy and the certainty of royal decree. A shrug, rolled eyes, or a snide remark from a person of influence can condemn a collection to the lowest *bolgias* of fashion Hell.

Nino made fashion interesting to me. His ideas were provocative and for a fellow who was new to European high culture and still burnishing his rough edges, Nino became a model of consistent dignity and kindness even in the bitchy swordfights that pass for conversations in haute couture. I observed in Nino's behavior a secular correlative of my Buddhist practice and marveled at the consistent manner within the vernacular of European culture with which he practiced kindness. His behavior spurred me to discover similar colloquial practices that might transform Zen Buddhism in America from an exotic mystique to something which might be perceived as available human behavior people might choose to commit to in their everyday lives.

NINO'S LEGAL WIFE, Chantal, had been introduced to me previously in his office. Though Nino continues to share their beautiful art deco home when he is in Paris, it is an open fact that he lives in Biella, Italy with his longtime companion, a dark-haired, good-humored German journalist named Sybilla Jahr. I have no idea if he and Chantal are divorced or still married, and while Chantal has undeniable authority within Cerruti 1881, Sybilla is the shrewd and astute woman of unforced charm with whom Nino chooses to spend the majority of his time. She has the confidence to sit watchfully in a busy room, or hover in Nino's shadow and keep her eye on the parts of the room he cannot see. It is my impression that she misses nothing and that her counsel with Nino carries great weight. There is also something about her contained solidity that gives me the impression that, should trouble occur, she would take no prisoners.

I was impressed that Nino had been able to create a stable relationship that allowed him to have his cake and eat it too. Without fuss or over-much pain, he had ordered his world in a way that worked for him. "The point is to do what you want in life without causing unnecessary distress and pain to others," Nino said to me once when we were discussing relationships. "Chantal is my wife, and the mother of my son. If our affections have cooled to some degree, I don't see that as a justification to deprive her of her social status and station. We work together quite effectively . . ." and he trailed off.

Apparently their relationship works for all involved including their son, Julian. It can't be that this success is due solely to Nino's skills or the more permissive mores of French and Italian society, but I suspect it has much to do with Nino himself. I had no idea how he had fostered such an easy mutuality among the women in his life and wanted to learn, because at that time Jean was no longer speaking to me, complicating the mutual raising of our son. Without such skills, I would be unable to protect myself or my children from the caustic consequences of divorce, and to date I had certainly failed to manage it in a way that ensured anyone's happiness.

─◄o►─

THE FOLLOWING YEAR, Nino asked me to model for him—manufacturing the winter- and spring-season garments for the coming runway shows in my size, creating a treasure trove of available garments, any of which I was allowed to claim after the show. His good friend, the fashion photographer Paolo Roversi, assembled an eight-page book of black-and-white photos of me in Nino's clothes, which was inserted as a small book in newspapers all across Europe and made me appear quite dashing, certainly not the self of my internal imagery.

The following year he asked me to represent his new cologne, using another Paolo image. In each instance, the most amusing part of these endeavors was the collaborative time we spent together. It required increasing effort to revert to my archaic "loser" identity when people like Nino and Paolo and a number of extraordinary women had lavished so much affection and attention on me. Trivial as I might once have considered modeling, the glamorized ME being celebrated in Nino's campaigns could no longer cohabit in the same doghouse with the moth-eaten old mongrel of my childhood. Two decades of meditation had weakened my attachment to that treacherous old hound and one day I dropped the chain and let him loose. In my mind's eye, he stayed a moment, unsure as to whether his freedom was real or an illusion. After a moment, he slunk off, slipped around a corner in my mind without ceremony, and has never returned for more than an occasional sniff, as if searching for food. Occasionally I recognize his tracks, but he seems to have finally understood that he will receive no more nourishment from me.

I don't want to create a false impression that this release was related to worldly "success." If success could heal, why do so many celebrity marriages end in divorce and celebrated artists wind up in rehab or the morgue? Why do people with a firm grip on the world's tail take their own lives or pursue suicidally risky behaviors? My newly-won equanimity had more to do with stubbornness and luck—a lifetime of unremitting struggle, refusing to give up, and the simple luck not to have died. Add to that the good fortune of discovering and *maintaining* a Buddhist practice, and the cumulative benefits of a long line of teachers and mentors over the entire course of my life. At the bottom of all of it is a mystery—why me? I have no better or more plausible explanation than *karma* or luck.

Nino's publicist informed me once that Nino was a count, and as I listened to her I imagined ancient traditions of aristocratic lore and pedagogy he might have soaked up from a venerable lineage. While I did not imagine it as actually written down anywhere, I did imagine a cumulative wisdom among the world's most privileged people, a how-to guide among elite peers. I was curious to learn about such lore if it existed. In truth, after hearing this, I went on a temporary flight of fancy, speculating that Nino's elegant manners might have been a precisely transmitted skill set handed down as training to ensure that "the little people" would continue to love the aristocracy and not set fire to their barns and fields.

There was a reason my mind veered off in that direction. I once had a brilliant, serious girlfriend, a well-known American actress who had married into an ancient Italian aristocratic family dating from the Renaissance. Her tales of the training she had undergone from her mother-in-law and her husband's mother and aunt to "learn how to behave" were fascinating and had led directly to my assumption that such knowledge existed. After hearing the publicist's assertion about Nino's lineage, I wanted to learn more about it but was afraid to approach the subject too bluntly. I eased an afternoon's conversation onto the question of manners and was surprised by the reflexive quality of Nino's response, which he summed up without pausing to think: "Finally, Peter," he said, "manners are simply kindness and consideration." The Dalai Lama was equally succinct when he said, "My religion is kindness."

◄○►

ONE DAY, WHILE introducing me to a friend, Nino described me in jest as his "illegitimate son." We are both roughly the same height and build, and though we don't resemble one another there is some physical and emotional consonance between us that others have noted. He was only being affectionately silly, but I was deeply affected by his joke, and embarrassed to reveal the degree to which I was moved.

Morris had been dead for over twenty years. He had lived into my adulthood—dying when I was thirty—but did not live into my maturity. He had never seen me outside of the counterculture; never knew me as a man of any worldly success or had the opportunity to brag honorably about my triumphs or to avail himself of the simple pride available to most fathers.

As a result of changes I had made since his death, my interior was a much clearer pool into which his face could sometimes appear in a startling fashion, like a body floating to the surface. Sometimes, when my life was good, his arrival was a comforting upwelling, but at others he arose as a scalding geyser lofting superheated spray into the air, burning me with bitterness or remorse.

Morris was too honest to fool himself, and Buddy Jones told me that he characteristically responded to inquiries about me by saying, "Pete's trying to find himself." Still, I know him like my digestion, like I know the coppery taste of sucking a penny, and I know he worried about me. He was too honorable not to have taken some blame upon himself for my behaviors he found worrisome. He was too aware to have missed the judgment implied by my absence and too cruel not to have flayed himself for being its occasion. My childhood had been too intense, too bullied, too self-conscious due to parental hyper-vigilance, and the stakes of virtually every decision too consistently high, so that when I once got the bit of autonomy in my teeth, I never returned to harness. What a shame.

I NEVER KNEW if Morris ever received any measure of peace from his life. Sharing my success might have been a small balm I could have offered him, that might have afforded him the joy, pride, and sense of redemption it did for my mother. I would have shaved years from my own life to offer such a gift to this impossible man who, in his last years, faced down his ruin and death without flinching or begging the least pity.

The most irresolvable loss about Morris's death was that it denied me access to his wisdom in circumstances when I could have used it most. I was an orphan in *his* world now—making serious money, traveling among rich and powerful men and women; the prey of agents, lawyers, managers, accountants, advertising people, and project hustlers all pitching for my business. Nearly everyone who approached me in those days (except my oldest friends) wanted *something*, and deciphering what it might be and how to best respond could be exhausting. Morris would have instantly separated the chicken salad from the chicken shit and his guidance would have saved me hours of rumination and indecision.

I picked my way through the minefields and hustle as best I could with minimal help and inevitable stumbles, but Morris, alone among all others, would have sidelined his self-interest and offered me objective guidance. No child can understand how valuable a resource such a gift is until he lives without it. My deepest source of pride these days is that my children often call me for advice or to talk out complex issues.

◄o►

NINO WAS FAR more famous, far more established than I was, and well-known on many continents. He had been dressing first-tier stars like Michael Douglas and Jack Nicholson for years, knew the politicians and power brokers in Milan, Rome, Paris, London, and New York. He had no idea how important a gift he had offered me by treating me first like a peer and then like a son—in jest—but a jest melded with obvious affection.

He was old enough to *be* my father and the warmth of his presence in my life called forth something wounded and wary, like the thrashing weasel I had once clamped in my trap. Whatever it was, Nino calmed it. After that remark, casual as it might have been, something deep in my interior relaxed for the first time I could recall. I moved in the world now with what, to me, was the novel feeling of being sheltered by a powerful and loving man. It's true that Morris had rescued and protected me after my marijuana arrest, but I was too humiliated and ashamed to experience his love operating beneath the exercise of his power. It barely mattered that Nino's joke about my being his "illegitimate son" was imagination or false. Imagination, after all, is the geography from which actors generate worlds more "real" than those we normally inhabit.

When I met Nino, I was in need of new tools and skills to live in this rarefied, high-status European milieu. My father had not learned to do it with grace, though he tried, and it was certainly beyond Buddy Jones's skill set. Furthermore, both those men were gone. My cranky, Commie-Jew, mordant humor and sophisticated Digger chic were entertaining when I put them to good use, but they were not going to be comprehensible at dinner with the Duke of Bourbon or the company that Nino and Roman kept. I needed to learn to discuss the world without allowing my resentments and passions to violate the harmony of the environment. If, as a Buddhist, I was to fulfill my vows to save the numberless beings, it would be necessary to erase my impediments to accepting them as they were.

Nino refined my observations about Europe even as Europe itself was reaffirming my earliest political instincts that societies *could* operate successfully by serving the interests of their citizens. I was under no illusion that Europe was heaven, but observing firsthand how the nations of Europe could afford healthcare, quality education, clean, convenient mass transit, and a safety net beneath which citizens were not allowed to fall, also reaffirmed desires and intention—consistent with my Buddhist vows—to struggle to establish such traditions at home.

One day over a coffee in the Café de Flore (my "office" when I am in Paris), Nino examined a critical difference between business practices in the United States and Europe. "In Europe, we make an agreement in principle," he observed. "We shake hands and then *we begin working together*. While we are working, the lawyers come in and draft the documents reflecting our understanding. In America, it is *very* different," he continued, with a wistful shrug. "There, nothing happens until the documents are signed, and then, *the moment they are signed,* lawyers are called in to examine them for hair-splitting opportunities to violate the understanding in their client's favor."

He stared out the window for a moment at the gathering dusk where rain was pattering on the bunched cars resting like schooled and glistening fish in the currents of the Boulevard Saint-Germain. The waiters in their black vests and white shirts flowed around us through the narrow aisles, trays at shoulder height, occasionally setting down a coffee, removing an ashtray, or adding a torn paper receipt to our growing pile on the table's corner. The interior lights snapped on, illuminating the wall mirrors and the tidal influx of end-of-the-day regulars began, stopping in for a drink, a snack, or an assignation. It was the hour when tourists were back in their hotels, and the French writers and readers reclaimed their favored tables. I was digging into my favorite salad, *Frisée aux Lardons* ("frizzy" lettuce, small chunks of thick bacon, and a soft egg), content to chew and listen as Nino continued:

"This is the reason that I place such importance on the European Union," he insisted. "If Europe fails, it will mean that the *only* model of capitalism available will be the American model, and that will make our world a *disaster*."

He went on to elucidate how Europe was an old continent that had fought many wars and survived many tragedies. "Our elites here have determined that by putting a modest cap on how wealthy they can become—and believe me Peter, it is a *modest* cap; you see the wealth in this country—by creating this ceiling for themselves, they manage to create a floor under how poor you can be. It is a concept of *solidarity,* adopted to create cohesion in society. Perhaps after so many wars and so much blood on our soil, stability and solidarity have become our primary values."

Walking home afterwards and considering what Nino had said, I speculated that Nino understood his work as, in some manner, an antidote to economic heartlessness and its reflection in the spheres of human relationships, aesthetics, and the general environment. *From that perspective,* even the frothy world of fashion becomes elevated. It was counterintuitive for me to think this way, but as I walked on enjoying the light rain it became apparent to me that there are only a few endeavors that could *not* be organized as vehicles for enlightened activity.[9] An enlightened intention *seeking the highest possibilities within its own realm* could transform even the trivialities of style into a nourishing pursuit. I had not considered that fully before, and another set of unexamined prejudices tumbled over.

I CHOSE TO walk back to my apartment after our meeting at the Flore. I always find the rain comforting, as if I carry a small tin barn roof over my head and not an umbrella. As I considered Nino's remarks about "the American model," Harry Palmer appeared in the emptiness behind my eyes. Memory led to memory as left foot follows the right and I recalled my last visit with my Uncle Bert, in which we discussed Harry.

I was in the living room, sitting across from where he was perched on a couch. I had been questioning him about Harry's tutelage of him as a young adult. Bert smiled slyly and confessed to me with tangible pride, "I'm *better* than Harry." I waited neutrally for him to continue.

"Harry terrified everyone," he said, as if the fact amused him. "They'd piss themselves when he entered the room. I don't do that . . ." and he smiled like Disney's magnanimous Cheshire Cat. "I've learned to make people feel they're doing me a *favor*," he purred, in a satisfied voice with the texture of grainy butter.

Bert went on to describe the restraint and delicacy required for a successful bribe to operate "ripple-free" and without blowback. "My business has numerous competitors," he explained, "and the products I manufacture are not unduly distinguished." Since his products were sold to various large retail chains, the fate of Bert's affairs, his family's well-being, and his expensive hobbies depended on cultivating the favor of the buyers for the chains and department stores that bought them.

"If my competitors buy the salesman a dinner, or tickets to a show, or a girl, I buy them a *house*," he continued brightly. "I put their children through school. I remember their birthdays and the names of their wives—and keep them separate from their girlfriends." He recounted this as if he were fanning open a deck of personal skills. He continued, explaining refinements in the art of receiving their "favors" with expressions of gratitude, dismissing as irrelevant any gifts he might be offering them. Bert's certainty, transmitted to him with demanding exactitude by Harry, was that *other men were available to be bought and/or manipulated for one's advantage.* Bert acquired and refined those skills and, along with them, contributed his own refinement of transmitting to his marks the *understanding* that he *appreciated* their "flexibility," as if it were a moral characteristic he prized. His skill lay in his ability to do so without once ruffling their pride.

Later that afternoon, I mentioned to Bert that I was toying with the idea of writing a book about Harry, long dead by then. Bert's response surprised me, "It's been done."

Shocked, I exclaimed, "Someone wrote a book about *Harry*? How could I not have known that?"

"It's better than a book," Bert answered, smiling mysteriously. I asked him what he meant, knowing well how deliberately details concerning Harry's life had been obscured. Bert asked if I had seen the film *A Bronx Tale*, featuring actor Chazz Palminteri. I answered affirmatively and told him how much I had enjoyed it. Then Bert inquired if I didn't consider Chazz's physiognomy and performance "the spitting image of Harry on every level, looks, behavior. . . ." I had to admit that it was as uncanny a resemblance as a doppelganger.

I was unprepared for what Bert said next: "I play that film with the sound off sometimes," he said, looking pointedly into my eyes. "I talk to him. To *Harry*," he stressed, as if I might have misunderstood. "I talk to him when I *need* him. When I have a problem."

He elaborated that when he was troubled, a moving, "living" Harry in the room, even on his TV screen, comforted him and relieved his anxiety (a family trait). Somehow, through this exercise, Bert's intuitions received a direct transmission of what Harry might have said if he was living. It was in that moment that I fully appreciated how precious Harry's mentoring had been for Bert. Completely unprepared for his father's death and the responsibilities it demanded of him, he'd been ripped from the womb of his academic life and delivered into the cutthroat maelstrom of business, suddenly responsible for his mother's and family's livelihoods, and Harry had been his only lifeline.

We talked about Harry long into the waning light of that autumn afternoon and Bert filled many gaps in my knowledge. As a child I had heard stories about Harry's service in the Treasury Department, disguised as a janitor and sweeping the toilets in Grand Central Station during World War II, eavesdropping for spies because of his fluent Russian. Nominally, the United States and Russia were allies, but hard-minded men in Washington understood that after the war a showdown would be pending over the spoils of Europe. Bert filled me in on further details about Harry's relationship with the New York State Boxing Commission and mentioned Harry's disappointment that some previous "trouble" had prevented him from being appointed its commissioner—a position he had coveted.

I wondered if the "trouble" might have had to do with Harry's work once, running the Corporate Fraud Squad at the IRS offices in New York City. As a result of his employment there, he knew where all the tax secrets of New York's corporate sector were lodged and could certainly have determined to whom those secrets might have been valuable. It was a scandal-ridden agency, where information was routinely sold or used to extort corporations. Harry left the agency before his name was ever tainted, but in 1947–1948, IRS scandals in the corporate division were big stories in the New York press, and the subject of Congressional hearings. Harry is explicitly mentioned in the minutes of those hearings . . . but *only* mentioned. He remains as enigmatic in those pages as he did in the bleeding and greedy world where he hunted the weak.

Near the end of our conversation, when the warm tones had been leached out of the light and a certain greyness that characterizes East Coast winter turned the classic heads and friezes on Bert's walls shadowless and dull, Bert muttered something nearly inaudible. I assumed I must have misheard him, and looked up, startled. He regarded me without flinching, confirming what I thought I heard. I held my breath, not wanting to disturb the intimacy of the moment. What he had said was, "Harry was a life-taker."

I sat quietly while Bert rummaged through some papers, until he found a yellowed newspaper clipping and handed it to me. It chronicled the daylight murder of two brothers in the street outside a burlesque theater on lower Broadway in Manhattan.

"Harry owned that burlesque house," Bert explained. "Those brothers were trying to take it away. Harry slept on the stage every night with a machine gun." There was a pause as he carefully refolded the column.

"This case was never solved," he said softly, replacing it in the file. "One day, I asked him, I said, 'Harry, why did you kill those two men?' He looked at me like I was an idiot, and he said, 'Because I *could*.'"

And there it was—"because I could"—the blunt expression of will, as stripped of rationale and obfuscation as a Kalashnikov. Behind the bunting and rumbling, below the cheers of crowds, braided into the invented rationales and shell game of "facts"—"*because we can*" is the eternal anthem of power; an homage to the will and to men like Jack, Morris, Bert, and Harry—the ham-fisted men. The decisive men. Those who will never accept frustration of their desires.

These men knew how to build empires and maintain what they had seized. They were hardheaded, immensely practical, strategic, and often fearless in the face of risk. I do not belittle or condemn such men any more than I would condemn a grizzly bear or a Bengal tiger. They are all "letters from emptiness" and from that perspective, equal beings in a universe that does not favor pity over cruelty.

I am not at all adroit in such matters. Since my earliest childhood vows "not to play" I have maintained no interest in bending others to my will or dismissing harm I caused others en route to a prize. In Morris's and Harry's cases, their power sponsored many acts of kindness and generosity and afforded me the blessings of comfort and protection within which I was able to reap the advantages of a broad and deep education. In Nino, however, I sensed an alternative path that did not leave broken men and women cast away along its track. It was a different way of operating—with high finish and broad reach—but promoted by kindness and persuasion, in addition to ambition, not threats and bribes. His intention was to create an antidote to the heartless materialism and shoddy values that he loathed. Such an intention changes the business practices it animates. I learned from him a quality of refinement and kindness that my mimetic skills absorbed as if I were a dry sponge and a bowl of clean, fresh water.

◄o►

WHEN I RETURNED to the States I had the feeling of having completed a major cycle. Simply stating facts, I had become an international film star. I had learned to be comfortable in three languages, travel easily, and move in international circles holding my own in every dimension that mattered to me. I felt as if I had mastered the worlds of Love and Power to the degree that I maintained interest in them, but my self-satisfaction and sense of peace at these accomplishments was still stirred by a restlessness I could not quite identify. It was not enough!

I was not ambitious for money, fame, power, or love, but there was something missing; something undone that I had neither accomplished nor abandoned; and trying to understand what it was made me vaguely dissatisfied.

◄o►

WHEN I REACHED my later sixties, I resolved that I would rather lower my standard of living than continue to hop planes to Bulgaria to make a sequel to *Return of the Living Dead 5* (which I had once done). My sense of my remaining time on earth was clarifying and each day was becoming more precious. I had evolved a career in voice-overs that could sustain me without film. My children were grown and independent and had completed their education debt-free. My second house was virtually paid for. I did not need the money I once did and I resented the demands on my time required to make more. Furthermore, whatever I lost from the world of film was more than compensated for by the fruits of a deepening Zen practice.

IN PRECISELY THE way that a falcon's "widening gyre" reviews familiar territory from a higher altitude, in 1994, four years after Jean and I broke up (but had not yet bothered to divorce), I was crossing the lobby in a local movie theater when a young woman hailed me. It turned out that we had a mutual friend, and in her eagerness to call out to me she had forgotten that I was a local celebrity and hailing me might make her appear an opportunist. I crossed the lobby to respond and say hello, charmed by the intense blush that had risen to her cheeks. Despite having hailed me, there was nothing brassy or forward about her and her beauty made the world stand momentarily at attention. Her name was Stefanie. There's an entire book in our courtship and the nineteen years we've spent together at the time of this writing, including our eventual marriage, but that book will never be written. She is, without a doubt, the most private person I have ever known and would be embarrassed and offended were I to reveal details of our personal life in a public manner. Suffice it to say that nineteen years after that casual meeting, we are still friends and she is the only woman to whom I have ever remained completely faithful.

—◁◦▷—

BY FEBRUARY OF 1999 Ruth was not doing too well. She had suffered for some years from emphysema, brought on by smoking and she had, by now, become frail and shaky. Her hair was thin and her eyes some-times appeared teary, unfocused, and startled. She trembled a bit when she moved, and her walk was precarious as if ball bearings under her feet might send her hurtling off in perilous directions for a moment's lapse of attention. It was becoming unfeasible for her to remain living alone, and yet she feared being a burden to her children.

My sister owns an 18th-century two-family farmhouse outside of Boston and she prepared the second unit to make Ruth comfortable. It was an ideal solution to Ruth's concerns. She would be living immedi-ately nearby to her daughter, yet her own apartment would offer her privacy and autonomy. Ruth moved in; the bird feeders were filled to attract the small feathered creatures she enjoyed so much, and with her comfortable and safe, it seemed like a good time for Stefanie and me to take a long-overdue vacation. We headed to Mexico for a week of rest.

My mother's sister Jeanette died the day we left. Their relation-ship had always been querulous and slightly impatient. They were extremely different from one another temperamentally and physiologi-cally and had never exhausted the residue of whatever childhood jeal-ousies and judgments had once divided them.

Ruth had not expressed much emotion about Jeanette's death though we could tell that she was shaken. Furthermore she was sim-ply too weak to travel to New Jersey for the funeral. I was in Mexico when I received her call. Her voice sounded hoarse and tired. She told me that she had a bad cold she couldn't lick and was going into the hospital "for a few days to recover."

"Mom, shall we come home?" I asked. "It's nothing, really, we'll just grab a plane and. . . ."

"No dear," she cut me off. "It's not serious." I asked to speak with a nurse who reiterated what Ruth said. "She'll be home in three days, enjoy yourself." She promised to call if the situation changed.

The nurse's call came the next day. "You better get here," was all she said.

Stef and I arranged cars, planes, taxis, calls to my daughter and son, and by the time my sister picked us up at Boston's Logan Airport, Ruth had slipped into a coma. The honor guard of her children and grandchildren gathered around her bed and our vigil was horrific. Every few minutes, with a heart-stopping gasp, Ruth would jerk upright, as if she'd been yanked aloft by a cable. Her unseeing panicked eyes stared into a void, and then she would collapse backwards, exhausted and gasping. I called the nurse, who assured me offhandedly that this happened "all the time" and that "it was just reflex." I watched this macabre ballet for about ten minutes and then began investigating. Tracing the tube from Ruth's morphine drip to beneath the bed, I discovered that the tube had slipped off of a cheap plastic connector, and her opiates were pooling on the floor.

I hit flash point immediately and snatched the nurse, propelling her to the bed. "There's your fucking reflex," I said, pointing to the useless narcotics wetting the linoleum. I was frightened by my own anger and how perilously on the edge of control I was teetering. I was ready to pitch her out the second-story window. My Zen practice had deserted me, and I was being shaken in the jaws of a large and very powerful dog again. The nurse was apologetic and frightened and within a minute had repaired the structure, after which Ruth calmed down and rested quietly at last. About two hours later, perhaps in an effort to appease me, the nurse, an attractive young woman of about thirty-five (shoot me for noticing her looks at such a time), took me aside and informed me quietly, "We can speed this up, if you like."

"Speed it up?" I repeated stupidly.

"Yes," she said, conspiratorially. "She's *dying*," she said, as if I hadn't noticed "It . . . doesn't have to take *so* long," she continued, regarding me significantly.

It took another moment before her meaning became clear to me. I took her by the arm (gently, so as not to frighten her again) and led her into the hall. She resisted a bit, like a goat being led to the killing floor. Coming close enough for her to hear my whisper, I said, "I don't know how many breaths my mother has left on this earth, but she put up with a monster of a husband and a monster of a son her entire life. The least I owe her is *every-single-fucking-last-breath she's entitled to.* I know you're trying to be kind, but if you ever even glance at me as if you are suggesting this again, if you raise an eyebrow in her direction, I'll have your ass in handcuffs and you'll be fighting off the bull dykes in City Prison *tonight!* Would that be *'quick enough'* for you?" She turned the color of salt, nodded a nervous assent, and I dropped her like a used Kleenex to return to my mother's bed.

Explosions like that had once been common in my life and had once infused me with a sense of power. Now it unnerved me. After years of hard work and discipline it was chastening to realize that I (like everyone) still rested just a hair's breadth away from a hurtful impulse. Each time I returned to normal from such a moment I renewed my commitment to mindfulness, to saving all beings—even that nurse—simultaneously despairing the fact that I was reaching for a goal beyond my ability; a goal for which it would be impossible *not* to fail at times. (It is the refusal to overlook even one living being that makes Buddhist vows so inclusive, and forces us to treat person after person *forever* in the most compassionate way we are able.)

There was nothing for me to do with my sorrow and regrets about Ruth, or with my apologies. There was nothing I could do to remedy the suffering she had endured from me. We tend to forget our own culpability when we are consumed by self-importance and deliver ourselves to indulgence. I am certain that I felt like Morris must have if he once considered his transgressions against me. There was nothing I could do but *be* there with her. Her children and grandchildren found places to sleep in the room and a nearby lounge, and early in the morning of the fifth of February, a night nurse woke me. "It's time," she said softly, as if she were saying good-bye to the words.

We stood by Ruth's bed and I chanted *The Heart Sutra*—the seminal text of Buddha's teaching; the clearest explication of the Buddhist concept of "emptiness"—the absolute common denominator of all phenomena. It ends with the ancient Sanskrit mantra, *Gate* (gah-tay) *Gate Paragate Parasamgate Bodhi svaha!* (Gone! Gone! Gone beyond! Completely, utterly gone. Enlightened! Thus done!). I held a sprig of cedar I'd taken from a tree outside as I chanted this four or five times and by then Ruth was no longer in the room—gone, gone, gone beyond—a week to the day after her sister's death.

THE RAINMAN'S THIRD CURE

M Y ENDURING INTEREST in spiritual matters over the years disappeared
and surfaced intermittently like a spring that dries up in the heat
of summer and reappears with the rains—rising and falling, disappearing for periods of time and then resurfacing, like a child's unsinkable
bathtub toy.

Even when I was throwing my own flesh into the pen of my junkyard dog there always remained some spiritual "glow" illuminating the background of my physical universe. I could access it when I
needed or remembered it, and it obviously served me or I would have
permanently forgotten it was there. The genuine problem was that
I only rarely dedicated myself to its demands. Nomads once carried
glowing coals smoldering in moss to be reanimated into campfires
at the next stop. Since I consider myself lucky, it is not difficult to
attribute that luck to some sort of spiritual counterweight I somehow
maintained even in my least conscious periods—the spark I carried.
Somehow, despite carelessness and inattention, it was never completely extinguished.

I continued my Zen practice with increasing diligence. I persevered through depression, through boredom, through colds and

discomforts, through doubts, and through my own speculations as to whether my practice was accomplishing anything at all. In intermittent weeklong *sesshins* as the hours stretched before and behind me, occasionally something in my body would "let go"—a ligament or a tensed muscle—and disgorge its freight of memories. I would be flooded with strong emotions as if the incident were occurring in that moment. They would evaporate and I would feel refreshed, renewed, and considerably lighter. It turned out that such experiences were simply coming attractions.

—◦—

IN THE FIRST week of December 2009, I was sixty-eight years old. Infirmity and dying were in the forefront of my mind. Forty-five years earlier I had contracted hepatitis C from shooting drugs. It had remained undiagnosed until the late 1990s, by which time the disease had been conscripting and destroying my liver cells for all those years.

My youth had left, snatching as it exited, the firm outlines of my body and my once distinct jaw-line and un-creased neck. The backs of my hands were dotted with liver spots, and shadows pooled below my eyes. My stamina had diminished and like most people who have aged beyond the notice of today's diversions for the young, my acting career had settled into a stasis with no promise of any breakthroughs. Sickness, old age, and death had become tangible to me in ways that had been only romantic posturing in my twenties.

It was now incontrovertible that in a conceivable future, everything I held dear, every memory and achievement, every treasure, including my own body, would be stripped from me. That is the central, unavoidable fact of human existence (and a fundamental tenet of Buddhism) and when it changed from a notion into a certainty, my perspective changed with it, particularly my ideas about time. Looking backwards, the lengthening succession of dead friends and family disappeared into emptiness like a black thread being unspooled into a tub of ink. The only uncertainty in my future now was speculation about how savagely sickness, old age, and death would claim their due. With these thoughts as unpleasant companions, I decided to sit another seven-day *sesshin*. It was December again, time for Rohatsu, the Great Cold *sesshin,* descriptions of which opened this book.

Sesshins are always rough, and this time the first three days were particularly difficult. Though my shaking and convulsions had subsided many years before and I could now sit as solidly as those senior monks I'd once envied, my body was forty years older. The pain in my knees was intense, debilitating, and distracting to the degree that during a private audience with my teacher on the third day, I confessed to him that I would have to quit the *sesshin* because I could not bear the pain any longer.

He was mildly critical of me for not paying closer attention to my body and for trying to bull my way through. "You're nearly seventy," he said. "It's hard to admit that all your cards are on the table now and that you have none left to draw. You'll have to play the ones you have as best you can. *That is the central fact of your existence.* That is reality and you'll have to adjust to that. You are *living* what we mean when we say, 'seeing without delusion.' You only have one set of knees and you need to take care of them. If you have to sit in a chair, sit in a chair. Don't cripple yourself trying to be tough or refusing to recognize the reality of your body or your age."

He was correct of course and had pinpointed the underlying depression amplifying my physical pain. After our conversation, I began alternating meditation periods between my cushion and a chair, calculating backwards from mealtimes so that the meditation period before a meal (which I preferred to take on my cushion) was done in a chair. This relieved the stress on my knees and the consequent reduction of pain allowed me to refocus and dedicate my efforts wholeheartedly. I aligned myself to the schedule without further resistance, and was able to focus my concentration on a question that had arisen for me on the *sesshin's* first day.

It was a simple question I had condensed into a short mnemonic phrase—"What is it?"—mental shorthand for the larger question— "What is it I'm missing or still searching for?" By the end of day four I was completely absorbed by it. It accompanied each inhale and exhale, and resided within me, simmering on a back burner, whether meditating, walking or eating. It floated through my dreams.

On the sixth day, in the late afternoon, the light outside was thinning and we began a period of rapid *kinhin* (walking meditation). Our route began by exiting a side door, circumambulating the rough porch girding the building, reentering through the door at the opposite corner, threading a path through the *zendo* and out the first door again. The wood underfoot was bracingly cold and its rough texture stimulating; the rapid walking increased my circulation and alertness and was a balm to my sore joints and muscles. The afternoon fog, creeping in from the ocean, was obscuring the edges of the hills, sending tendrils slithering through the grass like a vigorous living entity.

I had just stepped out the door onto the porch. Perhaps on the second or third round, but I had just begun my course down the building's long side. I remember that my hands were folded formally against my navel and my gaze was unfocused, and I remember a portion of the swishing black robe and flashing heels of the person in front of me. Several paces after passing through the door, a bird began to shriek from very nearby. It was as loud and startling as if it was sitting on my shoulder, and its plaint was unrelenting. Today, I know it was a Camp Jay, but I wasn't aware of that at the moment because my concentration was purloined by my question, and the bird's shriek was an irritant.

Eeek! Eeek! Eeek! Eeek! Eeek! it cried—strident, insistent, obliterating all thought. Suddenly, in that momentary emptiness, its cries were transformed and I heard them as "It!" "It!" "It!" "It!"—the indisputable answer to my question. I took one more step and the world as I had always experienced it ended.

I cannot describe what happened next because in that instant language and thought fell entirely away from my existence. The boundaries between "in here" and "out there" disappeared. The world remained recognizable, as it had always been, but completely stripped of descriptive language and concepts. Everything appeared to be a phantom of itself, luminous but without weight or substance. "I" had been replaced. The closest I can come to describing what I felt was as a part of an awareness with no physical location, inseparable from the entire universe. Everything was precisely as it had come to be. The world was perfect, without time, eternal, and coming and going as it had always been. Every doubt that I had ever harbored about Zen practice fell away. The timid fearful self I had been defending, aggrandizing, comforting, and trying to improve for my entire life had been relieved of duty and everything was fine without him. There was nothing I had to "do." I knew irrefutably that this was what I had been searching for since I first picked up a book about Zen when I was sixteen years old.

In the next instant, I understood that it was not all that important.

◄o►

WHEN I RETURNED to a more familiar state, I first became aware of a feeling of loss. My first conscious thought was, "Oh my God, what am I going to do *now?*" accompanied by a feeling of sadness as if the Universe were permeated with it.

Sometime later, reoriented to my normal reality, "I" was back, but neither as uniquely nor solidly as I had previously imagined. I appeared to have been demoted to my rightful place again as simply one among the world's phenomena. My sadness appeared to arise from two directions—first, from being forced to acknowledge that my previously conceived ideas were not quite right. The entire edifice of Buddhism, like the rest of the universe, now seemed to me to be like a shimmering, transitory phantom, no more (and no less) real than a dream. Then, the awareness that billions of people were suffering, struggling, grasping, scheming, dying, and killing each other for these "empty" rewards and reasons filled me with pity for "the millions of us useless to each other or the world."[1]

I had dedicated thirty-nine years to practicing Buddhism and pursuing an "idea" of enlightenment in the hope that achieving it would make me a master of the universe, exempt from "the heartache and thousand natural shocks that flesh is heir to." In the process I had constructed elaborate mental edifices of the Buddha's teaching that I had believed to be "real," had invested my faith and hope in them as the only reliable antidote to my personal suffering and the chaos of the world. Now, I was directly confronted with a much more visceral, experiential understanding that made it necessary to reconsider everything in light of the radical implications of the Buddha's insight— which implies that in an ultimate sense, these doctrines, despite having been immensely useful to me as guides and teaching, are not "real" either. I was overwhelmed and not at all certain of what to do with my experience. I certainly did not feel like a master of the universe or ready to announce myself as a teacher, despite the profundity of what I had experienced. A friend, a Sanskrit scholar, showed me a text that described the Buddha's initial reluctance to teach and his fears that the world was too defiled for his teachings to make any impression. I found it comforting to know that the Buddha struggled with doubt. This would not have been the first time in my practice that I had been forced to reconsider and reevaluate what I understood and to jettison previously held beliefs in the light of new insights. Looking backwards, it seemed to be the nature of practice itself. Even though I was shaken, this train of thought relaxed me and within that relaxation I reconnected to my commitment, and the momentum of long years of practicing settled me back onto my seat again.

◄o►

AT *SESSHIN'S* END I discussed my experience with my teacher, who acknowledged it and cautioned me, "Don't try to hold on to it."

I understood that he meant not to reify the experience or make a badge of it to paste on myself like fruit salad on a military tunic.

"You wouldn't have studied Buddhism all these years," he added, "if you had not already possessed some intuition of what this experience revealed to you. At the end of the day," he said, "*enlightenment is a verb. It is behavior.* If you're not kind, if you're not helpful to others, it doesn't matter what kind of personal experience you had."

My *sesshin* experience was the fruition of a lifelong quest pursuing intuitions and clues garnered from a long line of mentors—my parents Ruth and Morris, Susie and Ozzie Nelson, Jim Clancy, Buddy Jones, Harry Palmer, David Campbell, Gary Snyder, Karney Hodge, Nino Cerruti, and others from whom I might have received only a nudge when I needed it. While it may have been a personal experience I cannot call it a personal achievement.

For the remainder of the *sesshin*, I considered the Buddha's resolve to dedicate himself to relieving human suffering. He spent days after his enlightenment considering his experience, and while myth informs us that the God Brahmin urged Buddha to teach, lest the world be lost, it is more likely the Buddha realized that he could be helpful and reach some people. He pondered how to best speak of his experience so that others might understand and began his first sermon, The Four Noble Truths, quite simply, like a doctor, diagnosing a disease and offering its cure:

THE FOUR NOBLE TRUTHS
1) *Dukkha* exists

Dukkha is a Sanskrit word usually translated as "suffering," but it also includes nuances of "unease," "dissatisfaction," and "anxiety." Every one of these words had a personal reference to me, from my fears of growing old and losing my youth, to the years of anxiety growing up in my household. My commitments to a marriage and unbroken family had changed like ground shifting under my feet. I could certainly identify with dissatisfaction, from considering loss of life as I had once known it to disappointment with myself. It was reassuring to learn that these feelings were normal; a part of being human, not a neurotic aspect of the personality to be excised and thrown away. A teacher once said to me, holding his hands in a circle, "Human nature is half light and half shadow"—and he removed one hand—"if you take away the shadows, you no longer have a circle."

2) *Dukkha* has a Cause

It was also reassuring to learn that there was a *cause* for all these feelings. I could imagine how Louis Pasteur felt when he discovered that germs and not humors were the cause of disease. The Sanskrit word *tanhā*, identified as this cause, means "clinging to the pleasurable, craving, or desiring self-fullfillment." Part of what unsettles us in life is the feeling of ceaseless change. It inevitably involves losing something we are attached to. How many times have we heard someone say, "I like my life just the way it is?" Yet it is bound to change and that change will be experienced as loss. We will, in the end, lose *everything*. My mother's disappearance as a child; my father's absence; my anxiety about being incapable of running Turkey Ridge, or being able to make a living were all direct results of clinging to hopes and ideas about my life. My anxiety was the flip side of craving things to be different, or of wanting to be happy. In a world of constant change, it's obvious that we cannot *be anything* all the time. Happiness will come and go like sorrow, like weather, and everything else and our desire to fix it permanently is a craving that breeds dissatisfaction and unhappiness.

3) There is an end to *Dukkha*

Buddha's assertion that the self and the soul were an illusion was a startling and provocative assertion the first time I encountered it. It was a direct challenge to nearly every religion I had ever studied and every instinct that I and everyone I knew seemed to have, believing that some part of themselves will always continue. Whether they call it a self or a soul, it is nearly the same thing. This self defines itself in part by what we like and dislike. "I" didn't like athletics and loved to read. I loved the color blue and was pretty neutral about yellow. I tended towards liberal politics and thought that conservatives were uptight, harsh, and judgmental. My "self" has an opinion about everything and has constructed an entire world based on its three simple options— what I like, what I don't like, and what I'm neutral about. Since the universe has no mandate to make me happy or conform to my beliefs and wishes, the more rigidly I stick to a sense of self, the more rigidly I will maintain myself at odds with reality.

4) The way out of *Dukkha* is to follow the Eightfold Path.[2]

The Eightfold Path is the Buddha's prescription for repairing ourselves. It is a bit like the shop manual I bought for the motorcycle I repaired as a boy, which listed all the appropriate steps required to repair it. The Eightfold Path is a series of interdependent practices, some of which are wisdom practices like developing a deep understanding of the Buddha's teaching and developing a fixed intention to be truly helpful to all beings (by awakening oneself to be of use in freeing others of their attachments to and belief in a self) and to consider others' needs before oneself.

There are ethical practices that include making one's living in a way that does not harm others or the earth and its species; speaking of others in a kind and understanding way, without harshness or judgment; and behaving in a way that manifests kindness and treats life as precious. Finally, there are concentration practices, which include vigorous effort, developing single pointed concentration through meditation, and careful monitoring of one's own behavior moment by moment to ensure that one does not stray from the Buddha's proscribed path. This path itself *is a method* of liberation. One who lives in this way wholeheartedly and with total commitment is living the life of a Buddha. It is also important to note that from this very first sermon the Buddha indicated our responsibility to *others*, emphasizing that our struggles for awakening are not narcissistic.

PRACTICE IS NOT something done just for ourselves. We need a community of peers to help us stay straight and ethical and on track amidst the confusion, contradictions, and choices of everyday life. In the human realm the consequences of past decisions and actions we have committed with our body, speech, and mind, generated by positive or negative mental states, remain with this human body. An awakened Buddhist teacher who is not paying attention is just as capable of causing harm as any other being. Perhaps they are more dangerous because an absent-minded teacher may have a luster of achievement that can fool the innocent or unwary. There are also fine and conscientious Buddhist teachers who may not have had an awakening experience. When my teacher informed me that he wanted me to begin teaching and I demurred, he said, "There are people behind you that you can help, and people in front of you that you will learn from." The intention to be helpful is part of the Eightfold Path.

An awakening is not to be understood as a foolproof antidote for natural disasters, or the vagaries of an ever-changing world. It is not a fence to be vaulted so that on the other side one can glide through life on spiritual autopilot. Such misunderstanding makes us vulnerable to charlatans and sociopaths.

Awakening is not the "goal" of Buddhist practice. In some manner it can be considered a type of beginning. Suzuki Roshi once said, "to be enlightened may not be so difficult. To renew that enlightenment moment after moment is what is difficult." That understanding returns us, moment after moment, to "behavior."

It's common for people to malign the "ego" as the source of all problematic human behavior—anger, selfishness, showing off, and so forth, and regard awakening as a cure that succeeds by obliterating the ego. Spiritual seekers sometimes behave as if their advancement depends on taking their ego out into a field and shooting it. Of *course* there are problems associated with the ego. There are problems associated with water if you're under it and can't reach the surface. The "problem" with ego is not its *existence,* but our *attachment to it,* our *promotion of it* to supreme importance, and *our inability to step aside from it* and perceive the universe without its limiting filters.

If you place five dots in a circle on a piece of paper there is an implied center. Let the dots represent our sense organs—eyes, ears, nose, mouth, and mind—the implied center of those dots is the ego. We see, hear, smell, taste, touch, and *are aware of it* so we *imply* an entity that we imagine receives, experiences, and translates the sense-data from our organs. We assume that it is a fixed entity, separate from the rest of Creation, which we imagine as "out there." As long as we maintain this unquestioned belief in a physical "self" we remain unaware that we have sentenced ourselves to life within a very small chamber in the universe's immensity—the prison of our habitual ideas and beliefs which prevent us from seeing "things as it is"—Suzuki Roshi's lovely idiomatic expression of simultaneous multiplicity and oneness.

Hummingbirds were not created for human purpose or use. Neither were leopards, nebulae, octopi, weather systems, or the Amazon. Perceiving Creation only through the lens of what we like, dislike, or are neutral about has created our roiling, ruined, depleted world and the chaotic, murderous human affairs played out on it.

THERE ARE MANY services our "self" affords us, or it would never have survived the fine grinding of evolution. No matter how useful it may be, however, *we will never locate or grasp it.* It has no color, no shape, and no location. There is no organ in the body that corresponds to it or houses it. Yet because we all have the irrefutable experience of existing, we cannot say with definitiveness that it does *not* exist. Buddha himself would not choose sides in dualistic fool's game by choosing either—there is a self, or there is not a self. He described *all* objects, concepts, feelings, and perceptions as fundamentally *empty* of an *abiding* (permanent) self; but that is not the same as saying that it exists or does not.

The Sanskrit term *sunyata* is often translated as "emptiness," but this common English word can be problematic for Westerners who confuse "emptiness" with "nothing." Suzuki Roshi addressed this confusion when he once declared: "Emptiness does not mean annihilation; it means *selfless original enlightenment, which gives rise to everything.*"

"Selfless" means what it says. "Original enlightenment" is what exists before form, before thoughts and ideas, before language and concept. It is the Absolute—undivided, whole, and entire—the womb that gives birth to all phenomena.

The Vietnamese Buddhist teacher Thich Nhat Hanh offers us a useful alternative to "emptiness" with his phrase "inter-being," without connotations of nothingness. "Inter-being" implies some 'being' that may *feel* discrete and separate from the rest of the universe, but is constructed of non-being parts. Those parts are composed of other parts with which it is interdependent and so forth. Nothing exists without "all of it."

It doesn't take much thought to follow that assertion. No living creature has ever been *separate* from water, sunlight, microbes in the soil, plants, and the insects that pollinate them and the birds that control the insects. If we keep extending this list to include all the relevant interlocking systems and parts, we will include the entire universe. Even the earth's unique orbit in the solar system keeps it a critical distance from the Sun, where water neither evaporates nor freezes, making our dream of life possible.

◄o►

THE ANSWER TO my query, "What am I gonna do now?" resolved itself as a deepened commitment to practice. Within three years I completed my studies, spent six months sewing my robes, and then received ordination as a priest. Usually I practice invisibly in the world, without any identifying costume. Like most Buddhists the world over, I do not shave my head. Unless I'm requested to be the officiant for ceremonial purposes—weddings, funerals, memorials, naming children, or blessings—I don't wear my robes. I practice in the everyday world and struggle with its problems like most others. I have a job and the concomitant difficulties of juggling an economy, family, relationships, retirement, and fulfilling my vows. In this way my life is like most other people's, Buddhist or otherwise.

It needs to be clear that my recounting an awakening kind of experience is not a claim of any special quality for myself not available to everyone on earth, Buddhist or otherwise. Neither do I intend to imply that Buddhist practice holds any exclusive lien on wisdom. *Wisdom is the human birthright* but in order to avail oneself of it, a person must first understand that it is available.

If I were challenged to offer a description of wisdom, I would say, "Seeing things as they really are." If I were asked for a *working* description of it, I would say that it is the ability to migrate back and forth between three apparently contradictory ways of experiencing the world.

The world delivered to us by our five senses is a world of discrete unique entities—every blade of grass, grain of sand, leaf, and human being appears to be distinct and unique. Buddhist practice calls it "the relative view." This world is dominated by *intelligence*—a powerful reductive problem-solving mechanism that is responsible for our prosperity, long lives, wealth, and amusing toys. Intelligence has a shadow, however, and that shadow is its lack of a moral valence. Intelligence can create a hospital or a concentration camp; a new medicine or a bio-weapon. It solves problems without regard to the ultimate purpose of the solution.

The other common way of regarding the world, we could call the "Interdependent." It perceives reality as one interconnected entity. Too vast and complex to be "figured out" by intelligence, this perspective is ruled by *intuition*, an older survival mechanism composed of memory, emotion, and intelligence. Intuition triggers vast areas of the brain and leads very rapidly to action-oriented decisions. The shadow of this interdependent world is that in regards to the whole, an individual human life may appear insignificant; so too a single species. It can become too easy to make unethical sacrifices of other beings in pursuit of "larger" goals. I believe this is why the Buddha created his ethical constructs as central to his teaching, so that superficial understanding of emptiness or inter-being would not lead people astray and into potentially horrific acts.

Both of these views relate to the world that is delivered to us by our senses. There is a third way that Buddhist practitioners know as "Emptiness." This is the unseen, formless energy that extrudes itself as the myriad forms of the world, creating and then retrieving them back to the source. Suzuki Roshi suggested that we think of it as the white screen in a movie theater, the unseen background against which the shimmering movie of existence is played.

None of these modalities will solve every problem, but meditating is a particularly useful way to access the Absolute and to oscillate between the other perspectives. When we meditate we sit with an erect posture, in the vast emptiness that contains these other two views (and everything else). We do not choose between them; do not lean into or away from our problems or desires. We accept everything that arises, even the interruptions of thinking, because each part is a complete expression of the whole. Oscillating between them, accepting what comes—mind or mindlessness—gradually thins the imaginary membrane between them until it becomes porous. At that point we no longer lose awareness of independent existence or the Interdependent or the Absolute. Coursing between all three minimizes the harm that

occurs from ignoring the truths that relative and interdependent perspectives exclude from one another by definition.

Buddha observed that humans are already enlightened, and a
Buddhist teacher friend qualified his statement by adding, "The problem is that we don't believe it." It is this wisdom and the belief in it that
is the Rainman's Third Cure.

◄○►

I HAD NO conception of this at the age when I first head Dylan's song,
and perhaps he did not either. It takes time and loss to weaken the
hold our pet theories and indulgences have on us. Wisdom traditions are often obscured and pass unnoticed, particularly in wealthy
cultures filled with distractions because they inevitably carry an
unpopular message—*there are no panaceas* in a world in which everything changes and passes away. A useful Zen aphorism to this point
reminds us that "An iron Buddha cannot pass through a furnace; a
clay Buddha cannot pass through water, a wooden Buddha cannot
pass through fire."

Every fixed system, every ideology, every firmly held belief will
encounter circumstances in which it will be ineffective. To cling
rigidly to any philosophical or intellectual position—Capitalism,
Conservatism, Liberalism, Religion, Enlightenment—is to be an iron
or a clay Buddha.

FINALLY, BUDDHIST PRACTICE can be expressed as an *intention*, as the practice of fixing our intention on compassionate action and response so
firmly that it assumes the force of reflex. It is a difficult task requiring

dedicated practice if it is to become reliable and it appears counterintuitive in a world dedicated to speed and instant gratification.

Intention is not a train of thought. It is an animating impulse and must be grounded in the body. If the *body* is not capable of expressing kindness and compassion, the next time we are cut off by a thoughtless driver, we may have raised our middle finger at them without thinking. That impulse is perilously close to pulling a trigger. Such "leaking" of destructive, competitive, or hostile impulses like this causes havoc. It is often compounded by people who imagine themselves "good" (as opposed to human and therefore capable of any human emotion and act). Such assumptions tend to lead us to assume that everything we do is good.

Zen Teacher Norman Fischer elucidates a number of "practices," not necessarily Buddhist, that anyone can use to train their intention and tame their impulses. They are simple tasks like meditating, speaking kindly to everyone, gazing at the sky, practicing generosity, helping others, praying (whether or not you believe in God). All are practices that if diligently pursued help to calm our minds and focus our intention positively. Every one can be practiced invisibly without drawing attention to oneself. Once intention is reliably fixed, we can feel safe to improvise our attempts to help others. We can be who we really are.

◄o►

LIFE SEEMS TO move in large orbits. In May of 2014, one of my oldest friends (who enjoys working on vehicles as much as I do) flew with me to Iowa to pick up a 1952 Dodge Power Wagon truck that friends had restored and improved for me over the course of a year. Throughout my adult life I have remained a shade-tree mechanic; still partly the boy who assembled a motorcycle from a basket of parts. But ten years ago I had sold the Dodge Power Wagon that my girlfriend and I had driven from Turkey Ridge Farm to California in in 1973, after having owned it for nearly thirty years. I sold it because I no longer had a place to work on it and it deserved better care than I could give.

During the years I'd owned it, I'd bought parts and sought information from a concern called Vintage Power Wagons (VPW), a global repository of Power Wagon information and parts in Fairfield, Iowa. I had become telephone and email buddies with the folks there and for many years had a standing invitation to attend their Power Wagon Rally every June. I took them up on it in 2013, and so Terry Bisson, my friend since Grinnell College, and I traveled to the Midwest together. If you love trucks, it's a wonderful event, where men and women from far-flung locales congregate each year for a long weekend to show off their vehicles, winch one another out of tough spots, climb Iowa's short steep hills, collaborate on repairs, picnic, and renew old friendships. It all takes place under the umbrella of respect and love they hold for these virtually indestructible vehicles and the generous hosting of Vintage Power Wagons.

My disappointment at not having a truck must have been palpable, because by the time the rally ended, VPW owner Dave Butler, his son Jens, and their chief mechanic Matt Welcher—despite my complaints of having no garage to work in *or* money to spare—had convinced me that *they* would find and build me a Power Wagon and that "we'll make it so you can afford it." They clinched the deal by offering me parts and labor at such reasonable rates that they overcame my embarrassment at not building it myself, and I could not refuse their offer.

A year later, after triweekly emails, phone calls, photos, and numerous consultations, an old vehicle discovered resting in a Las Vegas garage for twenty-two years had been rebuilt from the frame up; modified and refined with modern disc brakes, power steering, and a new Dodge 360-cubic-inch V-8 engine replacing the original flathead six-cylinder motor. Bisson and I spent several days that May repairing or rethinking a few snafus with the VPW people, fired it up, drove it around Iowa a few days, reveling in the throaty rumble of the exhaust, and then began the long drive home to California.

Iowa was familiar to us from our time at Grinnell College together and, as I did as a student, I marveled at the richness and fecundity of Iowa. In other ways, the state appeared poorer and the people stressed and pedaling harder to stay in place. Matt Welcher had just lost his girlfriend (a mother of three) the week before we arrived when a tornado blew her barn down around her. Matt was immersed in palpable grief.

My practice afforded me some tools to be helpful and I was glad to be there and attempt to repay some of Matt's kindness to me. Speaking with people intimately and unflinchingly generally activates something deep in them and I found people during this trip ready to speak with me, often with surprising candor. It was not necessary to mention Buddhism or Zen, just to be fully present.

Terry and I drove hard and learned the first time we stopped that the truck was a celebrity. Whenever we pulled in somewhere to eat or refuel, people inevitably ambled over for a closer look:

"My father had a truck like that."

"I used to log with a Power Wagon."

"Wow, you don't see trucks like that anymore."

Each visitor offered an opportunity to converse, to learn something about their life and the values that they held. Each conversation
(and there were many) reaffirmed my confidence in the respect for craft
and honest labor that appears to be commonplace among Americans.
Tattooed bikers, farmers in shredded and dusty Carhartts, young cou-
ples in cars overflowing with camping gear, and families toting kids
approached the truck with surprised disbelief and an attitude akin to
reverence. I concluded finally that the most common opinion identified
the truck as a relic from an older, mythic, or once-remembered America
when values of thrift, self-reliance, repair, and pride in work had once
been universal hallmarks of our products and a wellspring of national
pride. In the aggregate these diverse souls appeared to share a common
vision of an earlier America they preferred, symbolized for them in the
moment by the reemergence of this sixty-two-year-old truck.

My work as an actor had accustomed me to being recognized on
the streets. On this journey there was no doubt that it was the *truck*
receiving the recognition. From their conversations I could recognize a
sense of loss touching the people who approached us; a nearly inarticu-
late sense that their world—our economy and political system—had
veered out of control and was no longer responsive to their wishes
or protecting them from predators. They clustered around the truck
as if it were a talisman of a better time, and it was clear that while
most of them were not rich, they were missing something more valuable to them than money. Time after time the phrase "What a great
truck" was directed at the Power Wagon and it was apparent that
people's regard was deeper than responding to its novelty or surface
charm. These people appeared to miss a life where they could depend
on employment, afford the rudiments of a house, a car, the ability

to educate their family, and protect themselves against catastrophe. Helping them in any way would be Buddha-work, and when I realized that this was what I had signed on to do as a priest, the shoe dropped and I understood why I was having these conversations.

AS I SLAMMED my driver's door, about to leave a gas station in Nebraska, an old-timer passed the pumps heading towards the convenience store behind them. He appraised the truck and shouted out, "That's a great vē-hicle!" His exclamation triggered a rush of associations.

In the early history of Buddhism, the Hinayana philosophy was dominant in Buddhist circles. It was known as the Lesser Vehicle, because its philosophy stressed enlightenment of the self, the relief of one's own sufferring and asserted that "emptiness" of a soul or a self applied only to human beings and only for their lifetime.

The philosophy that challenged and eventually replaced Hinayana is called Mahayana. The prefix *Maha-* means "great" and because its adherents labored for the enlightenment of *all* beings, it became known as *The Great Vehicle*. Mahayana asserted that *all* phenomena were empty of a fixed self. Furthermore it asserted that at death a compassionate *intention* to help others continues on to countless other world systems helping all beings. When that old-timer named it, I had to smile as I cranked the wheel and rode The Great Vehicle out into the highway's flow, heading west, all barriers broken, the future vast and free.

—MILL VALLEY, CALIFORNIA
OCTOBER 2014

NOTES

THE FIRST TWO CURES

1   http://isreview.org/issue/80/different-kind-teachers-union.

2   Fifty-five years later I applied for the U.S. Government pre-clearance program called GOES, which allows frequent travelers returning from abroad to avoid long Customs lines. I applied online, paid $100 and had an interview in which this arrest was referred to, but the officer told me that he would accept it as an error of youth, and that I'd receive my clearance. I returned home, elated. When I visited the website the following day to see the official announcement, I learned that I had been "refused" due to this "expunged" arrest. The email informed me tersely that "I did not meet their standards."

3   Raskin would eventually break with his boss, one of Kennedy's "best and brightest" technocrats, over the Vietnam war.

4   That photo is included in this volume's photographs, but all searches of *The New York Times* website for a better copy have proved fruitless.

5   Many years later, speaking with my friend, poet Michael McClure, an intimate friend of Duncan's, I recounted the story of my decision to stop working with Robert. When I told him about the students indicating their understanding by nodding, Michael laughed aloud and said, "They lied!"

6   Covered in detail in *Sleeping Where I Fall* (Berkeley, CA: Counterpoint Press, 2009).

7 I say "not a religion" because Buddha is not a god in the ordinary understanding of the word. However there are folk and other lineages of Buddhism that worship the Buddha as Divine. Not Zen.

8 This is what the attaché de presse informed me of at the time. But since the Festival was founded in 1946, it must have been the forty-first anniversary.

9 The Buddha enjoined people only against occupations that kill, intoxicate, or delude others. While austerity was dictated for monks, there are sutras where the Buddha talks about the advantages of wealth used wisely and to help others.

THE RAINMAN'S THIRD CURE

1 Gary Snyder, "This Tokyo."

2 Right Understanding, Right Aspiration, Right Speech, Right Action, Right Livelihood, Right Effort, Right Mindfulness, and Right Concentration. To evade the judgmental aspect of the word "right" in English, I prefer substituting "Buddhist," to imply this is how Buddhists do this, not to imply that others are wrong.